The
Great Catholic
Reformers

The Great Catholic Reformers

From
Gregory the Great
to
Dorothy Day

C. Colt Anderson

Paulist Press
New York/Mahwah, NJ

Jacket design by Trudi Gershenov
Book design by Lynn Else

Library of Congress Cataloging-in-Publication Data

Anderson, C. Colt.
    The great Catholic reformers : from Gregory the Great to Dorothy Day / C. Colt Anderson.
        p.   cm.
    Includes bibliographical references (p.   ) and index.
    ISBN-13: 978-0-8091-0579-3 (alk. paper)
    1. Catholic Church—History. 2. Church history. I. Title.
BX946.A53 2007
282.092′2—dc22

                                                                    2007019727

Published by Paulist Press
997 Macarthur Boulevard
Mahwah, New Jersey 07430

www.paulistpress.com

Printed and bound in the
United States of America

Contents

Preface ix

Introduction xiii

Chapter 1
Gregory the Great 1
    The Diagnosis 2
    Society's Effect on the Church 4
    Gregory's Plan of Attack 6
    Ecclesial Reform 8
    Administrative Reform 11
    Social Justice 14
    Discernment, Clericalism, and Ecclesial Authority 18
    The Apologetics and Polemics of Humility 22
    Gregory's Legacy 27

Chapter 2
Peter Damian: The Doctor of Reform 30
    Peter and the Papal Reform Movement 33
    Spiritual Incest 38
    Simony 45
    Collaborative Reform 49
    Peter Damian's Contribution to Catholic Reform 53

Chapter 3
Bernard of Clairvaux: The Impossible Reformer 56
    Progressive Reform 59
    Twelfth-Century Renewal 61
    Bernard's *Apologia* 64
    On Conversion 69
    On Consideration: Advice to a Pope 74
    Bernard of Clairvaux's Continuing Influence 77

CONTENTS

Chapter 4
Clare of Assisi: The Clear Mirror of Christ....................................79
    Clare the Franciscan Reformer 80
    The Crumbling Church of the Thirteenth Century 84
    Mary of Oignies..86
    Franciscan Reform 89
    Clare of Assisi's Understanding of Women and Ministry........93
    The Fight for Poverty 96
    The Bull of Canonization..100
    Epilogue 102

Chapter 5
Catherine of Siena: The Insatiable Reformer 103
    The Babylonian Captivity 106
    Penitential Reform 111
    Strategy 113
    Reform Rhetoric...117
    Conclusion 121

Chapter 6
When Reformers Collide: Jean Gerson and Jan Hus.................123
    The Great Schism..124
    Jean Gerson: Conciliarist..126
    From the Council of Pisa to Constance..............................131
    Jan Hus...132
    Council of Constance...140
    Conclusion 146

Chapter 7
Gasparo Contarini: Christ's Diplomat 150
    Abuses in the Early Renaissance Church (1475–1512).........152
    Contarini and the Catholic Reformers before 1517 157
    Ambassador and Statesman..164
    The *Consilium* 169
    Contarini's Legacy...174

Chapter 8
The Most Dangerous Man in England:
The Convert Cardinal Newman..177
    Reform after the Protestant Reformation 179
    Development of Doctrine...182
    On Consulting the Faithful..186
    Freedom and Infallibility 191
    Newman's Legacy...196

Chapter 9
Dorothy Day and the Catholic Worker Movement...................198
    Social Justice and the Papacy...201
    Genesis of the Catholic Worker Movement..........................206
    The Early Years of the Catholic Worker Movement.............209
    Dorothy Day and the Red Scare...213
    Conclusion 215

Conclusion..218

Notes 225

Index..259

Preface

Why write a book about the great Catholic reformers? It is a question I imagine many of my readers may have. I also expect that some of my readers may be suspicious of my motives. Others may see my work as a positive response to the sex scandal that has been traumatic for so many people. In fact, my interest in reform predates our most contemporary crisis. As for my motive, it can be stated simply: I want to encourage every Catholic to take up the difficult task of reform. My hope is that people will find a model to inspire them that will suit their own temperaments and spiritual dispositions. I intend to provide people with historical arguments, precedents, rhetorical strategies, and theological justifications for reform initiatives and movements. Finally, I want to broaden people's perspectives on what is or can be legitimate reform within a Catholic framework.

My mother inspired me to take up the study of reform. She died from cancer as I was working on this project. Joan Anderson worked for social justice by investigating cases of child abuse, assisting the poor, protecting the elderly, and fighting against discrimination. She was also the prayer leader for a large charismatic community in Savannah, Georgia, back in the heady days of the 1970s. My mother prayed for the sick, attended Mass regularly, tithed, took part in biblical seminars, and participated in the devotion of perpetual adoration. In short, she was devoted to living out the Second Vatican's call for a more active laity. Joan Anderson loved the church, but she never turned a blind eye to its faults.

In the late 1970s, my mother became aware of a scandalous and adulterous affair between a local priest and a parishioner. She decided to inform the bishop, Raymond W. Lessard, about the problem. As she loved to tell her friends, Bishop Lessard was not happy to receive this news and responded, "Who do you think you are? You are just a layperson, and you are only a woman." My mother answered that if God could speak wisdom and good counsel through Balaam's ass, then he could certainly use even a lowly laywoman like herself to give good advice. As we shall see, in one way or another, reformers always have to answer Bishop Lessard's question: "Who do you think you are?"

I am dedicating this book to my mother and to everyone who has stood up for what is right, only to be dismissed by people holding positions of power in the church. I intend to offer them consolation, encouragement, and theological resources. Since I am trying to reach as many people as possible, I have avoided highly technical language and have employed a narrative approach to the history of reform. The notes will lead the reader to more technical studies, translations, and critical editions of texts. Though there are references to studies in French, German, and Italian, I have concentrated the notes on sources written in English that are reasonably available. My hope is to make it easy for professors, teachers, and priests to use this book to create courses on reform. In the cases involving Italian scholarship, I have had to rely heavily on English or French treatments of the material because my ability to read Italian is limited.

The use of biblical citations also requires some explanation. The reformers covered in this book frequently use scriptural citations either to justify or to explain their reform work. When they quote scripture, I follow their citations, which frequently differ somewhat from the critical editions and standard translations we use today. This is crucial for preserving the integrity of their work. Because many of the reformers treated in this book draw upon scripture through liturgical texts, the writings of the saints, or from memory, we cannot assume that they always had a biblical text in hand when they quoted scripture. Actually, they were much more comfortable with the ambiguities in the scriptural texts than we are. (In instances where noted by NRSV, I have used the New Revised Standard Version translation.)

Since I want to reach as many people as possible, I have adjusted the translations I have used to gender-neutral language whenever it seemed possible. So when the Latin word *homo* appears in its various singular and plural forms, I have changed the translations to fit current standards; but in cases where such terms are clearly related to specific men, I leave the gender-specific translations in place. When the reformers used gender-specific language, I followed their usage because it is important for understanding their attitudes, cultural milieus, and objectives. Insofar as these usages reveal the sin of sexism in the history of the church, I believe it would be a mistake to obscure them.

As with any project of this scope, there are many people who helped me. My wife, Rose, who always provides honest and insightful feedback, has served as my first editor. She has also taken on more of the responsibilities for running our household, which was a sacrifice that helped to make this book possible. Christopher Bellitto, my editor, has helped me to stay focused and to keep moving even as I was adjusting to my new role as a father and grieving over my mother's losing battle with cancer. I am deeply grateful for his advice and encouragement. Several of my colleagues including Rev. Michael Fuller, Mary Ocasek, and Rev. Martin Zielinski read chapters and provided suggestions that I incorporated into the book. Marian Johnson and Anna Kielian, two of the librarians at the University of St. Mary of the Lake in Mundelein, Illinois, were very helpful in obtaining texts that I needed. Phillip M. Runkel, the archivist for the Dorothy Day Collection at Marquette University, saved me a great deal of time by sorting through Day's letters for reform-related themes. Two of my students, Randy Stice and Brian Carpenter, have helped me in the process of getting the text ready to send to press. Finally I would like to thank Rev. Michael Fahey, SJ; Dr. William Power; Dr. Wanda Cizewski; Dr. Ewert Cousins; Rev. Zachary Hayes, OFM; Rev. George Tavard, AA; and Dr. Bernard McGinn for their advice and moral support.

Introduction

In the twentieth century there was an active effort to recover a proper sense of reform in Catholic theology that ultimately found expression in the Second Vatican Council. The council declared that the pilgrim church is "holy and always in need of being purified" and that it "always follows the way of penance and renewal."[1] While the council was careful to avoid the term *reform* because of its historical association with the Protestant slogan that the church is *semper reformanda* (always in need of reform), admitting that the pilgrim church is *semper purificanda* (always in need of purification) is an acknowledgement of the need for ongoing reform.[2] However, the council did not present any clear description of how this purification or reform takes place other than the allusion to the way of penance and renewal. This lack of clarity has created a state of confusion within the church.

Because the council gave no clear guidelines for distinguishing reform from dissent, many people who have taken up the council's challenge to work for the purification, reform, and renewal of the church have been dismissed as dissenters or revolutionaries. At the same time, there are individuals and organizations that are seen as reformers, even though they advocate shrinking the church's catholicity by driving their neighbors out of our communion. While their goal of a smaller but purer church appears to be attractive to some, it runs contrary to the mission of a church that reaches out to incorporate sinners into its life-giving body. This idea of working for a smaller and purer church was condemned as the heresy of Donatism in the fifth century. Of course, some people who are dissenters pretend to be reformers.

When the council fathers were drafting the statement on the church's need for purification and reform, they were aware of the problem of distinguishing between true and false reform. In 1950, the Dominican theologian Yves Congar published what came to be a foundational work on the subject: *Vraie et fausse réforme dans l'église.* Congar's study influenced the Second Vatican Council's program and conditioned how the theologians and bishops at the council understood the nature of legitimate reform. Given its significance, Congar's work served as the theoretical starting point for this project.

Congar defined the Catholic understanding of reform as either a correction of abuses and problems or as an attempt to make things better. Nonetheless, he argued that the church's essential structure is irreformable. He identified the church's structure as being composed of three essential elements: infallible dogma (divine revelation), the sacraments, and hierarchical constitution.[3] The lives of the faithful are united to the life of the church through these essential elements, which he said is the meaning of being a communion. While the structure of the church provides a mystical unity that cannot be destroyed, there is also a lived unity brought about by the efforts of its members. Congar argued that the way people maintain or destroy community through their actions, the process by which people become holy, and all the other aspects of the life of the church can be corrected or improved.[4]

The preoccupation of Catholic theologians with the essential structural elements of the church was, in Congar's analysis, a serious impediment to the type of self-criticism necessary for any spiritual organism or institution to grow in holiness. He claimed that this tendency began in the sixteenth century, when the church came to see every criticism as proceeding from a spirit of opposition or dissent. Many Catholics began to employ an apologetic that Congar described as an attempt to defend everything. He explained that the result of this defensive stance required people to split the sanctity and perfection of the church from its historical reality. In other words, this apologetic led to a bifurcated church where the sinful actions of its members in history or in the present have absolutely no relationship to the essential nature of the church. He concluded that such apologists simply do not see reality as it is. Congar warned that an institution that failed to criticize itself was condemning itself to do nothing more than to survive.[5]

Anticipating the charge that such self-criticism would be seized by those who simply wished to denigrate the church, Congar cited Pope Pius XII's Christmas address to the sacred college in 1946. Pope Pius declared: "We are well aware that our words and our intentions risk being misinterpreted and distorted for the purposes of political propaganda. But the possibility of such erroneous or malevolent interpretations cannot cause us to stop speaking."[6] Congar was well aware that not every type of criticism is constructive, so he identified four characteristics of legitimate reform movements, which he saw reflected in the work of French reformers in the late 1940s: (1) Catholic reform must be frank and direct in presenting critiques; (2) Catholic reform entails serious intellectual foundations; (3) Catholic reform involves and empowers the laity; (4) Catholic reform method begins in a return to the sources of tradition *(ressourcement)*.[7]

The first characteristic, the frankness of the criticism, is linked to the final characteristic, a return to the sources. Congar argued that true reformers within the Catholic Church can present critiques that are so direct as to seem brutal or even revolutionary; nonetheless, he claimed that legitimate reform could never actually be brutal or revolutionary. Such strong criticism proceeds out of a love for and confidence in the church, but he admitted that it also comes from a deep resentment of the defects in the church.

Resentment occurs when people recognize that the church is straying from its tradition, which he understood as the church's way of responding to the problems posed by different historical and cultural contexts. It is important to realize that tradition, the process of handing down the revelation given in Jesus Christ, is better understood as a dynamic activity than as a static reality. Congar explained that tradition begins by maintaining received ways of proceeding and speaking, but it also recognizes authentic developments or improvements resulting from the necessities of the hour.

The reform method of returning to the sources, according to Congar, is what allows reform to take place without destroying the unity of the Catholic communion. He described the method as a return of theological and pastoral thought to the great rivers of a rediscovered and deep tradition. Congar asserted that tradition contains within itself the resources or the ability to adapt to new situations. Tradition is like a great river, which cuts new channels and forms new tributaries when it is faced with obstructions resulting from the buildup of sediment or from the process of erosion. If people were to follow the new tributary back, they would see that it came from the same source.

Congar explained that the second characteristic of true reform in the Catholic Church, the seriousness of its foundations, is related to tradition and to antecedent intellectual developments that "have incontestable value." He used the liturgical reforms instituted by Pope Leo XIII and Pius X as an example. The liturgical reforms had their source in the apostolic tradition, but the recovery of that tradition was preceded by new methods in history, advancements in textual criticism, archeological discoveries, and other scientific developments. Thus advancements in other sciences such as biology, sociology, psychology, anthropology, or philosophy help the true reformer see the ways that tradition can be more deeply understood and adapted to better fulfill its purpose.

Though Congar did not explicitly link the empowerment of the laity to tradition in his treatise on reform, it is clear that he believed such empowerment is rooted in the pastoral mission of the church. He argued that the oneness or unity of the church requires that all of the orders of the church collaborate in reform. Since all of the faithful are responsible for the welfare of the entire body of Christ, the laity must think about and respond to the problems of the church. However, he saw this action as always taking place under the direction of the hierarchy.

Congar used the relationship between priests and their bishop at a diocesan synod as an analogy to explain how the laity can collaborate in reform. At a diocesan synod the priests give their advice to the bishop, but the bishop is the sole judge and legislator. While Congar advocated the duty of the laity to identify and to call attention to problems and deficiencies in church life, he reserved the authority to effect change solely to the hierarchy, which he understood as primarily referring to the pope and the bishops. Whereas his position on the empowerment of the laity in *Vrai et fausse réforme* seems inadequate to many Catholics today, it represented a significant departure from the excessively authoritarian and clerical understanding of authority that emerged in the aftermath of the Protestant Reformation. To appreciate Congar in his context, we must recognize that many members of the clergy in the 1950s church still believed that the only role for the laity was to pay, pray, and obey.

Both Congar's theology and the field of reform studies advanced significantly after the Second Vatican Council, but it seems that the ideas in *Vrai et fausse réforme* still have a tremendous influence on the way the Roman curia judges reform initiatives or movements.[8] To a lesser extent these ideas have filtered down through intermediary sources into the ecclesiology classes offered in seminaries, which helps to explain why many bishops, who are willing to listen to concerns voiced by the laity, are at the same time steadfastly resistant to lay initiatives to reform the church. The same is also true of concerns raised by the lower clergy and the religious. Given the developments of the last fifty-six years, both in terms of scholarship and historical events, it is time to reappraise the validity of Congar's four characteristics of true reform.

In order to examine Congar's ideas about the four characteristics of legitimate Catholic reform, I began by following his example. First, I have adopted his definition of reform as either correction of abuse or as an attempt to make things better. Second, I have accepted his position that infallible dogma, the sacraments, and the hierarchical constitution of the church are irreformable. Third, the method I have employed is a *ressourcement* approach by studying the strategies, rhetoric, and careers of ten great reformers within the Catholic tradition. Obviously this is a very limited sample, so I am not attempting to present a comprehensive study on the subject of reform. Instead, I am trying to look at legitimate reform in widely disparate situations by members of the laity, religious, and clergy over a period of fourteen centuries. Further, I have included both men and women.

Since reform is a universal category that can be applied to any aspect of the church's life, I have restricted this study to reformers who were intentionally working for the reform of the entire church. While many reformers such as Teresa of Avila are important for the church as a whole, their efforts were primarily aimed at their own communities and thus they were not included. I have also had to exclude those who were primarily interested in reforming aspects of church life and discipline such as educational methods, preaching, liturgical concerns, and so on. Finally, I am not treating the work of the great reformers in the East like the Cappadocians, John Chrysostom, or Symeon the New Theologian because these sources were only known in the West through intermediaries if at all.

The most important source for transmitting the patristic reform tradition of the East to the West was Pope Gregory the Great. Gregory was not the first reformer in the Western church, but his work influenced everyone who followed, which is why he is the starting point for this study. I chose the eleventh-century monk and cardinal Peter Damian for two reasons: He is the official doctor of reform and he is suspiciously absent in Congar's *Vraie et fausse réforme*.[9] For the twelfth century I chose Bernard of Clairvaux, in part, because he was working to reform some of the consequences of Peter Damian's work.

In the thirteenth and fourteenth centuries, women rose to greater prominence in the process of reform. To represent this development, I chose to study Clare of Assisi and Catherine of Siena, but there were many other possibilities. I chose Clare because she represents the Franciscan reform agenda, which is very significant in the history of the church, and because she has the authority of sainthood behind her. Whereas Clare was a religious woman in the sense of having professed the vows and belonging to an enclosed community, Catherine of Siena was a laywoman. Catherine lived in the world, but she was also a third order Dominican. Thus Catherine serves to highlight the Dominican approach to reform and to provide an example of a reformer who was a laywoman. This was a period when there were many laywomen working for reform as third order members of the Augustinian Canons, Dominicans, and Franciscans. Catherine was an obvious choice because she has the authority of being a doctor of the church, she publicly criticized the highest members of the clergy with absolute fearlessness, and Congar referred to her as a prophetic reformer.

To illustrate what can happen when reformers disagree with one another, I chose to treat Jean Gerson and Jan Hus together. Both men were diocesan priests and both were deeply committed to reform. Unlike the earlier cases, these men have not been recognized as saints or doctors by the church, and many theologians view them with a degree of suspicion. Even so, Gerson and Hus are recognized for the important roles they played in the reform of the church. The ambiguity of their status is one of the primary reasons I included them in the book.

There were a host of possibilities to choose from in the sixteenth century, but I decided to highlight the career of Gasparo Contarini. Contarini spent most of his life as a layman before being made a cardinal priest. His experience as a Catholic layman informed his reform work. Contarini also represents an advance in understanding how systems within the church can create abuse. Many elements of his agenda were incorporated into the reforms of the Council of Trent. Further, his efforts to heal the divisions between Protestants and Catholics have influenced the ecumenical movement today.

Following the Council of Trent, reform became a four-letter word in the Catholic Church. John Henry Newman, a convert priest from the Anglican Church, helped to restore the place of reform in the church by recovering an appropriate sense of historical development. In fact, Newman's theology played a pivotal role in the emergence of *ressourcement* theology and influenced Congar directly. This recovery of the church's history in conjunction with philosophical developments in the nineteenth century opened the door for the idea of reforming unjust social structures. To illustrate this aspect of reform, I have chosen to study the efforts of Dorothy Day.

When I began research on this volume, I expected to more or less confirm Congar's thesis. I had just finished writing a book on St. Bonaventure that highlighted his approach to reform, which was quite consistent with the four characteristics of reform presented in *Vraie et fausse réforme*. I had hoped to find some identifiable and stable tradition of reform developing over the church's history. In the initial phases of research, I began to realize that I had set off on a quixotic quest. Reform is ultimately about the things that can change. Consequently, legitimate or true Catholic reform changes with the circumstances it is confronting.

The first three of Congar's four characteristics of true reform crumbled or had to be modified in the face of the historical evidence. Only Bernard of Clairvaux, John Henry Newman, and Dorothy Day met all of Congar's standards for true reform. Each of the reformers I have studied did seek to empower the laity in some way, but Gregory the Great, Peter Damian, and Jan Hus, for example, actively supported the duty of the laity to initiate reform agendas and to criticize, correct, and punish immoral clergymen. Insofar as they participated in a papal coup and created a new system for electing the popes, Peter Damian and his reform circle can be seen as revolutionaries, thereby violating Congar's first characteristic of true reform. By way of contrast, Catherine of Siena was adamantly against the idea that laypeople should punish the clergy for their crimes; and Jean Gerson went so far as to condemn the claim that the laity had the right to criticize their clergy at all. As we shall see, Clare of Assisi's Franciscan approach to reform was not particularly direct nor was it based on the serious foundations of scientific or theological research. Catherine of Siena was quite direct and frank in her criticism, but she primarily proceeded by means of personal revelations rather than by research. All of them, however, did attempt to show how their reform initiatives were consistent with scripture and tradition.

Given this state of affairs, I decided that it would be more helpful to look for models or exemplars of reform existing within the tradition than to attempt to establish definitive characteristics. Nonetheless, there is one common feature shared by all the reformers presented in this book that flows out of their shared commitment to scripture and tradition: They were all recognized as having authority because of their service to the mission of the church—the salvation of souls. One test for distinguishing true Catholic reformers from false is whether they seek to save rather than to condemn, to turn opponents around rather than to cast them down, to reach out to people rather than to cut them off. But Catholic reform also has a deep sense of accountability and discipline at its foundation.

As the great scholar of reform Gerhard Ladner has shown, the very idea of reform was initially understood in terms of the conversion and penance of the individual sinner.[10] The sacrament of reconciliation requires one to feel remorse for sin, to resolve to change behavior, and to make satisfaction. Satisfaction requires an effort to right the wrong committed; and it is a discipline necessary for maintaining community. Thus satisfaction, the element of the sacrament that holds people accountable, heals both the sinner and the community. Many of the reformers covered in this book were interested in establishing institutions or laws to better serve the mission of salvation by holding people accountable. Because they knew that laws and disciplines are meaningless if people are unwilling to enforce them, much of their work was the task of persuading people to recognize that God would hold them accountable for their failures.

The great reformers of the past warn us of the temptations facing today's reformers. Like the people they seek to convert, reformers can become oppressive and legalistic when they forget that their goal is to save rather than to condemn. When reformers fall into the sin of legalism, they become the sowers of discord. Some lose their way through impatient discouragement and others through imprudence. The desire for approval, pride, anger, and all the other sins that impede the life of the church transform reform from an act of conversion to one of perversion.

Since true reformers are also the true Christians, they recognize that they are engaged in a spiritual endeavor. Perhaps the best guide for true reform is how well it comports with our spiritual tradition. If spirituality is the measure we use, then the reformer must hold conflicting goods together within the greater truth of the analogy of faith. Thus true reform in the Catholic tradition requires a balance between mercy and justice. The mission of salvation demands urgency, but the process requires patience. The true reformer must be humble, but must also openly oppose injustice. The great Catholic reformers teach us that these dynamic tensions generate spiritual power, which is creative and unpredictable; but they also tell us that that the consequence for refusing to live in this state of tension is to reject reality for an abstraction, to choose ideology over truth, and to follow the path of vengeance rather than penance.

1

Gregory the Great

On the morning of April 25, 590, the city of Rome was filled with the sound of chanting. People streamed out of seven different churches, chanting the Kyrie eleison, in a procession that would converge at the Basilica of Santa Maria Maggiore. This grand liturgical event had been called for by the pope-elect, Gregory. However, the procession was not a joyous celebration of St. Gregory the Great's election; instead, it was a desperate plea asking God to remove the scourge of plague from the tribulations that had befallen the Eternal City. Gregory must have been moved by the faith of these people who had elected him to serve as their bishop. As the hungry and destitute worshippers moved through the ruined city, offering prayers of penance and supplication, members of the procession, overcome by disease and hunger, dropped dead in the streets. Witnesses report that at least eighty people died during this event. Still, the people continued to pray and Gregory continued to preach. After all, what is there left to do at the end of the world but to pray?

Pope Gregory I most certainly believed that he was living at the end of the world. Italy had been ravaged by war, disease, famine, and flood throughout his lifetime. Yet he was neither a fatalist nor a pessimist. If the end of the world was indeed coming, Gregory believed that it meant the mission of saving souls had to be pursued with a greater sense of urgency. As we shall see, he lived through some of the darkest times in human history. Even though this experience led Gregory to believe the Day of Judgment was near, he acted on the hope that God's mercy would continue to delay the *eschaton* so that more souls might be saved. The range and extent of his work, both in terms of his administrative and literary accomplishments, unveil the intensity and power of Gregory's sense of hope.

Both the terrible nature of his times and his sense of urgency for saving souls goaded Gregory to embark on the road to reform. The church he had been elected to lead was in a terrible condition, a reflection of his society that was infected with many social, cultural, and economic maladies. Since the barrier between the church and the society within which it exists is necessarily semipermeable, like the walls of a cell, it is not terribly surprising that the church was in desperate need of reform. Factors that influence society also influence the church; and the church, like a white blood cell, releases its healing message into society. Gregory's favorite way of understanding the role of the church was presented in medical terms. The church's mission was *cura animarum:* the cure of souls. However, before we can understand the treatments Gregory prescribed, we must briefly diagnose the patient.

The Diagnosis

Though the Edict of Milan had declared Christianity a licit or legal religion in 313, the society and the empire were still largely pagan. The empire continued to act as it had, using violence as the normal means of exercising power, preserving social inequalities such as slavery, and recognizing the law as merely a principle that indicated how rational rule should be exercised. The real source of the law was the will of the emperor. While the basic social principles and methods of government remained unchanged, Christianity did, however, begin to have an effect on Roman society shortly after the conversion of Constantine in 312.[1]

Roman society prior to the recognition of Christianity was brutally repressive and unjust. There was essentially no help for the poor. Desperately poor parents either abandoned their children or sold them into slavery. Child prostitution was legal and accepted. Criminals, political dissenters, slaves, military captives, and members of banned religious sects were routinely tortured for public amusement in the gladiatorial games. If one did not feel like going out for entertainment, one could legally torture slaves to death at home. This almost total denigration of human dignity led to a deep-seated sense of fatalism.

Shortly after Constantine's conversion, some of these aspects of Roman culture began to be outlawed. In the spring of 315, Constantine legislated that aid would be provided for hungry children. Of course, their parents would still have to fend for themselves. That same summer, he made child prostitution and pederasty illegal and punishable by death in the gladiatorial arena. While Constantine forbade the immoderate torture and murder of slaves in 319, moderate torture was still legal. Slaves who denounced their masters, however, were to be subject to crucifixion according to a law passed in 320. In 343, it became illegal to use Christian slave women for prostitution; nonetheless, it was still legal to use other slave women for prostitution. Although the church clearly had a reforming effect on Roman society in terms of law, progress toward a more just society was painfully slow.

There were also cases where the church's moral teachings concerning sin led emperors to legislate laws that were clearly unjust. For example, on August 6, 390, Emperor Theodosius passed a law stipulating that men who committed homosexual acts were to be burned at the stake. This is the same Theodosius who so famously submitted to St. Ambrose's demand for public penance in 390. Though many people would like to excuse the church because it was the emperor who passed the law, he did so as a preeminent member of the church with either the tacit approval or outright encouragement of the clergy. From this example, we can see the church's own movement toward holiness is not a straightforward or steady progression; instead, the church progresses much in the same way that the people Israel made their way to the Promised Land—with detours, delays, and setbacks.

Nonetheless, we must avoid the temptation to excuse members of the early and medieval church too readily. Early Christians knew slavery had no part in God's kingdom, they knew the rich should share what they had gained with the poor, they knew torture and forced conversions were wrong. Gregory declared in his letters that the use of violence nullified an act under its influence and that torture should not be used to extract confessions.[2] When he heard the bishops of Arles and Marseilles were forcibly converting Jews, Gregory demanded they cease the practice. The only way to true conversion, he declared, is through the sweetness of good preaching. Unfortunately, many later popes ignored Gregory's teachings on the matter, such as Innocent IV, who issued a papal bull authorizing torture as a tool for the inquisition in 1252. If Innocent IV had read Gregory, he would have recognized that abusive and oppressive behavior by the church repels people from the faith.[3]

Gregory was one of the theologians who transmitted the idea that God did grant people the right to hold property and positions of power, but he believed God gave these rights as a form of penitential punishment. This penitential order is disrupted and falls into sinfulness and oppression, such as racism or sexism, when people claim rightful preeminence over and against the good of others. Individuals, governments, and cultures are all prone to see their good as overriding the good of their neighbors. The result is injustice, which the church must seek to correct.[4]

Even though the injustice of Roman society was rooted in original sin, watered by personal sins, and cultivated by communal sins, the church had benefited enormously in terms of property when the emperors began to make Christianity the state religion. Just as the church was having some impact on Roman society in terms of justice, the Roman Empire began to have a dramatic effect on the church's property. Suddenly, being a cleric became a path to wealth, prestige, and power instead of the path to martyrdom. Even as the church formulated its stances on issues of justice, men drawn by the prospects of preference, "lovers of pleasure," slipped into clerical orders under pretext of piety. Gregory was well aware of the impact of Roman society on the prophetic nature of the church.

Society's Effect on the Church

The church's relationship with the empire was at once beneficial and detrimental to its institutional integrity. The flood of wealth the emperors, empresses, and prominent members of society poured into the church allowed it to build institutions that would survive the collapse of the empire in the Latin West. Unfortunately, the corollary was that clerical careers would become a means of advancement socially, politically, and financially. Clerical worldliness led to the first major reform movement in the church, monasticism. The monks sought to live out the evangelical counsels of poverty, obedience, and chastity.

Because they pursued spiritual and contemplative lives in contrast to the clergy, who were often involved in the affairs of the state, they began to have an increasing amount of authority as the true spiritual leaders of the church. Eventually, the monks began to have an effect on the clergy by pushing them toward a more ascetic form of life. Gregory's election, as the first monastic pope, was a watershed moment for the monastic reformers who wanted a clergy more focused on humility and service than on ruling over people as imperial bureaucrats.

If some people today think that the church has become too much of a social-welfare agency, they should consider that the early church had a practical monopoly on social welfare in the Roman Empire. The emperors gave the church control over all charitable institutions. By the fifth century, the church in Antioch provided clothing, maintained hospitals and dispensaries, and fed three thousand people a day. This meant that major sees in the large cities were receiving and distributing immense amounts wealth.[5]

Since the church distributed imperial funds, the bishops were given new judicial and political powers to facilitate their role in the imperial system. For example, Christians could submit legal cases to bishops instead of to the civil courts in cases involving religious issues. Many people chose to do so because the ecclesial courts were usually much more humane than the civil ones; however, once people submitted to an ecclesial court, they forfeited any right to an appeal. Clerics were also granted the extraordinary privilege of being exempted from civil courts. The ordained were given their own, independent, legal system. In fact, these types of privileges continued to exist throughout the medieval period, and the exemption of clerics from civil law was one of the greatest sources of scandal leading to the Protestant Reformation.[6]

All these factors had an adverse effect on the clergy. In the fourth and fifth centuries, theologians in the East had begun to develop a theology of reform in response to the new types of men who were coming into clerical office. Gregory of Nazianzus and John Chrysostom had written works describing the nature of ecclesial office and the quality of those men who should be called to it. Dionysius the Areopagite had provided a model of the bishop as the one who is upliftingly stooped—a man who bends down to promote and to help others. Gregory the Great drew ideas from these Eastern sources for his own reform agenda, but he had to adapt them to a setting where there was no stable empire.[7]

Gregory found the task of being a bishop in this chaos so daunting that when the emperor's letter confirming his election reached Rome, he tried to gather his belongings and to flee the city before he could be ordained. As Gregory packed his bags, he must have wondered why the emperor had confirmed his election. Gregory had written the emperor, whom he had gotten to know during an assignment as the papal representative in Constantinople, asking him to withhold his consent from the election. If John the Deacon's account can be trusted, Gregory's brother intercepted the letter and substituted his own letter as city prefect announcing Gregory's election as unanimous. Unfortunately for Gregory, news traveled fast in ancient Rome. Before he could make good on his escape, the people of Rome intercepted him and carried him to the Basilica of St. Peter to be consecrated as the new pope.[8]

In the prefatory letter to the *Pastoral Care*, Gregory explained that he felt the burdens of pastoral care were onerous and he feared the far-reaching responsibility it entailed. To be sure, this claim was part of Gregory's rhetoric of reform warning people from rashly aspiring to the episcopal office, but it also reflects the heavy demands placed on the clergy in the West. Many of these problems were the result of the Emperor Justinian's reconquest of Italy from the Arian Ostrogoths, who had conquered Rome in the fifth century.

It took Justinian roughly twenty years to drive the Ostrogoths from Italy, but the destitute and broken territory hardly resembled the fertile and rich imperial center it had been. His Byzantine forces looted and pillaged their way through Italy as they pushed their enemies back. In the wake of their war, the soldiers also brought the plague and famine with them. Seeing weakness, another Germanic tribe called the Lombards started to invade Italy in 568 and remained a threat throughout Gregory's papacy. The constant warfare led to a cycle of famine and plague. At the end of Gregory's papacy, more than a third of the population of Italy had succumbed to the plague, and still more had died as a result of the wars and famines.[9]

However, these were not the only problems facing the Roman pontiff. Beyond responding to poor relief, care for the sick, and refugees, Gregory knew he would also have to handle a multitude of ecclesial abuses in Italy ranging from offenses such as people buying their ecclesial offices (simony) to the desecration of Jewish synagogues. Given the scope of the problems faced by the Roman See, it is no wonder that Gregory wished to avoid the responsibilities of holding the office.

Gregory's Plan of Attack

Once Gregory had resigned himself to answering the church's call, he had to devise a strategy for handling the crisis in Rome in particular and in the Western church in general. At the end of the sixth century, the papacy was an office with little jurisdictional power and a lot less authority than it had possessed in the past or than it would possess in the future. Since Gregory had been involved in both secular government, as the prefect of Rome, and ecclesial government, as the papal ambassador to Constantinople, he was aware of the limitations faced by the Roman See. He saw clearly the need to act decisively in response to the famine and plague gripping the city. Gregory was about to set new precedents in terms of papal and episcopal responsibilities to the poor and oppressed, which he would have to justify for the clerical establishment in Rome and in the other local churches under his patriarchal authority in the Latin West.

While Gregory was concerned with what we would call social justice, he also embarked on a broader program of reform. His agenda included institutional, spiritual, and theological aspects of reform. Of course, he knew he would have to defend his initiatives against opposition and persuade people to follow his lead. If true conversion is only brought about by the sweetness of preaching, then certainly true reform is also born from persuasive preaching; however, when it was necessary, he was willing to use his jurisdictional authority against dissenters.

The dissenters to Gregory's policies were his own clergy. These men had an interest in the ecclesial system continuing to operate as it had been operating. They had served their diocese and now they had expectations about how much power and privilege they deserved. This sense of entitlement, this clericalism, was contrary to both Gregory's understanding of the gospel message and to his own spiritual constitution. Evidence of opposition can be seen in the archdeacon Laurentius, a powerful figure in the clerical establishment, whom Gregory deposed from office in 591 for his pride.[10] Acknowledging the ability of the Roman clergy to stall and to subvert his initiatives, Gregory rapidly created a circle of reformers drawn from the monasteries to help him achieve his goals and to dilute the influence of an entrenched diocesan clergy.

Given the entrenched and institutional nature of his opposition, Gregory justified both his immediate initiatives and his long-term goals in scriptural and traditional terms around two concepts: the care of souls and the fear of God. Since the purpose or mission of the church is to save souls, he argued that pastors and clerics should recognize that they will be measured by the number of souls they save. By linking the mission of the church to the Final Judgment, he concurrently offered an apologetic or defense for his initiatives and a polemic or critique of his opponents.[11]

Gregory disappears behind this rhetoric in the sense that he is making the claim that he is not acting out of his own desires. Rather, he is compelled to act by the fear of God. "To fear God," according to Gregory, "is to omit nothing from the good that should be done."[12] Since he and the rest of the clerical establishment are going to be judged in terms of the number of souls they save, all of their efforts need to be aimed at this goal. Gregory used this logic to bring the problems associated with clericalism to light. When bishops and the rest of the clergy forget that they are "worthless servants," they begin to neglect the good things they should be doing. Of course, when the church's leaders forget their role as servants, they set a bad example for the people as well. Gregory believed that it is the tendency to move away from humility that requires ongoing ecclesial reform.

Ecclesial Reform

Gregory saw the church as a collective individual or person. As Bernard McGinn notes in his history of mysticism, God speaks at once to both the individual soul and the whole church through the scriptures in Gregory's theology. Gregory's vision of the church as an individual is integrally tied to his reform rhetoric. Such an idea was hardly new. The New Testament refers to the church in a series of analogies to the individual person such as the bride, the mother, and the body of Christ. Seeing the church as a person, whether you mean a local church in particular or the entirety of the pilgrim church, was a well-established theological tradition by Gregory's time. The question Gregory had to answer was: "What kind of person is the church?"[13]

The opponents to reform frequently wrap themselves up in the language of perfection. Their answer to the question is that the church is the spotless bride of Christ or the sinless body of Christ. If there are problems, antireformers locate those problems strictly with individuals instead of being rooted in ecclesial institutions, disciplines, policies, or magisterial teachings coming from the bishops. Those who hold to this ecclesiology insist that change for the church can only be a movement toward imperfection. Gregory attacked such triumphalistic ideas about the church because they lead to self-satisfaction, which is anti-thetical to the path of penance that he believed the church must fol-low. It is not that Gregory had a pessimistic or cynical outlook on the church; instead, he firmly held that each day the sun of truth shines more clearly and that our understanding of God's self-revelation would increase with the passage of time.[14]

Gregory employed the exegetical tradition of interpreting multi-ple senses of scripture to explain how the church could be in need of reform. This tradition was grounded in the writings of John Cassian, who had described how the multiple senses of scripture could be applied to Jerusalem in an example that was already a classic formu-lation by the time of Gregory:

> And if we wish it, these four modes of representation flow into a unity so that the one Jerusalem can be understood in four different ways, in the historical sense as the city of the Jews, in allegory as the church of Christ, in anagogy as the heavenly city of God "which is the mother of us all" (Galatians 4:26), in the tropological sense as the human soul which, under this name, is frequently criticized or blamed by the Lord.

Gregory basically accepts this schema, though he slightly modifies it by collapsing anagogy into allegory. There are significant conse-quences to interpreting Jerusalem as a symbol of the church. If God addresses the church as a whole through these scriptural symbols, then God addresses the church in the way he addressed Jerusalem: as a spouse, as a whore, and as a mother.[15]

Reformers like Gregory interpreted those passages of scripture calling Jerusalem or Israel to convert and to turn away from evil as directly addressing the church's contemporary faults. One of Gregory's most significant symbols for the church was Job. Job can represent Christ or the church when he is interpreted through the allegorical sense. Gregory was simply echoing one of Augustine's exegetical rules. Some symbols apply to both Christ and the church, so Augustine argued it was important to learn what applies to the head and what to the body. Statements that indicate sin or imperfection should be inter-preted as applying to the body, which Augustine described as the "true and mixed body of the Lord." When Augustine considered the symbol of the spotless bride, he said that this refers either to the perfected church in the eschatological age or to God's eternal decision to save people through it. Following Augustine's admonition that Christians should have a "wide-awake understanding *(intellectorum vigilantem requirit)*" of the nature of the church, Gregory used the figure of Job to provoke people to take a critical and discerning look at what the church was doing.[16]

When Job is described as fearing God and as withdrawing from evil, Gregory interprets this as referring to the church. The church enters the path to righteousness in fear and is consummated in love. Here we can see how the salvation of the church as a whole and the salvation of the individual reflect each other in Gregory's theology. Both begin in fear over faults. Both withdraw from those faults by a firm intention of the will and by right thinking. Gregory went further and said that the church sins when it acts out of fear instead of love. This is true even when the church does some good deed out of fear, because it would continue to sin if it could do so with impunity.[17]

Worse, there are also those who claim to hold to the faith, but whose deeds deny it. These people are of two types: those who are wicked and those who do good deeds because they desire praise. Gregory described these people as members of the pilgrim church, but they truly belong to a different body—the body of the Antichrist. The first group believes they can be saved without works, but their manner of life destroys the faith they confess. Gregory presented Christ's admonition to the group seeking human praise, "Amen, I say to you they have already received their award." When Job is described as covered with wounds and oozing puss, Gregory said this shows how the church is wounded by its evil and tepid members. The puss represents the sins of the body, which are being painfully expelled. Gregory described this suffering with sin and evil as part of the ongoing passion of the mystical body of Christ.[18]

Gregory's use of imagery is graphic, but in this image the church is healing its wounds. This process of healing, symbolized by the excretion of puss, is not attractive; nevertheless, it leads to the restoration of health. He urged people not to be scandalized by the visible condition of the church, writing, "That there are many in the church who are bad and few who are good should not frighten you." Christians should imitate the saints and heroes of the faith such as Job or Ezekiel, who "did not refuse to bear with the bad." Actually,

Gregory believed that the effort to be patient with wicked people in the church was part of the process of honing the sword of our souls. As we shall see, patience becomes one of the distinguishing characteristics in discerning between the reformer and the schismatic.[19]

Of course, the most scandalous and deleterious examples of wickedness come from the clergy themselves. Given the behavior of the ecclesiastical leadership in the late sixth century, Gregory was worried about the consequences of triumphalistic ecclesiology for the church's credibility. Because the church was obviously flawed in many regards, Gregory thought claims to the church's perfection necessarily lead people to heresy and schism. If people believe the true church is the perfect church, then they become incapable of recognizing the wounded church, which takes the evils of the world into itself as the means to its own purification. In this way, they recapitulate or reenact the sin of those who rejected the divinity of Christ because of the scandal of the cross.[20]

Gregory provided a solid justification for reforming the church itself. The church is not perfect, though we have faith that it will be perfected. Gregory warned his people and subsequent reformers that the church contains another body, the cancerous body of the Antichrist. This reality means Christians have a duty to themselves and their neighbors to be vigilant and discerning when it comes to the church. At the same time, the only appropriate response to the wounded church is to work to heal it. Why did Gregory feel the need to warn the faithful about evil pastors and ecclesial leaders? The best way to answer this question is to begin with Gregory's use of his papal office to reform his own diocese and the dioceses under his jurisdiction as a metropolitan bishop.

Administrative Reform

Gregory crafted a theological critique of clericalism and triumphalism, but he was also actively engaged in the concrete work of reforming ecclesial institutions and leaders as well. Given the social and political chaos in Italy at the time, it is not surprising that Gregory had many problems with breaches of canon law and ecclesiastical discipline. While he urged people to have patience with the wounded church, he did not believe that the church should tolerate men who abused their ecclesial offices. The problems in the church were so extensive that Gregory organized the papal agents, the *defensores*, into a new institution with formal rights and privileges so that they could effectively investigate clerical abuses.[21]

As a metropolitan bishop, Gregory was required by canon law to call the clergy for all of the dioceses under his jurisdiction together twice a year. At this convocation, the metropolitan bishop would hear charges against clergy, including bishops. The metropolitan had the power to either depose the bishop or to sentence him to a period of penance in the monastery. Gregory firmly held that men who had been deposed for serious misconduct should never be restored to their pastoral office because it would subvert the church's discipline and harm the spiritual health of the faithful.[22]

The state of the clergy throughout Italy was truly scandalous for the faithful. Gregory deposed six bishops during his papacy. While we do not know the details, at least two of the bishops were deposed for their embezzlement of either church or state funds. One was deposed for unspecified crimes deserving of the death penalty. Bishop Andreas of Tarentum, who died before Gregory could depose him, openly kept concubines and even murdered a woman who was on the church's charity rolls in a fit of rage. In Campania, the bishops were using their offices to enrich themselves rather than caring for their clergy and protecting the oppressed and the poor. The lower clergy were also involved in scandalous behavior such as usury, simony, violence, homosexual acts, neglect of duties, and so on. Still, there was little Gregory could do to enforce discipline on bishops or other members of the clergy who were outside his jurisdiction as a metropolitan.[23]

There are several cases when Gregory involved himself as pope in the problems of dioceses outside his jurisdiction, but Gregory largely had to rely on his ability to persuade the bishops in these dioceses to reform their behavior. Hearing about simony in France, Gregory enjoined the bishops to recognize the canons of the church and Jesus' own words in Matthew 10:8: "You have received freely, freely give." If the bishops in France had refused, Gregory would have had little recourse to do anything about it. Though he could excommunicate bishops who flagrantly violated the church's canon law, he could not remove them from office. The pope's power over such situations was as the court of last resort. The papacy functioned as a type of ecclesial supreme court, hearing and adjudicating cases, handling disputed elections, and confirming ecclesial ordinations; but the popes did not have the executive or legislative power to intervene in the affairs of dioceses outside of their own metropolitan jurisdiction. A good example of this problem is the case of Archbishop Januarius of Sardinia.[24]

Gregory struggled throughout his papacy to reform Archbishop Januarius's diocese. As an archbishop in the late sixth century, Januarius had a great deal of independence from any ecclesial oversight. Januarius's own clergy had complained about his behavior, which is probably how Gregory came to be involved. One of the sources of discontent with Januarius was his lax enforcement of clerical celibacy and chastity. His archdeacon lived openly with women and he sold dispensations for clerical marriage. Lapsed clerics were celebrating the Mass. Perhaps the most offensive aspect of Januarius's leadership to his clergy was that he allowed the imperial authorities to extort money from the churches.

The complaints about Januarius were not only coming from his clergy. Gregory received complaints from the Jewish community in Sardinia because the Christians had desecrated and looted their synagogue. Monks complained that Januarius was allowing his clergy to plunder the monasteries. The laity charged Januarius with using a band of thugs to violently and illegally seize property. Gregory sent various missions to Sardinia and established a bureau in Rome with the sole purpose of investigating misdeeds in the diocese. Though Gregory had the legal authority to adjudicate these cases, he had no ability to remove Januarius from office.

Recognizing the difficulty of reining in bad bishops who held key sees, Gregory made every effort to ensure that the best men were ordained as bishops. Bishops were elected at this time by both the people and the clergy; however, we should not fall into the trap of seeing this as being equivalent to a more egalitarian church. Jeffrey Richards explains, "The actual electorate consisted of clergy, nobles (ordo) and people, but in general the chief clergy and the local nobles fixed matters among them." Since most of the higher clergy were also drawn from the nobility, this allowed for elections that served the interests of the nobility over the common good. Given his experience in both secular and ecclesiastical politics, Gregory was deeply aware of this problem.[25]

Gregory heavily involved himself and his administration in reforming the church by working to promote candidates who were suitable for the office. He often suggested his own candidates drawn from the reform-minded monasteries for vacant sees; or he threw his support behind local candidates whom he believed had the skills and integrity a bishop needs. As pope, he could also veto the election of a candidate on canonical grounds and he could decide tied elections. Gregory diligently sent his officials to investigate whether or not the men elected met the canonical requirements before ordaining them. Progress was somewhat slow; but, by all accounts, he was successful in restoring good episcopal leadership in many dioceses during his papacy. In addition to correcting the unjust behavior of the clergy, Gregory also sought to respond to the broader problems of oppression and abuse in his society.

Social Justice

All the seeds of the social-justice movement can be found in Gregory's theology. Nonetheless, Gregory was a man of his times who basically accepted the existence of unjust rulers, the institution of slavery, and inequality between the sexes as part of the everyday reality of his world. Still, he did not believe that this state of affairs was permanent or even desirable, because in the fully realized kingdom of God these evils will be wiped away forever. Reform in terms of social justice is largely a development of the nineteenth and twentieth centuries, so it may seem a bit anachronistic to talk about Gregory using these categories. When we think of a social-justice reformer, we tend to imagine someone who organizes people to reform oppressive social structures. Three great examples of this type of reform from the twentieth century are the suffrage, labor, and civil rights movements. Even when people recognize social-justice reform as a modern development or category, however, they must also recognize that it did not spring ex nihilo into the Catholic theological tradition.

In his *Homilies on Ezekiel*, Gregory listed the requirements for the active Christian life: to feed the hungry, to teach the word of wisdom, to correct people who are doing evil, to call proud people to humility, to care for the sick, to provide for the needs of all, and to ensure that everyone under Christian care or supervision has the means of subsistence. These requirements are not just for the clergy. The *vita activa*, the active life, is given both to the laity and the clergy. Of course for Gregory, the clergy would do well to remember they will be held to a higher standard on the Day of Judgment. "Since we have undertaken, however undeserving, a place of leadership," Gregory wrote to his deacon Honoratus, "it is our duty to help our people in need, so far as our power extends."[26]

Living the active Christian life makes both universal demands, such as providing for the needs of all, and local demands, such as ensuring the means of subsistence to those people for whom Christians are responsible—whether they are neighbors, employees, parishioners, children, or spouses. Unlike the social activism aimed at the very structures of society, which is how social justice manifested itself in the nineteenth and twentieth centuries, Gregory's aim was to get individuals in society to act justly by fulfilling the duties of the *vita activa*. The idea of changing imperial social structures was not part of his worldview because he shared the essentially eschatological orientation toward the kingdom of God held by the Christian community in the early church. The early and medieval church understood Christ's claim in John 18:36 that his kingdom was not of this world as an indication of the inevitable corruption of earthly kingdoms and societies. Gregory's concern was to call all Christians to be witnesses to the peace and justice of the eschatological kingdom.

Using Matthew's description of John the Baptist as a model for witnessing to the kingdom of God, Gregory taught his people that calling for reform and conversion is certain to engender opposition. Jesus stresses the distinction between John the Baptist, who was not a man given to wearing soft garments, and those who inhabit the halls of the kings. Gregory preached that these words indicated that John, who wears a garment made of camel hair, was not like those who avoid suffering troublesome things for God's sake. These people in soft clothes "are not fighting for a heavenly kingdom but for an earthly one."[27]

Knowing that most people could not adopt John the Baptist's radical witnessing and martyrdom, Gregory explained that they should recognize their duty to proclaim the gospel message. "Do as much as you can," he warned, "lest you be tormented for having badly kept what you have received." He exhorted his audience to recognize that even if they were given only one talent, they should share that talent rather than hiding it. Stirring his audience to participate in the mission of Christian witnessing, Gregory proclaimed, "You who are in God's tabernacle, in his holy church, if you cannot fill bowls with the wisdom of your teaching, give your neighbors ladles filled with a good word, as much as you have from the divine bounty." Thus everyone in the church has something to offer in terms of making the world more just.[28]

As a result of receiving the word of heavenly love in their hearts, Gregory insisted Christians have a duty, flowing from love, to encourage their neighbors in pursuing holiness and to discourage them from doing evil. In order to get people to act on this principle, he knew he would have to teach by example as well as by speech. So Gregory threw himself into the work of addressing the needs of the poor, the sick, and the disenfranchised. As the first pope to organize charitable operations, he left us an impressive record of his efforts to fulfill the duties of the *vita activa*. In addition to the free grain he distributed to the hungry, he reduced rent for the poor, subsidized refugee nuns, forgave debts to the church for those who would be bankrupted by paying them, and sent aid to other dioceses where people were suffering from famine. All of these initiatives burdened papal finances and engendered resistance from his clergy.[29]

Gregory had to justify why he was so involved in the "worldly" concerns of providing for people's physical needs to the diocesan clergy in the Latin West. In his *Pastoral Care*, he explained why it is necessary to provide aid to those who need food, clothing, and shelter:

> Some, on the contrary, undertake the charge of the flock, but wish to be so free for spiritual occupations, as not to give any time at all to external matters. Now, when such people wholly neglect to attend to what pertains to the body, they afford no help to their subjects. It is no wonder that their preaching is disregarded for the most part, for while chiding the deeds of sinners, and not giving them the necessities of this present life, their words certainly do not find sympathetic listeners.

He goes on to lay down this general principle: "Let pastors, then, give their entire devotion to the inner life of their subjects, yet not neglect to provide for the exterior life also." If a pastor has the material means or wealth to provide for the physical needs of his people, Gregory argued he must use that wealth to further the mission of saving souls by meeting those needs.[30]

Apparently, a great deal of wealth had been stored up by Gregory's predecessors, which he quickly began to disburse. He used the wealth as a source to fund relief efforts and to ransom hostages from the invading Lombards. Moreover, he used papal funds to provide the blind with beans and wine, of which no true Roman should be deprived. Gregory went so far as to return gifts when he felt that the Roman church was benefiting at the expense of others.[31]

As a witness to peace and justice, Gregory had to oppose violence and oppression. He interpreted the various forms of injustice and inequality he faced as occasions for him to choose to behave virtuously and to imitate Christ's steadfast opposition to evil. Gregory believed Christians had to be willing to resist evil to the point of their own deaths. Because the mission of the church is to save sinners, whether they are powerful or oppressed, rich or poor, free or subjugated, the perpetrators of injustice needed to be warned of the severity of the coming judgment as well. In fact, the rich and powerful are the ones who need the most help and instruction because their material blessings entail a duty to act responsibly, which they frequently either fail to recognize or fulfill. If the Christian could get the civil ruler, rich person, or slave owner to reform his or her behavior in light of the gospel, then the society would be more just.

One of the most important principles Gregory established was that the clergy had an obligation to involve themselves in politics insofar "as the necessity of defending the poor compels them." It would take generations of people lifting up this principle to bring this idea to at least a partial fruition in the nineteenth and twentieth centuries. Though he was not an advocate of the church acting as a revolutionary force, he did believe the church should stand in opposition to unjust laws, decisions, and actions. Such opposition to the wrongful judgments or legislation of secular authorities is not, according to Gregory, acting against the laws; instead, it is working to support the legitimacy of the law itself.[32]

While it is true that Gregory tried to reform society by reforming individuals rather than social structures, he believed the community bears responsibility for the sinful actions of its members and leaders. When he found out that the emperor Maurice was unfairly supporting the extortion of property from the people who lived on the islands off the coast of Italy, Gregory warned the empress Constantina that she, her sons, and the entire empire would be held responsible for these deeds. For Gregory, the ruler participates in the sins of those who act in his name and the entire people bear the sins of their rulers either by the oppression they suffer or by their tacit consent to injustice.[33]

For all of his success in raising the quality of life for the people, Gregory knew that this type of reform would only have power and life as long as the pope, bishops, and rulers remained committed to it. Law and policy are tools—not substitutes—for reformers. Tools are only useful if there is an active will to employ them. For a person to effectively use a tool, he or she needs to know how it is used and for what purpose. For example, if you apply sufficient force, a hammer will drive a screw into a wall, but the result is simply a damaged wall. Setting precedents, enforcing laws, and crafting administrative policies are one set of tools only available to those who hold high offices; but discernment, scripture and tradition, and rhetoric are accessible to everyone engaged in the work of restoring God's church. Gregory reached out to give people these tools and to teach them how to use them.

Discernment, Clericalism, and Ecclesial Authority

How is discernment related to ecclesial reform? Reform presupposes that someone has found the actions, teachings, or directives of an ecclesial authority to stand in need of reform. Reformers in the early church understood discernment as the means for measuring their institutional leaders and their teachings. Since discernment is rooted in the scriptures as one of the gifts of the Holy Spirit, it provided reformers with an ironclad justification for questioning their leaders. This notion of testing is consonant with the parable of the good shepherd, where Christ warns his followers to distinguish between his voice and the voices of thieves and hired hands (John 10:1–21).[34]

For the medieval church, the thieves and mercenaries were frequently seen as the scriptural symbols or types for bad clerics. The application of these types to ecclesial leaders was warranted by the pastoral epistles, which make it clear that it is every Christian's duty to distinguish between true and false teachers in the church. Gregory crafted his own justification for questioning ecclesial leaders from the materials he found in scripture concerning discernment.[35]

However, one must be careful not to confuse discernment with distrust. Discernment implies a critical openness that measures or tests what is being said or done. St. Paul tells us to test everything, but it would be absurd to interpret such a statement in terms of distrust.

Should we distrust scripture or Christ? A distrustful person does not discern because he or she has already made an assessment; therefore, the distrustful person is not open to hearing or receiving anything.

Gregory was concerned that bad bishops and pastors would lead people astray. He asked people to consider the implications of the prophet Hosea's words for their own lives: "Bad priests are a snare of ruin for my people" (Hosea 5:1; 9:8). Bad priests and bishops are called a "stumbling block of iniquity" (Ezekiel 44:12), he continued, because no one does more harm than the man who has the title of holiness though he is actually evil. Bad clerics either lead people to imitate their sins or cause people to fall away from the church. If the people have been armed with the sword of discernment, however, Gregory believed they could avoid being spiritually destroyed by bad pastors.[36]

In one of his early homilies, Gregory explained that in a discerning community these bad pastors are like the waters of baptism, which washes away the sins of the people and then flows down the drain into hell. Those who are discerning enter their heavenly reward purified by the work of even bad priests and bishops, in part by remaining steadfast as they see how priestly negligence is leading the clergy to perdition. In this situation, the bad clerics give an excellent illustration for the discerning Christian of what it means to "hasten to the torment of hell by their wicked lives."[37]

Gregory's works are suffused with points of discernment when it comes to the bishops, but there are three that were particularly important for reform movements aimed at the clergy. The three points can be framed in the form of the following questions: (1) Does the bishop exhibit purity of heart and exemplary conduct? (2) Does the bishop prefer the love and praise of the church to that of his Redeemer? (3) Does the bishop act like a servant or a lord? As we shall see, these three questions could be reduced to one: Is the bishop humble?

What does it mean for the bishop to have purity of heart and what should be considered exemplary conduct? Purity of heart can be described as moving beyond self-interest. Gregory says this is important for a bishop because the office requires him "not to seek anything for himself, but to regard the good of his neighbors as his own advantage." The ancient church held that the route to purity of heart is through self-denial or asceticism. They believed asceticism is the athletic training Christians need in order to win the race and take our crowns of glory (1 Corinthians 9:24–25)[38]

Purity of heart is more commonly expressed in terms of holiness today. In addition to self-denial, Gregory believed holiness requires meditating on the lives of the saints and taking time to contemplatively read scripture. Because these practices and disciplines are concrete actions that people can see, asceticism was seen as a sign of the probability of holiness. If the bishop trains himself through ascetic and contemplative disciplines, he will not make self-interested decisions based on favoritism or concerns over prosperity and adversity. Such decisions, whether they are for material gain or advancement, can be legitimately criticized and opposed by the people of the diocese.[39]

Concerns over adversity and prosperity flow into Gregory's second point of discernment, whether the bishop prefers the love of the church to the love of his Lord. Gregory wrote, "Often, indeed, incautious pastors, being afraid of losing human favor, fear to speak freely what is right, and, in the words of the Truth, do not exercise the zeal of shepherds, caring for the flock, but serve the role of mercenaries." He explained that such men are not shepherds; instead, "they are dumb dogs who do not bark (Isaiah 56:10)." These mercenaries do not stand up to defend their flocks from worldly and oppressive powers.[40]

Gregory describes this type of bishop or pastor as an adulterous servant of the bridegroom who wishes to take the bride as a spouse for himself. Because they fall into self-love or narcissism, they fail to correct the people who are important to them. One clear indication the bishop suffers from this form of rebellion is how he treats people whom he believes are powerless to act against him. Gregory wrote, "Indeed, persons who in their estimation can do nothing against them, they constantly hound with bitter and harsh reproof. They never admonish them gently, but, forgetful of pastoral meekness, terrify them in the exercise of their right to govern." He said these men love themselves more than they love God and, worse, they brag about their merciless actions against those they despise. "They have no thought for what they should do," Gregory continued, "but only for the power that is theirs. They do not fear the judgment to come."[41]

Bishops who act like this and want people to remain silent about their leadership are witnesses against themselves, for they wish to be loved more than the truth. A good bishop, according to Gregory, takes the free and sincere criticism of his people as respectful recognition of his humility. An evil bishop, on the other hand, reveals himself to be a rebel against God, who put him in office for the purpose of service instead of for tyranny.[42]

The third and final point of discernment, whether the bishop acts like a lord or a servant, is arguably the most significant of these measuring points. All bishops should avoid the trap of seeing the power of their rank in themselves; instead, Gregory said they should focus on the equality of their nature with those under their care. Bishops should find their joy in helping people, not in ruling over them. If a bishop focuses on his rank, Gregory said he would become conceited. This conceit will lead him to believe the praise of those who are under his authority rather than to inwardly judge himself. Gregory warned that such a bishop would eventually come to despise his people.[43]

Because of his ecclesiastical power, a bishop who falls into the trap of conceit, Gregory argued, assumes he has more merit and wisdom than those without power. The consequences for such a pastor are, according to Gregory, quite severe:

> He thus brings himself to be the likeness of him about whom scripture says: "He beholds every high thing, and he is the king over all the children of pride." He who aspired to singular eminence and disdained life in common with the angels, said: "I will place my seat in the North, I will be like the Most High." By a wonderful decree, therefore, he finds within himself the pit of his downfall, while outwardly exalting himself on the pinnacle of power. A man is made like the apostate angel when he disdains, though a man, to be like other people.

In other words, the bishop who acts like a lord is a reflection of Satan and cannot therefore be considered a true hierarch, though he can still validly perform the sacraments. To follow such a bishop's example leads to damnation. Gregory charged such bishops with ignoring Christ's command: "Whosoever will be the greater among you, let him be your minister; and he that will be first among you shall be your servant. Just as the son of man did not come to be ministered to, but to minister" (Matthew 20:25–28).[44]

Gregory firmly grounded Christian and ecclesiastical authority on service. This rhetoric proved to be a powerful tool in the hands of reformers. In the following chapters, we shall see that many bishops and popes who did not recognize their role as servants were confronted with the charge of being the ministers of Satan. Some of the reformers who employed this rhetoric and rationale were tremendously successful, like Jean Gerson, and others, like Jan Hus, found their agendas and themselves going up in flames. While Gregory taught people to be discerning when it came to the leadership of the church, he also instructed those who held "lesser" positions how to measure themselves when they felt it was necessary to admonish and correct their ecclesial "superiors."

The Apologetics and Polemics of Humility

There is a real ambivalence in Gregory's theology when it came to the question of someone who holds a subordinate position in the hierarchy correcting a superior. This is partially due to the fact that Gregory knew such behavior could be dangerous, but it is also because reformers who lack discernment fall into the same errors as the people they want to change. Like ecclesiastical leaders, those who hold lesser positions in the hierarchy, which includes the laity and the religious for Gregory, also make their progress through humility. Just as the authority of the bishops is based on humility, which is visibly manifested in service, the authority of the rest of the church rests upon the same foundation.[45]

Though Gregory was worried about opening the door to unending and unreasonable criticism of the bishops and clergy, he crafted a theological justification for people to admonish and to correct their ordained leaders. It is the humble Christian who has the authority to correct bishops. This may seem to be a counterintuitive claim because the opponents to reform generally charge reformers with a lack of humility. Gregory was aware of this problem and he explained how people who are humble could legitimately correct those who hold higher positions in his *Moralia*. Gregory gives the examples of Moses warning Pharaoh, Nathan accusing David, Elijah rebuking Ahab, Peter defying the priests and elders, Stephen chastising those who martyred him, and others to show that being humble does not mean being silent and passive. This willingness to criticize or admonish superiors is the result of true humility, which grows out of the fear of God.

People who are humble or who fear God do not fear those who are exalted with honors or who hold important offices in this life. Fear of God drives out all other fears and considerations that hold us in bondage to the opinions of people. Gregory wrote that humble people will not "spare the powers that are contrary to the truth, and those whom they see to be inflated with pride, they abase by the authority of the Holy Spirit." In other words, Gregory taught that the humble person, having stripped away his or her own pretensions, does not give credence to the pretensions of others. Nonetheless, he reminded people that while the saints and heroes of the faith did speak out against their superiors, they also demonstrated their merciful humility by their deeds. Gregory gave several examples of this, but perhaps the most significant example is the relationship between David and Saul.[46]

Gregory used the story of David and Saul to illustrate how the reformer can correct a superior. Saul had set out to kill David because he feared his popularity with the people; but when David had a clear opportunity to kill Saul, he refrained from doing so. Arguing that God had delivered Saul into his hands, David's men urged him to strike down the king. However, David simply cut off a piece of the king's mantle and told his men that he should not strike down the Lord's anointed one. He was struck with remorse for having come to the point where he needed to deface the mantle of the king. David then showed Saul the piece of his mantle and confronted him with his wickedness saying, "Since I cut off an end of your mantle and did not kill you, see and be convinced that I plan no harm and no rebellion. The Lord will judge between me and you, and the Lord will exact justice from you in my case." Saul responded, "You are in the right rather than I; you have treated me generously while I have done you harm." In the story, David balances his resistance to an unjust king with his mercy. Gregory explained that the way he found mercy for his enemies was through being pierced by compunction or penitential grief, which led his heart to "reflect on itself." David both admonishes and corrects Saul, but he leaves the judgment of Saul to God alone.[47]

David's display of humility, his demonstration that he was not a rebel, was a sign of authority that even his enemy was forced to recognize. Gregory believed such a display of humility was essential for Christian reformers. People who lack humility are not reformers; instead, they are dissenters, schismatics, or heretics. Those who wish to correct the evil deeds of others must begin by applying the principles of discernment to themselves. "For holy people do not speak freely out of pride, nor are they submissive out of fear," Gregory continued, "but whenever justice lifts them up to speak freely, remembering their own weakness preserves them in humility."[48]

The church is a type of school of humility for Gregory. It is by humility that we make progress toward salvation. Gregory describes a type of spiritual dynamic operative in the church whereby we are saved by those we despise. The incarnation of Jesus Christ, the Suffering Servant, sets the pattern. Gregory also saw this dynamic repeated throughout scripture. He loved to incorporate stories of those who were despised or seen as unimportant saving those who were important and even those who were, in fact, holy. Gregory prodded the faithful to acknowledge how God frequently uses wicked people in the church to teach them patience, fortitude, humility and hope.[49]

How do wicked or evil people help us learn these virtues? Gregory reminded people that virtues like patience or perseverance are only manifested through adversity. By proving from experience our inability to predict how anyone will be tomorrow based on his or her behavior today, God teaches us humility. Gregory explained, "One who comes after us may frequently pass us by through the swiftness of his [or her] good works; tomorrow we may with difficulty follow one today we appear ahead of." His example was St. Paul, who participated in the sin of those who stoned the first martyr, Stephen, and who became the Apostle to the Gentiles. For Gregory, it was clear God uses the evil members to teach us that we should not be presumptuous about either our status or the status of others in the church. Further, Gregory employed this idea of the mixed body to console his audience. How is such an idea consoling? It allows us to see that we may never despair about the salvation of a neighbor or family member, even if they are steeped in murderous sin like St. Paul, because we can never know the riches of divine mercy.[50]

False reformers forget that they do not know when God may lift someone up with his grace. They presume to usurp God's judgment and to condemn people themselves. Some who claim to be reformers are simply rebelling against the ascetic disciplines of self-denial so they can indulge themselves. They decide they are superior to or holier than the church and reject its decisions. In this way their only guide becomes their own self-interest. Others desire the love of the church over that of Christ. When this happens, they behave just like the unreformed bishop, but they play to a different constituency. In this case, the reformer has no patience for the weaknesses of opponents and overlooks the faults of supporters. Just as the bishop who lacks humility becomes diabolical, reformers who forget their equality with the people they are criticizing also tear apart unity.[51]

Gregory warns people not to allow their just criticisms of what is wrong to plunge them into the lower depths of themselves by pride. In other words, like the false bishop who locates his ecclesial rights and authority in his own person, the false reformer grounds his or her authority in self-righteousness. Gregory advised people to avoid becoming insolent and to refrain from striking their leaders with the sword of public disparagement and denunciation, though he did recognize that there are times when good Christians simply cannot refrain from speaking out against some excessively wicked act by a priest, bishop, or pope.[52]

As members of the hierarchy, the laity and the religious also have a duty to lift up and to promote sinners, even when those sinners are bishops or priests. Gregory firmly held that we are not called as Christians to strike people down while simultaneously maintaining that scandalous men must be removed from office absolutely and permanently. This may seem contradictory, but it is not. Removal from office is not equivalent to damnation. At the same time, forgiveness of sin is not equivalent to worthiness for office.

Gregory taught the medieval reformers that by struggling with these issues they would learn to balance mercy with the duty to oppose evil. The clergy, like the laity and the religious, must be treated with the medicine of sin, mournful humility; but, like the bishop, the lay or religious reformer must recognize that too much medicine at any given time can kill the patient as well. Gregory believed the Christian reformer must temper zeal with discernment if he or she wishes to heal rather than to destroy. "We cannot help the fallen to stand," Gregory declared to his monastic brothers, "if we are not first willing to bend down from our rigid height."[53]

The apologetics and polemics of humility are a double-edged sword. They provide a justification for people to reform an imperfect church. At the same time, they justify the existence of an imperfect church. Bishops and priests who lack humility certainly need to be reformed, and reformers who lack humility need to repent from their presumption. Gregory urged everyone to recognize that the people they despise are the very people God will use to save them. This is the way we, as human beings, come to learn humility. Since he believed that the goal of a hierarchy is to imitate God by reaching down to promote the lowest members, he concluded that the task of reforming the clergy must be guided by love and must be understood in terms of saving people.[54]

This idea of hierarchy was already traditional, but Gregory used the concept of hierarchy to attack the growing problems associated with clericalism. Though a cleric can hold a high office, if he lacks a sense of humility and charity, he actually holds the lowest place in the church. Gregory wrote:

> So, then, in the case of humanity there are some who, though of higher rank, are inferior, and others who are in a lower estate, are better, because the latter by their good way of life transcend the character of the lower estate, while the former fall short of the merit of their higher estate by not living up to it.

In a homily that was probably delivered to the bishops, Gregory applied this idea to them, writing, "I think that God suffers greater outrage from no one, dearly beloved, than from bishops. Those he has placed to correct others he sees giving an example of wickedness in their own lives." Such bishops hold both the highest office and the lowest spiritual state in their diocese. When this happens, it is clear those who hold lesser institutional positions, but who have been given greater personal holiness through the gifts of the Spirit, should try to correct the bishop.[55]

Gregory used the distinction between office and person to open up the possibility for the laity and the religious to reform their ecclesiastical leaders. The office of the bishop must be respected as a part of Christ's sacramental dispensation to his church; but as a person, a bishop has no automatic claim to superior holiness, knowledge, or wisdom. The duties of a bishop's or pastor's office, however, demand that he strives to be an example of holiness. When a bishop fails to strive for holiness, he fails to fulfill the duties of his office. At this point, it becomes the duty of those who have been subjected to the "stench of their wickedness" to warn their bishop of his spiritual peril.[56]

Gregory's Legacy

Gregory established the basic framework for reform in the church. His institutional and administrative reforms set precedents that would eventually find their way into canon law. As we shall see in the next chapter, his papal register became a primary source for the reforms of Pope Gregory VII in the eleventh century. A cursory reading of Gratian's *Decretals* reveals the profound impact Gregory the Great had on the development of canon law. Over the centuries, social reformers, humanists, and popes would draw upon Gregory's portrayal of the *vita activa* as necessarily entailing a duty to feed the poor, to educate people, to provide for the needs of all, and to oppose injustice in order to ground their own initiatives in the church's theological tradition. Most importantly, Gregory provided a theological rationale for reform itself.

By pointing out the imperfections and even sinfulness of the church, Gregory provided later reformers with a theological justification for their critiques. Given his status as a pope, as a saint, and as a doctor of the church, Gregory's theological authority lent strong support to subsequent reform movements. His polemics against the growing problem of clericalism gave people categories they needed to respond to those bishops who wished to transform their magisterial office into an imperial one. He not only taught Christians they could question the actions and teachings of their ecclesial leaders, but he also urged Christians to see that it is their responsibility to be discerning. When the clergy become rebellious, he charged the laity and the religious with the duty to admonish and to correct them.

While admonishment and exhortation can be bitter, Gregory insisted reform must be governed by merciful humility. Everyone in the church must remember that the goal of the church is to save souls—not to condemn them. For Gregory, reforming the church is essentially the task of calling individuals and groups to follow the example of Christ and the saints by their humble service. He clearly articulated a principle that became central to Catholic reformers: Christian authority rises out of service to others. In this way, he taught reformers to be discerning when it came to their own motivations. Borrowing from traditional theologians like Augustine and John Cassian, Gregory developed what can be called a spirituality of reform that balances the need to reform with the need to maintain the unity of faith, which he called the bond of love.[57]

The essential virtue for maintaining unity, according to Gregory, is patience. Impatience with the imperfections and sinfulness of the church is the source of presumption, heresy, and schism. Impatience agitates the mind so that it does not know what it is doing, which later leads to regret when the mind is calm; and it is counterproductive for reformers because it overthrows the good things they are trying to accomplish. Since charity or love is patient (1 Cor 13:4), Gregory concludes the lack of patience shows that people lack love. Thus they reveal their ignorance about themselves and about the way to salvation.[58]

In order to teach others the meaning of the faith, it is necessary to know how to bear the evils of others with equanimity. Gregory believed that the church provides us with opportunities to learn how to bear with the evils of others as it moves us toward salvation. Like Christ, the pilgrim church bears the evils of the world even as it works to purify them. This is the way the church and its members come to holiness. Gregory insisted that people should not expect to bring the church to perfection, because the reality is that the church brings us to perfection by stirring us to reform ourselves, our communities, our leaders, and our world.

The imperfect and wounded nature of the pilgrim church is not, for Gregory, a sign that the Holy Spirit has lost his way guiding the church toward sanctification. Nor did he believe it was the role of the reformer to separate the wheat from the chaff or the sheep from the goats. Only the Son of Man has this right. Though he believed it is always the time for renewal and reform, he recognized that the process shall be completed only at the time set by the will of the Father. The only pious or appropriate response to the wounded body is to work to heal it.

Of course, Gregory knew all too well that the church does not always appreciate the bitter medicine of humility. He anticipated that his own clergy would undermine many of his efforts when he died, so he armed reformers with the rhetoric and theology they needed to defend themselves against a patient who frequently lashes out from pain at those who are trying to help. Though his own clergy were successful in suppressing his writings in Rome immediately after his death, he had disseminated his works beyond their reach. Largely due to the influence of the Irish and Spanish clergy and missionaries,

Gregory's ideas gradually spread throughout Christian Europe. By the ninth century, Charlemagne had made the study of Gregory's *Pastoral Care* obligatory for all the bishops in his empire. Like most of the reformers we are studying, Gregory only saw partial successes in his own lifetime, but the seeds he planted by his efforts bore fruit that sustained and consoled those who followed him down the straight and narrow path of Catholic Reform.

2

Peter Damian: The Doctor of Reform

St. Peter Damian (1007–1072) has been officially designated the doctor of reform by the Roman Catholic Church, but he could just as easily have been the doctor of discipline. His interest in discipline extended from the life of the individual believer to the enforcement of ecclesiastical laws. The primary problems he faced included the buying and selling of ecclesiastical offices, clerical sexuality, and the lack of order in the collections of canon law. Without any uniform standards of canon law, the bishops were able to rule their dioceses absolutely as they personally saw fit.[1] Because they tended to treat the church as their own property, many of the bishops were not doing a very good job of maintaining ecclesiastical discipline. Since the vast majority of them had bought their offices, it is not surprising that they would see the church as a form of investment.

The idea of the church as a community had almost disappeared in the eleventh century.[2] One of the key goals of the reformers was to root out simony and to recover a more communal understanding of the church. Whereas prohibitions against simony were recognized to carry the force of tradition, the reformers were attempting to move people away from local customs. Additionally, they had to contend with the traditional status of the secular laws stemming from the proprietary church system established by Charlemagne and his heirs. Under this system, ecclesiastical positions were related to benefices associated with particular churches, dioceses, and abbeys. These benefices provided income to support the work of the monks and the clergy as well as resources for poor relief, but it was often the local nobility who held the right to install someone into a benefice. What had started as a means to provide income to the clergy had gradually led people to see churches as buildings that could be either owned or leased in the same way as a mill or an orchard. The resulting sense of entitlement, both on the part of the laity who held the rights to the benefices and the men installed into these positions, opened the door for more serious abuses.

The most serious of these abuses had to do with clerical sexuality. Like simony, the ecclesiastical laws calling for clerical celibacy had been well established in the Western church for centuries. Nonetheless, most of the clergy in Europe had concubines. This state of affairs was possible because the culture assigned no value to the idea of male virginity, and concubinage was an accepted institution in society.[3] Of course, concubines did not have the rights and protections granted to married women, which meant they were totally at the mercy of their clerical patrons. Both Roman law and Germanic custom favored personal property for women and in many places it was customary for a wife to have control over her dowry and inheritance. In a society that had no status or protections for landless and unmarried women, the imbalance of power between the clerics and their mistresses led to much abuse; but most of the people who objected to clerical concubinage were not concerned at all about the treatment of these women.

Most of the reformers were solely interested in the issue of ritual purity. The prohibitions against clerical marriage had originated out of concerns surrounding the purity of the priest or bishop, who was expected to abstain from sexual intercourse before performing his liturgical duties. Another concern was that many of these clerics had found ways to steal the communal property of the church in order to provide land for their illegitimate children. Even so, there was little discussion of the need to make the clergy personally more devout or to demand better pastoral care for the laity. Peter Damian's efforts against clerical concubinage shifted over time as he began to move beyond ritual concerns to seeing the inherent abuse of power involved in these relationships.

The worst problem with clerical sexuality was the large number of priests and bishops who were seducing or compelling boys and adolescents to perform acts of sodomy. This was true even though clerical concubinage was widespread, so the problem was neither the result of celibacy nor of homosexuality. Today, we would identify such behavior as child molestation. Certainly, there were also problems involving coerced and consensual sexual acts between adult clergymen as well, but many of these men also had mistresses. Since the term *homosexual* was the product of the modern science of psychology, we have to be careful not to use the term anachronistically. The medieval writers focus on acts rather than tendencies, desires, or identity issues when it comes to sexuality.

Peter Damian attacked all forms of sexual abuse committed by the clergy throughout his career, but he found the church unwilling to face the problem. His words of warning to Pope Nicholas II have an eerie resonance:

> Indeed, in our day the genuine custom of the Roman Church seems to be observed in this way, that regarding other practices of ecclesiastical discipline, a proper investigation is held; but a prudent silence is maintained concerning clerical sexuality for fear of insults from the laity. But this is something that badly needs correction, so that precisely what all the people are complaining about should not be hushed up in council by the leaders of the church…. Therefore, because of the ignominy involved, I do not see how something that is everywhere publicly discussed can be suppressed at the synod, so that not only the offenders be properly branded with infamy, but also those whose duty it is to punish them be found guilty.[4]

He goes on to say that when the law was enforced in these matters, it was not enforced impartially. "For we indeed punish the acts of impurity performed by priests in the minor ranks," he complained, "but with the bishops, we pay our reverence with silent tolerance, which is totally absurd."[5]

When the clergy failed to reform themselves, Peter Damian believed it was the duty of the laity to discipline the clergy. Although he was completely in step with the papal policy of his day, Deacon Hildebrand, who had been one of Peter's colleagues, would eventually work to erode the idea that the laity could or should take any initiative to reform the church. Hildebrand, who would become Pope Gregory VII, was primarily concerned about the attempts of the nobility to dominate the church and to use it for its own ends. Even so, Peter Damian's collaborative model of reform between the laity, religious, and clergy was widely read and distributed throughout the Middle Ages.

Like Gregory the Great, Peter Damian provided a standard by which later reformers could evaluate their clergy and a justification for the laity to punish either lax or immoral bishops. Peter applied the idea of reform in ways that Gregory the Great could not have imagined. Whereas Gregory's reform method aimed primarily at reforming individuals or local institutions, Peter Damian extended the idea of reform to the church as a whole in order to check the tyranny of undisciplined bishops. Further, he was also one of a handful of medieval theologians who supported the idea that the common people have a right to rebel against unjust rulers. As we shall see, Peter was a supporter of the principle that all leaders must be held more accountable before the law than their followers.

Peter and the Papal Reform Movement

The papal reform movement in the eleventh century grew out of a collaborative effort to reform the church by the laity, the monks, and the clergy. The goals of the movement were to root out the sins of simony, clerical concubinage, and other forms of clerical sexuality. In order to achieve these goals, the reformers sought to strengthen the papacy, which was the only institution in medieval Europe that could claim to have authority over the church as a whole. Such a central authority was necessary to check the power of the bishops and archbishops, who were generally opposed to reform because they benefited from the status quo. Even the papacy and the curia were deeply involved in the sin of simony.

Like so many reform movements, this one was only able to establish itself because the church had reached a crisis point. When Henry III went to Rome to be crowned emperor, he found three rival popes. He deposed all three and appointed his own candidate, which he could do because of political instability in Italy. The power vacuum allowed Henry to exercise control over events in Rome.

Henry cared deeply for the church. He and his father had been actively engaged in reforming the church within the empire. They had promoted the establishment of cathedral schools in Liège, Bamberg, and Magdeburg, which had become prominent centers of learning. Henry was so committed to reform that he only appointed as bishops men who had gone through these schools.[6] Because of his reputation for upholding the laws of the church, he was called the *Linea Iustice*, "the measure of righteousness."[7]

Henry's first pope was almost immediately assassinated. His next choice, another reform-minded bishop, was also poisoned. Henry's third appointment was Pope Leo IX, who was a relative with a reputation for fighting simony as the bishop of Toul. Immediately after his election, the new pope surrounded himself with a group of reformers whom he brought into the curia. It may have been a decision that saved his life. Many of these new cardinals were drawn from monasteries and dioceses outside Italy, which helped to promote the idea that the papacy was indeed an international institution.

Peter Damian was thrilled with these developments. With his fame as a preacher and crusader against simony and the sexual sins of clergy growing, Peter was swept into the service of the papal reform movement. He shared the goals of Leo IX to restore clergy to the apostolic life that was described in the Acts of the Apostles and in the prescriptions of canon law.

There were significant problems facing the reformers in terms of this strategy. First, there was no single authority in Europe that could enforce canon law. Second, there was not a consistent code of canon law. The collections that did exist, such as the one produced by Ivo of Chartres, often contained more examples of dispensations from the law than authoritative texts.[8] This reflected the attitude that the law was too demanding. People were in the habit of seeing dispensations from canon law as the normal course of action rather than as emergency measures aimed at some particular crisis. The third problem resulted from the apparent contradiction between canon law and the description of apostolic life found in the Acts of the Apostles. Whereas the Acts of the Apostles supported the canonical prohibitions against simony, they undermined the laws against clerical marriage.

The first task facing the reformers was to strengthen the papacy. They were helped by the fact that all the new collections of canon law contained the decisions of the contemporary popes, which reinforced the claim that the pope was the supreme legislator in the church.[9] Pope Leo IX and his immediate successors tried to turn the idea of a universally structured church, under the leadership of the papacy, into a reality. They worked on multiple fronts to convince people that the pope had universal jurisdiction over the church. For example, Leo IX began to hold synods outside Rome to reinforce this idea, and he sent papal legates to areas outside the Roman dioceses. With the support of the local secular authorities, these papal legates were able to appoint and depose bishops. In some cases, they were even able to divide or merge dioceses. Still, the papal legates had to persuade people that they had the jurisdictional authority to support these actions.

Peter Damian helped to formulate the rhetoric the reformers needed. He disarmed his opponents by admitting that the various rights, privileges, and ranks of the different sees had been established by the emperors and kings in the past. Nonetheless, he maintained that the authority of the Roman See was not dependent on the decisions of emperors for its authority:

> But only he who granted the blessed custodian of the keys to eternal life the powers of earthly and heavenly dominion founded the Roman Church and built it on the rock of faith that would soon emerge. It was no ordinary earthly utterance, but the Word by whom heaven and earth were made, and through whom the elements of all things were structured, who founded the Roman Church. Clearly, it enjoys his privilege and is supported by his authority.[10]

Peter concluded that the person who opposed the privileged position of the bishop of Rome was a heretic. However, this comment applies to the office and not the officeholder. In other words, a man who holds the office but fails to fulfill its duties or who misuses it can be legitimately opposed and even deposed. Of course, he had to maintain this position because the papal reform movement had begun with Henry III deposing three rival popes.

While this type of papal apologetics was convincing for some, two extraordinary events in Pope Leo IX's reign had more influence than any of these rhetorical arguments for papal primacy. Leo declared a ban on simony and clerical concubinage at his first synod in Rome. When the bishop of Sutri, who had been charged with simony, dropped dead before the assembly as he began to defend himself, people saw it as a divine confirmation of the new pope's policy. Shortly thereafter at a synod in Rheims, the bishop of Langres was struck mute, perhaps by a coronary stroke, as he tried to defend himself.[11]

Stories about miraculous events had more than a little authority in the eleventh century. The belief that these bishops were struck down by divine wrath for their opposition to canon law as it had been proclaimed by Pope Leo IX in his encyclical helped to elevate the authority of canon law, which was particularly important as the reformers worked to end clerical marriage and concubinage. Their arguments for demanding celibacy were almost exclusively based on the authority of canon law.

Though the papal reformers were actively changing the law themselves, they did not see the inherent problem with ascribing absolute authority to the disciplines and laws of the church. Because canon law is constantly changing throughout the history of the church, it cannot have absolute authority. The idea that canon law had equal authority to scripture or tradition would cause chaos in the latter part of the Middle Ages as people began to realize that many of the canons stemming from councils, synods, decretals, and papal bulls are irreconcilably contradictory.[12] Further, there was no way to settle which canons were the "correct" canons. Thus the position of the eleventh-century papal reformers on the authority of canon law would have to be reformed at the Council of Trent.[13]

The papal reformers were, however, wrestling with a more immediate problem. The movement stumbled and almost collapsed as it started out of the blocks over sacramental concerns. The question of the validity of simoniacal ordinations became a divisive point among the reformers. A group of rigorists, led by Cardinal Humbert, argued that these ordinations were invalid. At the Roman synod the Italian bishops warned Leo that such an interpretation would mean that the entire clergy of the Roman dioceses were invalidly ordained. Further, all their sacramental acts would have been invalid.[14]

The reformers broke into two camps, each led by men who either were or had been monks. Of course, the monks had been the primary reformers since the fifth century. Cardinal Humbert, who had been a monk, led the group that was primarily concerned with the issues of ritual purity. Their supporters publicized their ideas and were very active in attacking clerical simony and encouraging the laity to rise up against impure clerics. A second group of reformers, led by Peter Damian, argued that the ordinations were valid. Of course, Peter felt that the men who bought their offices should be removed from office if it was feasible, but he insisted their sacramental acts were valid. As we shall see, Peter formulated a response that settled the matter for all but the most extreme rigorists.

While the cardinals Peter Damian, Humbert, and Hildebrand have been described as the triumvirate behind the movement to reform the papacy, the lay triumvirate of Empress Agnes, Duchess Beatrice of Tuscany, and Duke Godfrey of Lorraine was just as important.[15] The election of Nicholas II by the cardinals could not have taken place without the political support of Agnes and the military support provided by Godfrey and Beatrice. With the aid of Godfrey's army, Pope Nicholas II was installed into his office on January 24, 1059.

Nicholas II called for a Lateran synod after his installation. The synod was attended by 113 bishops and its decrees were published by the pope in an encyclical letter titled *Vigilantia universalis*. The letter included measures against simony, clerical marriage and concubinage, and a decree on papal elections. The papal election decree was the most striking piece of new legislation because it justified the procedures followed in the election of Nicholas II, it secured the reformers' hold on the Roman Church, and it sought to ensure that papal elections were carried out according to the principles of canon law.[16] Certainly there were violations of this law following the papacy of Gregory VII, but it became the standard by which subsequent elections were judged. In fact, the way popes are elected today is based on this important institutional reform.

The measures against clerical sexuality and simony were less effective. There are several factors that undermined progress in these areas. First, the bishops were unwilling to publicly acknowledge the sexual behavior of their clergy because they were afraid of scandal. Further, many members of the clergy had little desire to oppose what had become customary, especially when it was a custom that made their lives easier. Finally, Pope Alexander II and Pope Gregory VII reversed the policies of their predecessors in regard to the laity. The popes became opposed to the nobility taking a leading role in reforming the church, which they feared would open the door for political leaders to dominate the clergy. In the end, this was a shortsighted strategy because the papacy did not have the means to enforce discipline on the dioceses outside the territory governed by Rome in central Italy.

Increasingly, Peter's influence and role in reforming the church were marginalized by Alexander II and Gregory VII. Still, Peter's theology was widely distributed through his letters. As the papal reform movement shifted away from collaborating with the laity, except when collaboration was defined in terms of obedience, Peter began to publicly defend the laity's involvement in reform. In his arguments against clerical sexual abuse and simony, he raised the principle that the clergy must be held accountable for their crimes. If the bishops would not enforce canon law, then they would become accomplices to the crimes of their priests. He urged the laity to act when the clergy failed to uphold the teachings of scripture, tradition, and canon law. We can see the development of this line of thought in Peter's attacks on what he calls spiritual incest.

Spiritual Incest

In 1049, Peter Damian wrote his first treatise concerning the problem of sexual abuse among the clergy and sent it to Pope Leo IX. Peter saw the problem as resulting from a lack of discipline in the church. He reminded Leo that the mission of the church was *cura animarum,* or the care of souls, and warned that laxity on the part of the bishops was leading people to destruction. Initially, Peter framed his attack on clerical sexuality in terms of ritual purity, canon law, and the abuse of power. While this first attempt to address the issues surrounding clerical sexuality concentrated on priests and bishops who were using the power of their offices to seduce or to rape boys and young men, he also highlighted the abuses of power associated with clerical concubinage.

According to Peter, the problem of homosexual acts among the clergy and with the laity was pervasive in the church of his day. "Unless immediate effort be exerted by the Apostolic See," he warned, "there is little doubt that even if one wished to curb this unbridled evil, he could not check the momentum of its progress."[17] Peter explained that boys and adolescents who entered into the lower ranks of the clergy found themselves "enslaved under the iron rule of Satanic tyranny *(diabolicae tyrannidis mancipari)*" because they were commanded or seduced into performing sexual acts such as masturbation, mutual masturbation, fornication of the thighs, and anal intercourse.[18]

While Peter admitted that there is a distinction between one who pleases himself and one who involves others in his sins, he complained that many of the bishops would only depose men who had committed acts of anal intercourse. His inclusion of masturbation in the discussion indicates that Peter was not concerned with homosexuality as we understand the term. While all four of the activities he listed were related to questions surrounding ritual purity in the eleventh century, Peter was not particularly concerned with a person's desires or tendencies.

Like many of his contemporaries, Peter did not believe that the sacramental or the ministerial acts performed by impure priests and bishops were valid when he first embarked on his career as a reformer. Thus he concluded that the failure to discipline men who fell into any kind of impurity, which could include nonsexual sins such as simony, was dragging entire communities into the depths of sin. Since such men are supposed to act as intercessors for their community, he argued they could not perform this duty effectively. Peter asked Pope Leo, "Therefore, if one is embarrassed to act as intercessor with a man with whom he is not at all acquainted, how can one dare to act as an intercessor for the people before God if, in view of his life, he knows that he is not on friendly terms with the grace of God?"[19]

Worse still, Peter was worried that God would not accept sacrifices from impure hands, which called into question the validity of the Masses performed by impure clerics.[20] While the eminent scholar of monasticism Jean LeClerq argued that Peter Damian never changed his theological doctrine, Peter did abandon this position.[21] He shifted his thinking in this regard as he became more familiar with both Augustine's and Gregory the Great's arguments with the Donatists. As we have seen, the Donatists had denied the validity of the sacramental acts performed by clergy who were involved in serious and public sins. When Peter Damian began to recognize the pastoral implications of such a position, he reformed his theology. In brief, he came to see that the people of God cannot be dependent on the personal morality or quality of their clerics because they cannot know such things with certainty, which would place an impossible burden on the members of the church.[22]

Peter shifted the argument away from sacramental concerns and toward the questions of church governance and discipline. By failing to maintain proper order through the use of discipline, Peter claimed the bishops were stimulating the growth of sexual abuse in the church. Because an erotic cleric is more afraid to be despised by men than to be judged by God, he argued that such men would do anything to avoid losing their clerical identities. When such a man knows he will not lose his status, Peter argued he would continue with his daringly illicit acts. Therefore, the bishops who had refused to depose erotic clerics, he concluded, were providing these men with opportunities to prey on the people under their authority.[23]

Why were the bishops behaving this way? Peter suggested that they were motivated by a shortage of men who were able to celebrate divine services, which he identified as perverse thinking. He argued that it was better to leave the ecclesiastical office empty than to install the wrong person into it. Peter asked the bishops to consider that even in recent history, there had been extended periods of time when the Apostolic See had been vacant until the right candidate could be installed. An unworthy man who is arrogant enough to presume a position of honor in the church, he explained, will not provide good pastoral care by following the commandments and by practicing the disciplines prescribed for clerics.[24]

The destructive plague of sexual abuse was raging throughout the church because of the lack of leadership. Peter offered the following admonition to the bishops of his day:

> Listen, you do-nothing superiors of clerics and priests. Listen, and even though you feel sure of yourselves, tremble at the thought that you are the partners in the guilt of others; those, I mean, who wink at the sins of their subjects that need correction and who by ill-considered silence allow them license to sin. Listen, I say, and be shrewd enough to understand that all of you alike "are deserving of death, that is, not only those who do such things, but also they who approve those who practice them" (Romans 1:32).[25]

He went on to explain that the bishops who did not correct their clergy were just as guilty as the priests who were seducing boys and adolescents. Even worse, Peter tells us there were bishops who were sexually abusing their own clergy as well. These men would either seduce or compel the priests under their jurisdiction to have sex. In order to avoid scandal, the bishops would then either confess to these poor men or have them confess to him, so that they would be bound by the seal of confession from revealing what had happened.[26]

Drawing on the spousal model for the relationship between the bishop and the church, Peter charged the bishops with spiritual incest. If the bishop is the husband and the church is the bride, then he argued that all who are reborn in the church could appropriately be called the bishop's children. In fact he was using this image as a way of talking about piety, which is based on an analogy to the relationship between parents and children.[27] Peter also extended this metaphor to anyone who had pastoral duties and authority over others in the church. Even godfathers who abused their relationships with their goddaughters in order to have sex with them were guilty of spiritual incest.[28]

Whereas an actual father who betrays his relationship of power and trust with his children by sexually molesting them was subject to excommunication and exile under the canon and civil laws, Peter argued the bishops who betrayed their spiritual children deserved a harsher punishment. His reason for the harsher sentence was that the betrayal involved in spiritual incest ran even deeper than familial incest. Even if the bishop never personally commits such a deed, Peter concluded he was still guilty of the crime of spiritual incest if he allowed his clergy to sexually abuse boys, young men, concubines, and even prostitutes.

Peter exhorted Pope Leo IX to enforce the canons of church law on the scandalous matter of priests seducing boys and young men. The law clearly prescribed the following penance:

> Any cleric or monk who seduces young men (*adolescentium*) or boys (*parvulorum*), or who is apprehended in kissing or in any shameful situation, shall be publicly flogged and shall lose his clerical tonsure. Thus shorn, he shall be disgraced by spitting into his face, bound in iron chains, wasted by six months of close confinement, and for three days each week put on barley bread given him toward evening. Following this period, he shall spend a further six months living in a small segregated courtyard in the custody of a spiritual elder, kept busy with manual labor and prayer, subjected to vigils and prayers, forced to walk at all times in the company of two spiritual brothers, never again allowed to associate with young men for purposes of improper conversation or advice.[29]

In other words, such men were supposed to be confined to monasteries where they could be supervised for the rest of their lives. Since these sins require such a degrading, public penance, Peter argued they were grounds for deposing men from holy orders because canon law forbade men who had to perform public penance from assuming ecclesiastical offices.[30]

Pope Leo IX was not moved by Peter's arguments. Leo informed Peter he did not believe clerics who had seduced boys and young men to commit acts of mutual masturbation and other sexual acts should be automatically deposed. In the name of acting humanely, Leo said that these men could retain their offices as long as they had not engaged in such behavior for long periods of time or with many people. The pope did concede, however, that any cleric who had anal intercourse should be deposed.[31]

As far as Peter was concerned any sexual act on the part of a clergyman with others, including contractual sex with prostitutes, was a form of sexual abuse that demonstrated the offender was not fit for holding a priestly office. This was true because of the imbalance of power and social standing between the participants; but Peter was more concerned about the spiritual impact it had on their victims, who were being seduced into mortal sin. Of course, he knew that he could not hope to raise these other issues with the pope and the bishops if they were unwilling to act against clerics who were essentially raping boys. So Peter continued to work for reform in other areas and waited until he had a more sympathetic ear in Rome to raise the sexual-abuse issue again.

In 1059, after Peter had become a cardinal bishop, he returned to the issue again and vented his frustration at a man whom he had helped to become pope. Writing to Pope Nicholas II, he made the following promise to the bishops who had either participated in the sexual abuse of anyone or who had allowed it to occur in their jurisdiction:

> The day will come, and that certainly, or rather the night, when this impurity of yours will be turned into pitch on which the everlasting fire will feed, never to be extinguished in your very being; and with never-ending flames this fire will devour you, flesh and bones.[32]

Then he shifted his attention to Pope Nicholas II and admonished him to remember that he would be subject to divine punishment for his inertia in the face of this evil if he failed to discipline his subjects, the bishops.[33]

Even when the laws concerning clerical sexuality were being enforced, Peter complained they were not being applied impartially. Those who held the higher offices of bishop and archbishop were able to escape punishment and even criticism for their crimes. Peter argued this way of enforcing the church's discipline stood proper order on its head. The pope and the archbishops should imitate the way the Lord himself imposes discipline on his people. He appealed to the examples of two Old Testament priests, Phinehas and Eli, to show proper discipline and to illustrate the consequences of laxity.

Peter said Phinehas represented how the metropolitans should act in enforcing the laws of the church and Eli represented how the metropolitan bishops were acting. Phinehas was a priest who found one of the most prominent Israelite chiefs having sex with a Midianite princess, which was forbidden. As Peter told the story, Phinehas seized a spear and transfixed the pair through their genitals before all the people. Though many of the Israelite men were having sex with women in the worship of Baal, Peter explained that Phinehas only struck down the most prominent and socially elite offenders. This action demonstrated to the rest of the people that the laws would be enforced. Certainly, it cooled their ardor.[34]

From this example, Peter formulated the principle that the sins of more highly placed people must be more vigorously prosecuted than those of the anonymous and powerless. He argued Phinehas was simply imitating the way that God punishes sinners. Peter wrote:

> This is why the Lord himself, while the whole Israelite people were no less guilty of this crime, was silent regarding commoners, but vented his fury in condign punishment only on their leaders. "And the Lord was angry and said to Moses, 'Take all of the leaders of the people and hang them on gallows in the full light of day, that the fury of my anger may turn away from Israel'" (Numbers 25:4).[35]

Thus the eminent must be punished more harshly and more publicly both to set an example and to turn away God's wrath. Whereas this example fit in well with Peter's rhetorical style, it was a bit too gruesome and too graphic for later reformers. However, his use of Eli as an example of laxity and its consequences became a standard piece of reform rhetoric in the church's tradition.

The priest Eli was charged with honoring his sons more than God. The sons of Eli were spoiling the sacrifices to Yahweh, and Eli failed to punish them. Though Eli had not actively participated in the sins of his sons, Yahweh declared a death sentence upon Eli with his sons. Just as the one who had corrected sins was worthy of a blessing, Peter concluded, so too the one who fails to punish sinners is likely to be cursed by God. To justify his position, he cited Gregory's interpretation of this passage: "He who fails to correct, when it is possible for him to do so, makes himself guilty of the other's fault."[36] He asked the pope and the other metropolitan bishops how they thought God would judge them if they remained silent when they were confronted with the sins of the clerics under their jurisdiction.

Peter saw their failure to enforce ecclesiastical discipline as bringing the dignity of ecclesiastical office into disrepute. Interpreting 1 Samuel 2:30–31, where God told Eli he would lop off his limbs, Peter wrote:

> With these words, he said, as it were, "Since by granting you the dignity of the pastoral office I strengthened your arm against my enemies, although you refused to use force in punishing them, I will now cut off your arm, that is, I will take away the power of the priestly office, so that as you were lacking an arm in fighting for me, you will now be without a hand to defend yourself."[37]

Because of their failure to exercise appropriate episcopal oversight, he believed that God would strip the bishops of the one thing they truly prized, the power associated with their ecclesiastical offices. Since they had refused to fulfill the duties demanded by the pastoral office, he argued the bishops lost the rights associated with those duties.

This argument also applied to the pope. Since the papacy itself had been strengthened by the reformers for the purpose of correcting ecclesial corruption, Pope Nicholas II would have seen how Peter's warning was most directly aimed at him. What Empress Agnes, Duke Godfrey, and Duchess Beatrice had given to the papacy, they could also take away. Peter had developed strong arguments for papal primacy and fought to free papal elections from political influences, but he also maintained that the pope could be corrected and even deposed for malfeasance by lay authorities.

Though they might escape a just judgment for the moment, Peter warned the pope and the bishops that they would never be able to escape the sentence of the heavenly judge. Over the course of his career as a member of the papal reform movement, Peter came to see that people had to be persuaded to follow the law. Increasingly, his rhetoric shifted away from legal categories to spiritual ones like the fear of God. Nonetheless, he worked to establish universal standards when it came to canon law and the enforcement of the church's discipline, but he learned reforming the laws of the church meant little if bishops were too weak or apathetic to enforce them. Strengthening the institutional power of the papacy was a means to clean up these abuses, but only if the man holding the office had the will and fortitude to act.

The primary reason the bishops were unwilling to act was their sense of entitlement. Peter saw this sense of entitlement, which is one manifestation of the sin of clericalism, as growing out of the sin of simony. As he worked on the difficult questions surrounding the validity of simoniacal ordinations, Peter closely linked the juridical powers and legal privileges that came with ecclesiastical offices to their duties.

Simony

When it came to simony, Peter found himself in the position of having to reform the reform movement. The reformers took over Gregory the Great's description of simony as buying an office, making a promise of payment, or obligations resulting from ordination.[38] All the reformers agreed that simoniacal clerics should be deposed, but they had to consider the impact it would have on pastoral care in the church. Cardinal Humbert and his circle of rigorist reformers argued that even the ordinations of men who were innocent were invalid if they were performed by a bishop guilty of simony. Of course, this implied that most of the sacraments performed by these clergymen were invalid as well. Since the laity earnestly believed they needed valid sacraments to escape hellfire, this put a great deal of pressure on them to oppose and to punish the offenders.

While Peter had considerable sympathy with the rigorist position at the outset, he quickly realized that this argument went too far. In a sense, it represented a misunderstanding of the nature and mission of the church as a sacramental institution. What is the value of having a visible, institutional church if the faithful have to rely upon the hidden moral quality of officeholders? How can the church fulfill its pastoral mission of healing souls *(cura animarum)* if it has to rely so heavily on the purity of sinful men? Peter realized that the rigorist position was in fact a form of clericalism because it rooted sacramental power in the person rather than in the office. The implication was that the pure priest has a right to perform the sacraments because of his personal qualities.

If the clergy believe they are indebted to a man and not to God for divine favor, Peter warned they would wither away in their ministry. This admonition applied to both the clerics guilty of simony and to the rigorists. If priests and bishops forget to look to God as the primal source of life-giving grace, he said they would not be able to produce grace from themselves.[39] Peter argued that Christ delegates to his ministers the office of ecclesiastical ordination but Christ retains within himself the sacrament of all orders. Drawing upon St. Augustine, he explained that Christ does not transfer the right itself or the power of ordination to men.[40]

Even though the bishops seem to ordain people by virtue of their office, Peter taught that it is only Christ who invisibly confers the Holy Spirit. To those who held otherwise, he wrote:

> There is one, indeed, who prays but another who hears the prayer; the one who asks, differs from him who approves the petitions. What man dares to compare himself to Peter and John? And yet it was said of them that when they went to Samaria to impose hands on those who had been baptized, they prayed for them and they received the Holy Spirit.[41]

From the case of Peter and John, he concluded that it was not a result of their gifts but of their prayers that the Holy Spirit entered into the faithful. Since there is only one high priest from whom all priesthood is poured out upon the members of the church, Peter argued that bishops should be seen as servants or ministers of the sacrament of holy orders.

Why was Peter so concerned with upholding the validity of the ordinations and other sacramental acts of evil bishops? Peter explained that if a bishop was simoniacal and all his ordinations were invalid in the past, then all the clergy who followed would have been invalidly ordained. The result would be that all the sacramental ministry in the diocese would have been invalid ever since. After citing Christ's statement that people need to receive the Eucharist to have life in them (John 6:53), Peter wrote:

> For if those men were not priests and therefore were unable to consecrate or administer the sacraments of the Body of the Lord, how could we believe that their followers, as the dead *(mortui)*, crossed over to life which they did not have when they were among the living? But if we admit this, we must also believe that all who were burdened with grave sins passed without the sacrament of penance.

The consequence would be that many, if not most, of the faithful departed are completely deprived of hope.[42]

Even if the sacramental acts of simoniacal clerics were valid, there remained the question of how to punish them for their manifest crimes. Whereas Peter had advocated deposing all such men in his early career, he came to see that it was not always the best course of action. Peter was sent on a mission to Milan as a papal legate with Bishop Anselm of Lucca in 1059 to help settle the unrest in the city over both simony and clerical concubinage. A deacon in the city named Ariald had begun preaching against clerical marriage in 1057. Apparently Ariald's preaching resonated with the laity, who rose up against the clergy on May 10, 1057. Ariald and his followers became known as the Patarines. For two years, the Patarines terrorized the unreformed clergy. They would enter priests' homes, drag them out of their beds and away from their concubines, and force them to sign pledges that they would be both celibate and chaste.[43]

Ariald then began organizing people against simony. The laity had been striking the Masses and sacramental services of the unreformed clergy, which was a tactic they learned from the papacy, but now they were becoming violent. The popes in this period encouraged such resistance on the part of the laity against unreformed clergymen.[44] Because the popes had always served as the final arbiters of ecclesiastical disputes in the West, civil unrest also served as a pretext for papal intervention in dioceses that had not been under Rome's jurisdiction. By resolving these disputes through papal legates, the popes in this period reinforced their claims to universal jurisdiction. Nonetheless, the clergy in these dioceses had to be persuaded to accept the authority of Rome and the decisions of papal legates. Peter was sent on this mission to Milan because he had credibility as a reformer, he was an excellent rhetorician, and he was flexible in how he applied disciplinary decrees to concrete situations.

When Peter arrived in Milan in 1059, he found that all the clergy in the diocese were guilty of simony because they had to pay a tax in order to be ordained. If Peter's account can be taken at face value, the clergy were agitated to the point of violence over Rome's involvement in their diocesan affairs. In a letter to Cardinal Hildebrand, he wrote, "Finding myself in a difficult position because I was unable to correct the practices of the church on the mere authority of the canons, I strove at least to put an end to its evil customs, and to make promotions to orders free in the future."[45] If he had attempted to strictly apply the law, he knew the Archdiocese of Milan would have simply rejected Roman authority altogether, which would have been a significant defeat for the papal reform movement. At the same time, the reform movement needed to demonstrate its ability to apply the principles of canon law in order to clean up church abuse and to truly and publicly punish the offenders in a way that would satisfy the laity's legitimate demand for proper order in the church.

Although Peter found that canon law did not provide for an adequate solution, which would have meant deposing these men from their offices, he framed his response in a manner consistent with the law. He found a canonical opinion from Pope Innocent I stating that when many have sinned the crime cannot be punished. Of course, this was far too lax for Peter and the laity in Milan, but he found a papal decree from Leo IV that stated fallen clerics could be reinstated if they admitted their errors and made satisfaction for their sins. Further, Leo IV had said that such men could never be promoted beyond their current rank.[46] Finally, Peter also drew upon Fulbert of Chartres' citation from the Council of Toledo, which said that it is possible to readmit a man guilty of simony to holy orders, to make his decision.[47]

With his legal precedents in order, Peter decided to allow the clergy to retain their offices if they publicly swore to end simony and clerical concubinage and if they performed the penances he imposed upon them. The archbishop was given one hundred years of penance, though some of it could be, interestingly enough, redeemed by a money payment. The archbishop also had to make a pilgrimage to the tomb of St. James in Spain. The clergy were given either five- or seven-year penances, depending on the severity of their crimes. They also had to make pilgrimages to either Rome or Tours.

For the proscribed period, the archbishop and his clergy had to fast on bread and water for two days out of the week in the summer and winter months. During Lent and Advent, they would fast three days a week. For those with seven-years or more penance, there was the additional penance of fasting for the rest of their lives on Fridays. This decision did not completely satisfy all of the laity in Milan, especially the Patarines, but it proved to be a workable solution until the assassination of Ariald in 1066 by the antireformers. Peter revealed his deep ambivalence toward his solution, writing, "Whether I have erred in reconciling these men, I do not know."[48]

Peter Damian's centrist stance on the validity of the sacraments of simoniacal priests and his balanced application of the laws were approved at the Easter Synod in Rome in 1059. Concerning Peter's work on simony, R. I. Moore, the great scholar of popular medieval movements, wrote:

> The judgment which Damiani gave at Milan and its subsequent confirmation are therefore of momentous importance, for it affirmed, at the critical moment, that the apostolic succession was incorruptible by the vices of the successors, and that the church's capacity to assure the salvation of the faithful was not compromised however great the imperfections of those by whom it is transmitted.[49]

Peter's sense of the role of persuasion and collaboration in reforming the church was, unfortunately, the road less traveled by the popes and the cardinals. With the papacies of Alexander II and Gregory VII, the notion of collaboration between the laity and the clergy in the ongoing task of reform gave way to the idea of the subjection of the laity and everyone else to the will of the pope. Peter was aware of the change and he began to more vigorously defend the laity's role in reform at the end of his career. Certainly, this is one of the reasons his work fell out of favor in the post-Reformation Catholic Church.

Collaborative Reform

Peter saw reform as involving all the orders of the church, which was something of a progressive attitude for a man of the eleventh century. It's clear that Peter believed the monastic and eremitical form of life is superior to other Christian vocations and that the clergy officially hold places of leadership. As we have seen, he was arguably the strongest supporter of papal primacy; but we have also seen that he believed popes could be legitimately deposed by lay leaders. Further, he knew all too well one cannot assume officeholders and those who have vows either fulfill the duties of their offices or observe their vows. Peter's experience of the church led him to oppose the idea that the bishops or the popes stood above the law, which was a position justified by a forged collection of canon law popular with the clergy, the *Pseudo-Isidorian Decretals.*[50]

Peter argued that everyone is subject to correction. He applauded Henry III's deposition of the three popes he found when he went to Rome for his coronation, calling the imperial intervention a strike against the "multicephalous hydra" of the simoniacal heresy.[51] Though he encouraged lay authorities to uphold the laws of the church when the clergy failed to do so, he did not believe that the laity should manipulate the church or write canon law. Peter went so far as to argue that a ruler who failed to respect the will of God as established by the canons could be rightfully overthrown by the people.[52]

In 1058, Peter wrote a letter to his secretary Ariprandus asserting the idea that no spiritual institution could survive without correction. He argued that St. Peter's willingness to accept correction from St. Paul, who certainly held a lower hierarchical place than St. Peter in the minds of medieval Christians, was a model for all human institutions. Lifting up St. Paul's example for imitation, he showed his medieval contemporaries that sometimes it is appropriate to publicly reprove superiors. While this idea was not new, Peter Damian went further and set out to refute the scriptural arguments the clergy cited against ever publicly speaking out against superiors.[53]

There were basically two primary texts that were used to discourage people from speaking out against their superiors. The first text was Matthew 18:15–17 when Jesus said:

> If another member of the church sins against you, go and point out the fault when the two of you are alone. If the member listens to you, then you have regained that one. But if you are not listened to, take one or two others along with you, so that every word may be confirmed by the evidence of two or three witnesses. If the member refuses to listen to them, tell it to the church....[54]

This was difficult advice for a medieval Christian to follow. Bishops, abbots, abbesses, and nobles had tremendous power over the people under their jurisdiction. To think of confronting such a person privately, especially if they were wicked or abusive, was more than most people could do. In effect, it was asking people to privately confront the very people who had abused or wronged them. If the poor person survived the encounter unscathed, it was unlikely that he or she could find two or three others to privately accuse their superiors of a crime. Thus he or she could never fulfill the requirements to justify making a public charge.

The second text that discouraged open criticism was drawn from St. Paul's advice to Timothy. St. Paul categorically states: "Never be harsh with an elder (presbyter), but speak to him as a father (1 Timothy 5:1)."[55] Peter asked how Paul could ignore his own advice and the command of Jesus. How could Paul heap rebukes on St. Peter, who had the right to govern the whole church, in the presence of everyone?

Peter Damian's answer was that St. Paul could do so in the service of obedience. St. Peter had fallen away from maintaining the "orthodox" position he had formulated at the Jerusalem Council in Acts 15:10–11, namely, that Gentiles should not be forced to follow Jewish observances. He wavered because of pressure from James and the other Jewish Christians in the Jerusalem community. By publicly shaming St. Peter, Peter Damian claimed St. Paul helped the "first pope" to recover the resolve he needed to properly lead the community.[56]

In other words, Peter Damian was arguing it is legitimate to harshly and publicly correct superiors when they fail to follow the guidelines of scripture and tradition. By defending the gospel and the decisions of the Jerusalem Council, St. Paul was being obedient. Of course, Peter Damian had to defend such action because he was frequently correcting his superiors in exactly this way. One of the most interesting aspects of his work is that he particularly argued that the duty to correct eminent clergymen also applied to women.

In 1064 Peter wrote a letter to Duchess Adelaide of Turin justifying the idea that women could correct and reform even the most preeminent members of the clergy and urging her to reform the dioceses in her territory. Peter knew this idea would not be well received by his fellow clerics, especially since he was writing about clerical concubinage. He claims to have hesitated in writing the letter because he feared the "calumny" of "insulting clerics."[57] So first, he wrote to the bishop of Turin in order to deflect criticism. Peter seemed apologetic for his delay, writing:

> Indeed, they would have complained and said, "See how shamefully and inhumanely he acts while preparing to destroy us, he who is unwilling to discuss this matter cautiously and discreetly with bishops or with other men of the church, but brazenly publicizes to women what should have been handled in the sacristy."[58]

Since the bishop of Turin only had one diocese under his jurisdiction and Adelaide controlled the kingdoms of Italy and Burgundy, Peter argued it was not improper for him to write to her concerning clerical sexuality. He knew Adelaide had the means to clean up the behavior of the clergy by force.

For Peter, sexuality did not determine a person's virtue or power. These are gifts that come from God. Peter praised God for making Adelaide as strong as a man and for endowing her with more goodwill than temporal power. He urged her to follow the Old Testament example of Deborah, who sat in judgment and who ruled without the help of a man. Peter affirmed Adelaide's own justification for her power over men. Defending her power to a petulant priest or bishop, she had said, "Why should one wonder, father, that almighty God saw fit to grant me, his unworthy servant, some small degree of power over men, since at times he endows even some despicable herb with wonderful qualities."[59]

Though Peter urged Adelaide to collaborate with the bishop of Turin, he did not expect the bishop to be very cooperative. This is why he concentrated on the relationship between Deborah and Barak as an example for how she should behave. Deborah had commanded Barak to battle against Sisera, but Barak refused to go unless Deborah went as well. According to Peter, Barak represents the bishops whose reform efforts begin with zeal but do not endure because they are weak and lazy. Sisera represents clerical impurity. Because of his reluctance, Barak did not slay Sisera. In the end, it was a woman named Jael who killed the enemy by driving a tent stake through his skull. This story shows that sometimes God "uses women to achieve a more glorious triumph."[60] It also justified unilateral action on Adelaide's part if the bishops failed to act.

Peter provided Adelaide with an arsenal of scriptural citations justifying her action in cleaning up the male clergy. He pointed to the example of Judith, who was afforded the glory of cutting off Holophernes's head by God as a reward for the harsh rebuke she gave to the weak and fearful priest Ozias (Jdt 8:12—13:20). He also cited the deeds of Esther who caused Haman to be hanged (Esth 7:9–10), the wise woman who cut off the head of Sheba and threw it to Joab (2 Sam 20:16–22), the woman Thebez who threw a stone that crushed the head of the general Abimelech (Judg 9:53; 2 Sam 11:21), and Abigail who disobeyed her husband and thus saved her family from destruction (1 Sam 25:14-35).[61] Peter promised Adelaide, "You can also turn away the sword of God's anger from your own house and from the ones you have under your authority in these areas, if you strive to overcome impurity that is supported even in the highest circles of the church by bishops who do not pay attention to it."[62]

Peter's position on the right and the duty of the laity to correct the clergy was increasingly at odds with the papal reform movement as envisioned by Gregory VII. Nonetheless, his justification for everyone, including women, to correct their "superiors" continued to influence reformers well into the sixteenth century. Peter's theology provided a counterbalance to the increasingly outlandish claims of papal authority. Since temporal privileges such as wealth and coercive power were not inherent to any pastoral office, he argued the laity could legitimately take these away from the clergy. Over time, this aspect of his theology was ignored even as his arguments for papal primacy were frequently repeated by Catholic apologists.

Peter Damian's Contribution to Catholic Reform

In his life and his letters, Peter Damian can be seen as following Gregory the Great's advice on how to effectively reform the church. He began his mission by seeking purity of heart through ascetic disciplines. Peter made an effort to show that he was not a rebel by entering into the service of the church. Like Gregory, he grounded both Christian and ecclesial authority on service and maintained a strong distinction between those who held offices in the church and the offices themselves. He warned his contemporaries and his medieval heirs against the uncritical acceptance of clerical authority; but he only spoke out publicly against their worst abuses and most wicked acts. Finally, he imitated Gregory's efforts to create a record of his efforts and principles by preserving them in letters and sermon collections.

For Peter, proper order particularly demands that the worst offenses need to be made public. On one level, he was simply echoing the penitential disciplines of the ancient and medieval church; but on another level, he was arguing that publicly revealing the worst sins was the means to preserve the credibility of the church. This course of action was warranted by the scriptural examples of Phinehas and Eli. By exposing the worst offenses, the church shows that it will expose all sins. Conversely, when the church is lax in its discipline and hushes up the worst sins of its members, it signals that it is not serious about its own laws, tradition, and mission. By setting a bad example in terms of Christian order, Peter believed the institutional church was impeding its ability to save souls by undermining its own authority. This laxity, he argued, stood in direct contradiction to Jesus' teaching on the importance of following the law in Matthew 5:19.[63]

Observance of the laws and disciplines of the church, however, is not an end in itself for Peter. The real goal of Christian law is to save souls, which means the law has to be applied judiciously. He began to recognize the problem with holding to the law so rigorously, like cardinals Humbert and Hildebrand, that the church lost sight of its mission to provide pastoral care. The church could not, for example, legally declare that the sacramental acts of impure priests and bishops were invalid. Nor would Peter accept the idea that the church leaders could legally exempt themselves from all accountability to the laity. He recognized the spurious nature of the canons that exempted the clergy from correction and pointed out their inconsistency with scripture.

The tension between Peter's claims concerning the authority of canon law, especially when the canon came from a papal decision, and the authority of scripture and tradition was never formally resolved in his theology. While we can see a shift in his emphasis from issues of law and purity to spirituality and pastoral care, Peter always maintained the absolute authority of canon law. In the end, it would take the crisis of the Protestant Reformation and the resulting Council of Trent to resolve this problem.

Peter's greatest contribution to the idea of reform was that the church could be reformed as a whole. He stands out as one of the greatest institutional reformers in the history of the church. His efforts to expose what he considered to be false canons and his work at strengthening the papacy and reforming the curia had a lasting impact on the church. The new method of electing popes he had helped to establish, though it was not always followed, allowed more reform-minded popes to be elected in the twelfth and thirteenth centuries. Increasingly, pastoral concerns dominated the reform agenda of Peter Damian's successors. Further, reform movements began to set up their own institutions, like the Cistercian Order, which operated outside the bounds of individual dioceses and answered to the pope as the universal head of the church. As we shall see, the way Peter linked pastoral care to institutional reform increasingly became the standard norm for Catholic reformers in the succeeding centuries.

3

Bernard of Clairvaux: The Impossible Reformer

Like all his reforming predecessors, Bernard had to defend him-self for raising scandalous issues. In a letter to the abbot of St. Denis monastery, he wrote:

My fear is only lest I offend anyone by speaking openly of what is disturbing me, for the truth can sometimes breed hatred. But I hear the Truth that breeds this sort of hatred, comforting me with the words, "It is necessary that scandals come," and I do not consider that what follows applied to me at all: "But woe to the person through whom it comes." When scandals come through vices being denounced, it comes through those who are blameworthy and not through those who blame it. And I do not set myself up as being more circumspect or more discreet than he [Gregory the Great] who said: "It is better that there should be a scandal than that the truth should be compromised."[1]

Bernard told the abbot that he was a reformer and, as such, he did not call evil good; but instead, he called evil for what it is. Yet he also explained that the person who fails to praise what is good is a mere detractor rather than a reformer, a person who would rather complain about evil than remedy it.[2]

No figure in the twelfth century was more involved in the life and concerns of the medieval church than Bernard. Born to a noble family in 1090, Bernard entered the monastery of Cîteaux in 1112 at the age of twenty-two. Three years later he was sent to found his own monastery in Clairvaux. As abbot he went on to establish sixty-eight other Cistercian monasteries. In addition to being an influential abbot, he was a literary giant, a maker of popes, and an advisor to kings. Although scholars have recognized how Bernard and his Cistercian brothers were working to reform the corruptions they saw in some of the practices of the Benedictine monks, he is generally not seen as being actively involved in reforming the broader church.[3]

Bernard's lack of recognition as a reformer points to the limitations inherent in interpreting reform primarily through legal and political categories. If this is our standard, then Bernard's critique of the centralization of power in the hands of the curia, of an overemphasis on a canonistic understanding of the faith, and of the church's involvement in secular politics would not register as a coherent reform agenda. On one hand, Bernard was renewing the concept of reform in light of its original meaning—of calling individuals to a conversion of heart. On the other, he was extending and stretching the concept of reform to include the idea of progress.

One of Bernard's foremost concerns was to reform the work of those who had followed the path of Gregory VII. These men have come to be known as the Gregorian reformers and should not be confused with the movement surrounding Gregory the Great. The Gregorian reformers employed Gregory VII's methods of using legal, coercive, and institutional means to clean up abuses in the church. Roughly forty years later, some of the legal and institutional reforms associated with the curia and the power of the papacy, for which Peter Damian and Gregory VII had fought, were creating unforeseen corruptions in Rome. Men seeking coercive power and the wealth and privileges associated with it flocked into the curial offices. Bernard's struggle with papal and curial ambition is an example of a repeating pattern in the history of the church: Programmatic and institutional reforms that solve one set of problems for one generation often become the source of scandals for the church in later generations.

Not surprisingly, the Gregorian reformers of the twelfth century and the Benedictine houses associated with Cluny labeled Bernard and his Cistercians as upstarts and as austere literalists. Bernard's exhortations to the clergy asking them to refrain from involving themselves in secular politics and affairs must have seemed a bit naïve to the battle-hardened Gregorian reformers and their allies at Cluny. These veterans seriously doubted that a man who eschewed reliance on canon law or juridical power would be successful advancing the reform of the church. Bernard, who simply grounded his message in the persuasive power of Christian spirituality, understood reform as a renewal that belonged to the sphere of grace.[4]

The primary analogy Bernard used for reform of the church drew upon Gregory the Great's notion of the reformer as a physician. Bernard described the problems in the church as a chronic illness, writing, "Today a foul corruption permeates the whole body of the church, all the more incurable the more widespread it becomes, all the more dangerous the more it penetrates inwardly." What was this disease? In short, it was a plague of ambition and self-interest manifested most spectacularly in the diocesan clergy. While everyone was claiming to belong to the church, he complained that no one was a peacemaker. "Called to be ministers of Christ," Bernard wrote, "they are servants to the Antichrist."[5]

Times of peace and prosperity are the factors that Bernard identified as triggering the outbreaks of this chronic disease. Using the analogy of a chronic illness allowed him to explain why reform efforts must be ongoing. In effect, reform is like the body of Christ's immune system, which responds to various outbreaks of disease in the body. Because chronic and intestinal diseases are neither fatal nor permanently disfiguring, Bernard's analogy allowed him to present criticism even as he maintained that the church will be the spotless bride at the consummation of history.[6]

If Gregory the Great came up with an apologetics of humility, then Bernard established the apologetics of love. "I speak confidently," Bernard proclaimed, "because I love sincerely." He continued to explain that true love drives out suspicion and doubt, which allows the lover to speak frankly.[7] By linking criticism and correction to love, he offered a justification for his reform efforts. According to Bernard, frank and direct criticism is a sign of love and not of rebellion or dissent.

Often Bernard speaks out of motherly love and actually assumes a motherly voice. Writing to Pope Eugenius III (1145–53), he described his relationship to the pope in maternal terms because Eugenius had been one of Bernard's monks. He wrote, "You were once in my womb, you will not be drawn from my heart so easily." Whether Eugenius ascended to the heavens or descended into the depths, Bernard said there was no escape from his maternal love. This belief had an impact on his reform method and rhetoric. He explained, "Therefore, I will instruct you not as a teacher, but as a mother, indeed, as a lover. I may seem more the fool, but only to the one who does not love, to the one who does not feel the force of love."[8]

As a lover or as a mother, Bernard worked to reform the church through literary sermons, letters, and lives of the saints. In this sense, he was following the path of his predecessors. We will concentrate on Bernard's *Apologia to Abbot William, On Conversion,* and *On Consideration* because they reveal how he appealed to different audiences with his rhetoric and because of their influence on later reformers. Most significantly, these sources illustrate how Bernard was one of the first reformers to defend the idea that new or better forms of life, ministry, and worship can develop in the church.

Progressive Reform

Bernard had to respond to those who accused the Cistercians of being presumptuous because they sought to do something new and better in the church. This attitude reflects the spirit of those who obstinately defend and blindly observe human traditions. His rhetoric pointed to the need to discern between what is part of the divine revelation and what is merely human custom in canon law and church teaching. For Bernard, the argument that some practice, observance, or law is the way that the church has always done something holds little weight. While scripture may warn us against being wiser than is proper for us, he pointed out it never says, "Be not overly good." He reminded the opponents of progress that St. Paul "was not content, but gladly stretched forward to those things that were before, forgetting those that were behind, striving ever to be better."[9]

The people who claim they "do not want to be better than their fathers" are proclaiming themselves to be, according to Bernard, the "sons of lax and tepid fathers whose memory is accursed because they have eaten bitter grapes and the teeth of their children have been set on edge." In other words, those who do not want to be better than previous generations are more likely to be imitating the sins of their ancestors than the virtues. He gave this warning to those who opposed progressive reform:

> Jacob saw angels ascending and descending the ladder, but he did not see any standing still or sitting down. A fragile hanging ladder is no place for standing still or sitting down. A fragile hanging ladder is no place for standing still nor, in the uncertain condition of this mortal life, can anyone

remain in one fixed position. We have not here an abiding city nor do we yet possess it, but we are still seeking the one to come. Either you must go up or you must come down, you inevitably fall if you try to stand still. It is certain that the one who does not try to be better is not even good.[10]

Bernard advised his reforming brothers that the new Pharisees were looking for an opportunity to attack them. He asked his brothers to avoid confrontation or conciliation with modern Pharisees, the opponents of progress, because he said they were blind and incapable of much more than spitefulness. "It is not your concern," Bernard wrote, "to cure the scandal of those who will not be cured unless you too become sick."[11] This became an important principle to help the Cistercian reformers discern between what can be compromised and what cannot. For those who could be cured, Bernard cast his rhetoric in the language of the heart. His emphasis on the affective dimension of the person, which includes feelings and desires, reflected the quickening of a new spirit of humanism that was reinvigorating European culture. Bernard's preaching and theology is both carnal and erotic. In this sense, we can say he reformed a theology that attempted to ignore the beauty and the power of carnality.[12]

Bernard chose this strategy as a response to a growing sense of legalism, which he believed was corrupting the church. The most damaged diocese was Rome. He claimed that the greed and ambition in Rome had made it "more a pasture of demons than of sheep." This greed was compounded by an unhealthy interest in canon law, which was studied by ecclesiastical climbers who perverted the law for their profit and advancement. Claiming the law should be judged by its fruits, Bernard worked to reform the idea that canon law had the authority of tradition.[13]

In the half century between the end of Peter Damian's career and the beginning of Bernard's, Europe experienced an intellectual and spiritual rebirth. Bernard, like all reformers, is a reflection of the promises and the anxieties of his times. We can see how the new attitudes toward the natural world, the human person, and the idea of progress are incorporated into his work. Similarly, Bernard's distrust of methods of the new schoolmen mirrored the perspective of many of the monks. Bernard was not, however, opposed to all the new masters of theology and he certainly cannot be legitimately called anti-intellectual. For example, he supported the efforts of Peter Lombard and John of Salisbury, both of whom were important in the development of scholasticism and in supporting ideas that led to the development of the universities.[14] To appreciate Bernard's expansive agenda and methods, we must first come to understand the issues facing a twelfth-century reformer.

Twelfth-Century Renewal

There were several parallel reform movements taking place in the twelfth-century church. It was one of the most fertile periods in the life of the church, but it was also a time of corruption and dissent. Simony and clerical concubinage continued to be sources of scandal. The reform movement that Peter Damian had helped to foster had been subordinated to papal apologetics surrounding the investiture controversy. The investiture controversy, which was essentially a question of who had the right to install a man as bishop, set the pattern for the relationship between the church and the state for much of the later Middle Ages. It also squarely raised the issue of papal jurisdiction.

Like Peter Damian, Bernard was both an advocate for universal papal jurisdiction and deeply concerned with the way Gregory VII and his successors understood their authority. In particular, he was concerned with the growing power and corruption of the Roman curia. As Leclercq noted, Bernard was alarmed over a certain "historical realization" of papal claims to secular and political power.[15] Because of Peter Damian's and the other papal reformer's success in strengthening the papacy, people increasingly turned to Rome to settle disputes and to win privileges. This state of affairs required a larger staff, bigger budgets, and an ever-widening scope of activity.

Papal claims to possessing the authority to depose secular princes had the unintended consequence of making the manipulation or control of the pope and the curia an irresistible temptation for political leaders. The easiest way to influence the new papal administration was to bribe a curial bureaucrat or to put an ally or relative into a curial position. Suddenly, the cardinals became men of enormous influence and power on the stage of international affairs. People began to identify the "Roman Church" with the "Roman curia." The corruption was so acute that the German theologian Gerhoh of Reichersberg called the curia the mother of anxieties who "breeds evils." In 1148, the cardinals began to assert themselves over the rights of the bishops and episcopal synods. The cardinals complained the machinery of the church should be left to them exclusively. Not satisfied with making outrageous juridical claims, the cardinals went so far as to claim they were the axis around which the church revolves.[16]

The Roman See was not the only institution that had become increasingly secularized. Many of the monastic houses, particularly those associated with the monastery in Cluny, had become both wealthy and influential. Beginning in the second half of the eleventh century, there was an enormous increase in the number of monks and a corresponding expansion of monastic properties. This growth was due, in part, to societal forces and a population explosion. Because the society was based on holding and owning land, population growth presented a serious dilemma of how to provide for children who would not inherit the family estates. Landholding families resolved this conflict by sending some of their children to the monasteries.[17]

As the cities and towns grew, the monks found their land to be increasingly valuable. Instead of selling their property, they would lease it for building and development. They were also gaining control over the benefices associated with individual churches as a result of a restitution movement led by the popes of the period. Since the reformers had made it illegal for laypeople to hold the benefices to churches, laymen and laywomen frequently "sold" or donated these rights to monasteries in order to spite their bishops.[18] More and more churches were coming under the control of the monasteries, which created tensions with the diocesan clergy. The monks began to staff these churches with their members and thus set the stage for a series of conflicts over who had the right to preach in a diocese.

The new orders, like the Cistercians, believed the Benedictines had become corrupted by their growing wealth and secular involvement. As a new order, they had to defend their particular form of life and to explain how they fit in with the church as a whole. The twelfth century is punctuated by the apologetics and polemics of the reformers and antireformers. In particular, reformers had to distinguish themselves from the growing number of dissenters, schismatics, and heretics. This led many of the reform movements to attack each other, making the twelfth century a time of incredible contention.[19]

The church also had to contend with the Cathars and other heretical groups. Though they were perceived as heretics, the Cathars were really a competing religion that had come from the East. They were dualists and anarchists who argued that all institutional religions are necessarily corrupt. The Cathars also believed that the material and carnal world was evil, so they abstained from sex, took up lives of poverty, and followed a path of simplicity. When the local bishop passed through town on his fine horse with silver stirrups and jewel-encrusted saddles, wearing the most sumptuous robes, and looking the part of the prince, the poor and struggling townspeople began to find hope in Catharism.[20]

The initial response by the church was either to ignore the Cathars or to repress them, but Bernard argued that the bishops should strive to convert them through preaching and by providing a good example. He asked Pope Eugenius these piercing questions:

> With what feeling of assurance, with what kind of conscience do we fail to offer Christ to those who do not possess him? Or do we restrain the truth of God in our injustice. Indeed, at some time it is necessary for the full number of Gentiles to come in (Romans 1:18). Are we waiting for faith to fall upon them? To whom has belief come by chance? How shall they believe without preaching?

He told Eugenius that preaching is useless when it is corrupted by the lives and deeds of the clergy. Because of the corruption of the clergy, he concluded, "we are oppressed by the stronger and we in turn oppress those who are weaker." The injustice of the church and its members simply provided ammunition for the Cathars. Bernard even suspected that many of the bishops in southern France were so greedy that they had accepted bribes from the Cathar movement to ignore the fact that Cathars were active in French dioceses.[21]

While there were anxieties over heresy, the twelfth century was equally a period marked by openness to new ideas. Gerhard Ladner, one of the seminal Catholic scholars in reform studies, has pointed out how the language of reform was expressed in the language of "vitalistic" metaphors related to birth, rebirth, growth, flowering, spring, warmth, light, and life. This language lent itself to a developmental understanding of the church and of our understanding of the faith. The shift between Gregory the Great and Peter Damian was one where reform was expanded from the realm of the personal to the institutional, but in the twelfth century the shift was from an idea of reform that was strictly backward looking to one including a forward-looking perspective.[22]

Bernard's *Apologia*

Who was the source for Bernard's forward-looking perspective? The answer is St. Augustine, who had understood personal reform in terms of change for the better. By applying the category of reform to the entire church, theologians such as Peter Damian and Gregory VII had opened the door to the idea that the church as a whole could change for the better. Still, this idea existed side by side with the older notion of looking to the past for models of behavior and of reform.[23] Bernard's *Apologia to Abbot William* reveals how a new reform movement like the Cistercians defended innovation even as they held to tradition.

The Cistercian Order introduced several innovative reforms into monastic life. They were the first true religious order in the sense that they were a unified body of houses tied together in a constitutional form of government. Interestingly enough, the Cistercians are one of the earliest international organizations to have a representative government. Second, they allowed members of the middle and lower classes to enter into monastic life as *conversi*, or lay brothers. This opened up new possibilities for people to pursue a spiritual life, which had largely been restricted to the nobility. Finally and most importantly, the Cistercians refused to accept oblates.[24]

In the Middle Ages, many if not most of the members of the various Benedictine houses had entered as oblates. An oblate was a child, usually around the age of six, who was being offered up for monastic life by his parents. The result was that the monasteries were full of men who had no personal commitment to live a life of renunciation. Because of the misdeeds of these men who had monasticism imposed upon them, there were frequent scandals concerning the monasteries ranging from sexual abuse to simony. All the Cistercians, by way of contrast, entered having had the experience of living as adult laymen in the world. In addition to cleaning up abuse, their experience of living as laymen in the world made them extremely effective preachers.

While these innovations reflect the progressive aspect of reform in the twelfth century, the Cistercians also returned to the sources of Western monasticism for their inspiration. Bernard McGinn has called the Cistercians men who "strove to obey what they conceived to be the spirit of the *Rule* [of Benedict] in as literal a fashion as possible."[25] The Cistercians were literalist in the sense that they wanted to return to the practice of manual labor and of poverty, but this pursuit of poverty was also expressed in the simpler architecture and liturgies they promoted.

Not surprisingly, some of the Cistercians began to claim preeminence for their own form of life and to detract from the other orders, particularly the Benedictines, as having fallen away from the purity of the *Rule*. Of course, the Cistercians were responding to the charges of being innovators whose asceticism was aimed at winning human praise rather than divine approval.[26] Many of the Benedictines saw the very existence of the Cistercians as an insult against their time-honored traditions. To avoid the charge of being detractors and sowers of discord, which could have serious legal ramifications for new orders in the twelfth century, Bernard had to diffuse the situation.[27] He did so by pointing to and defending the legitimate diversity of forms of life, devotions, and liturgical observances.

Bernard began by addressing the conclusion that his decision to be a Cistercian demonstrated disdain for the Benedictine Order. If this was the case, he responded, then the Cistercians should take insult from all of the Benedictines who did not adopt their form of life. He then drew out the perverse implications of such a perspective:

> By the same token, we would have to take it for granted that celibates and married folk are at variance, simply because their lives are moderated by different church laws, and that monks and regulars are always at odds due to differences in observances. We would never guess that Noah, Daniel, and Job share the same kingdom, since we know they followed very different paths of virtue. Finally, we would have to affirm that either Mary or Martha or both failed to please the Lord, since their efforts to do this were so very unlike.[28]

If this were true, there could never be peace and harmony in the church. Bernard concluded that God gave all of these diverse observances because people are diverse in their spiritual needs.[29]

The seamless robe of Christ, according to Bernard, is multicolored like Joseph's robe. Unity does not imply uniformity. To prove that the church must maintain legitimate diversity, Bernard cited 1 Corinthians 12:4: "There are varieties of grace, but the same Spirit; there are different words, but the same Lord." The different charisms that St. Paul listed are, according to Bernard, the different hues of the robe. "It is not I by myself, nor you without me, nor a third person on his own, who can form this one robe," he explained, "but all of us together, provided we take care to maintain the unity of the Spirit in the bond of peace." He asked why people should be worried about the pilgrim church's diversity, if Christ taught there will be supreme unity and diversity in the heavenly kingdom when he spoke about the many rooms in his Father's house (John 14:2).[30] If there are different forms of equality in heaven, he concluded, then it is legitimate and even praiseworthy to have different forms of equality on earth.

Having affirmed legitimate diversity, Bernard turned his attention to his overzealous monks. He argued that the men who ignored St. Paul's command in 1 Corinthians 4:5 to leave judgment to Christ were not truly members of the Cistercian Order. Chastising his brothers for judging everyone by Cistercian standards, he wrote:

> Instead of submitting to God's justices, such people wish to set up their own. This being the case, they belong neither to our Order, nor to any other. They may live orderly lives, but their haughty language makes them citizens of Babylon, which means "disorder"; they are sons of darkness and children of hell, where there is no order but unending chaos.[31]

This was an important step in winning over the Benedictines. Bernard showed that he was not a partisan or an ideologue defending his own party at the expense of the truth.

Bernard continued with a lengthy discussion of his brothers who focus on their external acts or works as a sign of their holiness. Citing 1 Corinthians 6:10, Bernard warned them to consider that detractors will not inherit the kingdom of heaven. He chastised them for forgetting that Christ said the kingdom of God is within you (Luke 17:21), which means it consists in interior virtue rather than outward observances. Referring to those who boasted about the stringent Cistercian dietary practices, he wrote, "We fill our stomachs with beans, and our minds with pride."[32]

Of course, Bernard expected his brothers would try to defend themselves by attacking him. To ward off the attack, he presented it himself. He admitted that some would argue he so downplayed the material observances in favor of spirituality that he was, to put it in our own polemical categories, a type of cafeteria Cistercian, picking and choosing his observances. Bernard composed one of the most eloquent responses to this concern in the church's history. After assuring his brothers about his commitment to the rules and observances, he wrote:

> At the same time, if it happens that one or other element must be left aside, it is important that it be the material. For, just as the soul is more important than the body, so spiritual practices are more fruitful than material ones. But as for you, if you have become so complacent about your bodily observances that you look down on those who cannot follow suit, then it is you who are the real transgressor. You lose your grip on more important things, and cling to trifles, whereas Paul tells us to "seek the better gifts" (1 Corinthians 12:31). In this matter of disparaging your brothers, humility is lost when you put yourself up on a pedestal, and charity when you trample on others, and surely these are the great gifts.[33]

Having first corrected his own, Bernard turned to address some of his concerns about elements within the Benedictine Order. He further softened the blows to come by writing, "Though such abuses are in the Order, I hope they are not of the Order." By distinguishing between the institution, for which Bernard professed his love, and some of its manifestly corrupt members, for whom he had ready rebukes, Bernard hoped the men who truly loved the Benedictine Order would not be angry over what he had to say.[34]

According to the logic of Bernard's apologetics and polemics of love, one can expect some pretty candid criticism following a profession of love. In this case, he began the critique gently by drawing on common exhortations and admonitions concerning excesses in eating and drinking, monks who shirk their duties by pretending to be ill, brothers who are followers of fashion in their clothing, and lax superiors.[35] When Bernard turned to offer his more pointed critiques, he made it clear that many of the Benedictines had also fallen into being overly concerned with externals. His most acerbic criticism was over the amount of gold, silver, jewels, and other riches that were being brought into monasteries and were being incorporated into Benedictine liturgies.

The very thing that Catholic romantics lovingly look back to for inspiration, the grand medieval churches, Bernard described as extravagant and unnecessary. He claimed their expensive décor and art captured the people's attention but dried up their devotion. Concerning the churches and their art, he wrote:

> Cupidity, which is a form of idolatry, is the cause of all of this. It is for no useful purpose that we do it, but to attract gifts. You want to know how? Listen to the marvels of it all. It is possible to spend money in such a way that it increases; it is an investment which grows, and pouring it out only brings in more. The very sight of such sumptuous and exquisite baubles is sufficient to inspire men to make offerings, though not to say their prayers. In this way, riches attract riches, and money produces more money. For some unknown reason, the richer a place appears, the more freely do offerings pour in.[36]

According to Bernard, these "monstrosities" only served to open purses and not hearts.

This fund-raising strategy was, according to Bernard, a vanity that was only rivaled by its insanity. While the church was ornamented with gold and jewels, resplendent with its stained-glass windows, and graced by artistic finery, he complained its children were left hungry and naked. He scolded the great builders of churches and collectors of fine liturgical art: "The food of the poor is taken to feed the eyes of the rich, and amusement is provided for the curious, while the needy do not even have the necessities of life."[37] Like the detractors among the Cistercians, some of the Benedictines were also overly concerned with externals.

With his *Apologia*, Bernard provided an important example to later reformers about how to preserve unity and how to reform without becoming judgmental and narrow-minded. Bernard framed his criticism in a way that attempted to reconcile the Cistercians and the Benedictines. He balanced his charges in a way that called both parties in the dispute to recognize their faults. He wrote to the abbot that he hoped his apology would stop the more austere monks from belittling others and restrain the lax monks from their excesses. "In this way, both sides can maintain their own values," he explained, "but without passing judgment on those who think differently."[38]

Many of Bernard's concerns about the overemphasis on the external aspects of the faith became recurring themes in his writings. When confronted with clergymen who obsessed over the finest clothes, who sought to create heaven out of stone and glass, and who only had the most precious materials for their sacred vessels, he reminded them that the voices of the poor will cry out against them in judgment. Because the poor are the clergy's brothers and sisters in the heavenly kingdom, Bernard admonished the clergy this way: "See now: your brother's portion serves the pleasure of your eyes, our lives have less worth than your superfluous goods, your vanity grows to the extent that our basic needs are stripped away."[39]

Bernard's rhetoric became much more pointed as he turned his attention to the higher orders in the church's hierarchy. It also became more intimate. On the one hand, he adopted Peter Damian's principle that the leaders should be corrected more harshly; but, on the other, he softened the blows through his apologetics of love. For example, he explained his criticism of bishops this way:

> I can see two cruel she-wolves, vanity and a taste for luxury, hurling themselves at the shepherd. I tremble with fear and bleat, believing that someone will run to the rescue of this man in danger. What will they do to a poor sheep like me if they can attack the shepherd himself with such ferocity? And if he does not want me to cry out for his sake, will he not allow me to do so for my own?[40]

Bernard, the lover, the poor lamb who loves the shepherd, stretched the limits of reform rhetoric in his sermon *On Conversion*, which was squarely aimed at the clergy. As we shall see, the comparison of his criticisms to the bleating of a frightened lamb is so incongruous as to be funny.

On Conversion

Bernard's original sermon *On Conversion* was intended to call members of the clergy to reform themselves and, ultimately, to enter the monastery. Bernard delivered it in 1140 to clergymen who were either teaching or studying in Paris. The sermon was very successful and led twenty-three members of the audience to take up the Cistercian form of life. While the later literary version retains elements calling men to the monastery, it also outlines vices of the clergy and contains a description of the model pastor as well. These concerns with the nature of priestly ministry suggest Bernard wrote the literary version with the intention of disseminating and preserving his reform ideas. The intensity of his admonitions and exhortations in this sermon became a model for later reformers. By studying his rhetoric, we are better prepared to hear the words of Catholic reformers like Catherine of Siena and Jan Hus as well as Protestants like Luther.

Prior to presenting his criticisms and admonitions, Bernard employed standard techniques to win over the goodwill of his audience. He began by giving a brief lesson on the need for conversion, the role of grace and reason in conversion, the consequences of failure to repent, explaining why some seem to be able to easily convert to God's will, and the role of the vices in creating resistance to God's will. Bernard was clearly attempting to appeal to the interests and concerns of these schoolmen.

As he delighted them, Bernard used the Beatitudes to introduce the Beatitude of being a peacemaker as defining the nature of priestly ministry and as providing a standard for discerning the quality of the clergy. He argued that there are three types of peacemakers corresponding to the three orders of the church. The first type of peacemaker, corresponding to the lay state, is the person who "renders good for good" and who wishes harm to no one. The second form of being a peacemaker corresponds to the life of the monk, who can patiently bear evil. The priests and bishops make up the third type of peacemaker. This is the one who returns good for evil. Praising the priesthood in light of its peacemaking role in the sacrament of reconciliation, Bernard wrote: "He, then, is deservedly blessed with the name 'son' (1 John 3:1), because he does the work of a son, for, grateful for his own reconciliation, he reconciles others to his Father too."[41]

After praising the priesthood, Bernard gave one of the most powerful critiques of the unreformed clergy that one can find within the Catholic tradition. He began by employing eucharistic allusions and common experience. Based on common experience, he argued there is no one who deserves more anger than the person who pretends friendship. The biblical example is Judas, who betrayed Jesus with a kiss, which of course is the sign of peace. So Judas is representative of those who are not reconciled with God but who ambitiously seize the rank of peacemaker. Because Judas also took meals with Christ and dipped his hand into the same dish at the Last Supper, which recalls the eucharistic ministry of the priesthood, Bernard used Judas as a type for all the priests who pretend to love their people but betray them by their deeds.

The Judas priest, according to the saint, has no part in the prayer of Jesus: "Father, forgive them; for they do not know what they are doing" (Luke 23:34 NRSV). These men take away the key of knowledge and of authority from the people by their bad examples and prevent people from entering into communion with the Lord. Bad priests and bishops are "vessels fit for destruction" (Romans 9:22). Interpreting John 21:15–17, Bernard argued the true or reformed priest demonstrates his love of Christ by feeding the Lord's beloved sheep. To the priest who does not love and feed Christ's sheep, Bernard warned:

> Woe to the unfaithful stewards who, themselves not yet reconciled, take on themselves the responsibility of recognizing righteousness in others, as if they were themselves righteous men (Isaiah 68:2). Woe to the sons of wrath (Ephesians 2:3) who profess they are ministers of grace. Woe to the sons of wrath who are not afraid to usurp to themselves the name and rank of "peacemaker." Woe to the sons of wrath who pretend to be mediators of peace, and who feed upon the sins of the people. Woe to those who, walking in the flesh, cannot please God (Romans 8:8) and presume to wish to please him.

These Judas priests sin through their ordination; and Bernard argued they continue to sin as long as they exercise their ministry. Because it is almost impossible for "the sweet fruit of love to ripen from the bitter root of ambition," he concluded that ambitious bishops and priests are likely to be kept from salvation as long as they retain their offices.[42]

To make sure that people could recognize these vessels of destruction, Bernard described their behavior. First, they have no spirit of gentleness with sinners. They also have no sense of their imperfection and they feel no remorse. These priests, he continued, desire money and not justice. The eyes of such a man are captured by anything showy and they hunger for human recognition and praise. This type of priest or bishop has no mercy, rejoices in his anger, and "behaves like a tyrant." Before turning to discuss the state of the clergy in the church, Bernard gave his audience a breath of reassurance: "While we do not accuse everyone, yet we cannot excuse everyone. The Lord has left himself many thousands" (Romans 11:4). If this was not the case, he concluded, the church would have been over-whelmed in the distant past like Sodom and Gomorrah.[43]

The ill-fated cities provided Bernard with a transition into the sexual abuses of the clergy. At this time the church was growing and the number of vocations to the priesthood was swelling. Assessing the situation, he wrote that the rise in vocations was directly proportional to the decrease in merits. Bernard saw the ambition and greed of the clergy as establishing lust as the clergy's principal ruler. To those who were considering the celibate life, he warned:

> Would that those who cannot contain themselves stood in fear of rashly professing a state of perfection or taking the name celibates. It is a costly tower indeed, and a great word, which not all can accept (Matthew 19:11). But it would undoubtedly be better to marry than to burn (1 Corinthians 7:9), and to remain in the lower rank of the faithful people and be saved than to live a worse life in the high rank of the clergy and be judged more severely.[44]

For Bernard, the health of the church cannot be reduced to the number of men entering the priesthood. The church would do better to try to discourage people from pursuing this form of life if they lacked the prudence to consider the cost of the vocation or an awareness of the difficulty they would certainly face.

To those who were peacemakers in fact as well as in speech, Bernard tried to encourage them even as he warned them of the poor state of the episcopacy. He repeated the Beatitude for the peacemakers in contrast to the hirelings. The hireling in John 10:12 flees when the wolf comes, showing how persecution and tribulation distinguish between the blessed peacemaker and the faithless cleric. The problem with the contemporary bishops, about whom Bernard complained, was even worse:

Oh, that those who are not shepherds today would show themselves to be hirelings in charge of sheep and not of wolves. Would that they did not themselves injure the sheep and flee when no one was pursuing (Proverbs 28:1). Would that they might not expose the flock to danger when they see the wolf coming. They had to be endured when they were found, especially in a time of peace, receiving their pay and, if only for the money (Matthew 6:2, 6:5), working to guard the sheep: as long as they did not disturb the sheep and drive them away from the pastures of truth and righteousness for nothing.[45]

Bernard advised people to expect their tribulations from faithless and wicked bishops. He assured them, however, that they have nothing to fear from these men "if no wickedness" had them in its control. Further, he encouraged them to be mindful of the fact that the tribulations of the righteous are signs of an abundant reward in heaven. As long as Christ remained their cause, Bernard advised reformers and peacemakers to take solace in the Lord's promise that in him "the patience of the poor will never perish" (Psalms 9:19).[46]

Bernard's oddly consoling admonition about tribulations became an important piece of reform rhetoric for later movements. His idea that true peacemakers, who also have to be true reformers, are certain to face opposition from established authorities is well grounded in the scriptural stories of the prophets, in the gospels, and in the Acts of the Apostles. Bernard had effectively appropriated the pattern of the Suffering Servant to explain the ministry of the reformer. When reformers met with opposition, whether it was ecclesial or secular, they began to see the opposition as a confirmation of their cause. In the latter part of the twelfth century, Bernard's belief that true reformers would face tribulation was interpreted in light of apocalyptic expectations. The fusion of these horizons produced creative and progressive ideas, but they also tended to foster radical and revolutionary groups.

Even so, we must keep in mind that the Cistercian abbot was not a revolutionary, seeking to change laws and governmental systems. By reminding people that the laws serve the mission, he was calling people away from relying so heavily on juridical and legal categories. Bernard was not anti-institutional, but he believed that people easily fall into a type of institutional idolatry that made them insensitive to the leadings of the Holy Spirit. Nowhere does Bernard make this tension more evident than in his letter to his former disciple, Pope Eugenius III.

On Consideration: Advice to a Pope

Bernard wrote *On Consideration* directly to the pope, but he was aware that it would be read by others. The work was intended to have general applicability to the whole Christian people, which is evident from the spiritual questions it raised. He expected that these spiritual issues would remain consistent throughout the body of Christ over time. Still, the elements addressing the abuses of his day reveal the ways Bernard was trying to respond to corruptions resulting from the institutional and canonical reforms advanced by Peter Damian and the reformers of the eleventh century. The very reforms that were aimed at strengthening the legal powers of the popes and cardinals became the source of new temptations in the form of legalism. Recognizing that he could not overcome the unhealthy emphasis on canon law and jurisdiction by appealing to legalistic arguments, Bernard began his letter to Pope Eugenius by showing his sympathy.

The problem Eugenius faced, according to Bernard, was the way that mundane affairs harden people's hearts. When he wrote this small treatise, the papacy had experienced significant political victories in Germany, England, France, Portugal, and much of Spain. It had finally achieved the political means to build an international ecclesial government with the cardinals constituting its bureaucracy. As Elizabeth Keenan has noted, the problem was "to prevent administration from choking charisma."[47] Bernard opened the treatise by sharing in the pope's grief over all the affairs associated with the papal office. Clearly, Bernard was concerned that his former disciple had been harmed by his time in office. Like a wound that becomes more insensitive as it becomes more incurable, he argued that hardness of heart is the result of constant suffering. Bernard asked Eugenius to consider: "Is there anything that habit cannot pervert? Anything that is not dulled by frequent occurrence? Anything that is not overcome by repetition? How often do people dread something disagreeable which later becomes agreeable through habit?"[48] The various distractions of the papal office, Bernard feared, would lead the pope where he did not want to go.

Bernard's language is reminiscent of the legend of St. Peter being led to martyrdom, which threw the contrast between the early popes and Eugenius into stark relief. Instead of being led to martyrdom, Eugenius was being led to a hard heart. Bernard described a hard heart this way:

> One that is not torn by compunction, softened by piety, or moved by entreaty. It does not yield to threats; it becomes obdurate with beatings. It is ungrateful for kindness, treacherous in its advice, harsh in judgment, unashamed of disgrace, fearless in danger, inhuman toward humanity, brazen before divinity, unmindful of the past, neglectful of the present, improvident toward the future. This is a heart which recalls nothing at all of the past except injuries suffered, retains nothing of the present and makes neither provision nor preparation for the future except perhaps in vengeance. To encompass all of the evils of such a heart in a single phrase: it is a heart that neither fears God nor respects humanity.[49]

Bernard warned the pope that he was heading toward a hard heart if he continued to devote all his energies to the administrative demands of the papacy without taking time for prayer and study.

In a forceful way, Bernard directly charged the pope with wasting his time on "things which are nothing but a spiritual affliction, a mental drain, and a squandering of grace." The pope was so busy with legal issues that he was failing to teach the people, to build up the church, and to meditate on the law. "Oh yes," Bernard conceded, "every day laws resound through the palace, but these are the laws of Justinian, not of the Lord." He asked the pope to consider the propriety of allowing secular laws and politics, the laws of Justinian, to echo about while God's law was relegated to silence. To the papal apologists in the curia who claimed the pope had the right to be involved in politics, he cited 2 Timothy 2:4: "No one who fights for God entangles himself in secular affairs."[50]

Bernard argued that the pope's involvement in secular law and politics overstepped his ministerial authority and distracted him from his mission. By extension, the argument he presented also applied to the bishops as well. Bernard dared the pope and his curial apologists to demonstrate from scripture any account of the apostles sitting in judgment over people, distributing lands, or surveying boundaries. Citing Luke 12:24, Bernard reminded Eugenius that even Christ did not involve himself in judging secular affairs. Given the Messiah's example, Bernard asked why the pope thought he should judge everything. "Clearly your power is over sin and not property," he explained, "since it is because of sin that you have received the keys of the heavenly kingdom, to exclude sinners not possessors."[51]

The pope and the bishops cannot, according to Bernard, claim apostolic rights to things that the apostles did not have. The apostle Peter had responsibility for the churches, but Bernard emphasized the fact that he did not possess wealth or dominion. He asked the pope to listen to the words of 1 Peter 5:3: "Not in lording it over your charge but making yourself a pattern for the flock." Since Christ absolutely forbade the apostles from acting like the kings of the nations and lording it over the people, he concluded: "It is clear: dominion is forbidden for Apostles." The apostles, following the example of their Lord, imposed the ministry of service. Bernard reminded the pope that St. Paul had described his ministry in terms of labors, beatings, imprisonment, and the threat of martyrdom (2 Cor 11:23).[52]

Was Bernard trying to forbid the pope from exercising rule? Yes. He said so unequivocally. He explained himself this way:

> Is not an estate made subject to a steward and a young lord to a teacher? Nevertheless, the steward is not lord of the estate nor is the teacher lord of his lord. So also, you should preside in order to provide, to counsel, to administer, and to serve. Preside so as to be useful; preside so as to be the faithful and prudent servant whom the Lord has set up over his family. For what purpose? So that you may give them food in due season; that is, so that you may administer, not rule.[53]

In short, magisterial authority is not equivalent to imperial power. Ecclesial leaders should teach and administer, but they should leave legislation and governance to others. If the pope and the curia were to exercise their jurisdiction and power, Bernard argued it should be on behalf of the poor and the powerless, widows and orphans, and not for the wealthy and influential.[54]

Following the examples and doctrines of Gregory the Great and Peter Damian, Bernard understood the magisterial and ministerial role primarily in light of teaching and service. He insisted the authority and the power of the papacy are conditional and subject to limitations, though he did not proceed into a legal discussion of remedies.[55] Instead, Bernard framed his critique within spiritual and pastoral terms. When the pope, or a cardinal, or a bishop oversteps his bounds and becomes involved in secular affairs, he sets a pattern for his flock. Such behavior tells the people that politics, property, and current affairs are more important than serving by example, studying scripture, evangelization, and prayer. Taking his own advice to serve by example, Bernard closed his treatise with a call for prayer: "He [God] must still be sought who has not yet sufficiently been found and who cannot be sought too much; but he is perhaps more worthily sought and more easily found by prayer than by discussion. Therefore let this be the end of the book but not the end of the search."[56]

Bernard of Clairvaux's Continuing Influence

Because Bernard put so much emphasis on the carnal, he also saw the dangers inherent in an unhealthy preoccupation with externals. While his preaching left people burning for Christ's touch, stoked with the fires of eroticism, he decried the rouging of Christ's bride by the men who wished to sell her like a prostitute in their pursuit of offices, privileges, and wealth. Many of the reformers had been seduced by their love of laws and institutions. While Bernard was not opposed to the structures, laws, and disciplines that are necessary for an incarnational church, he believed these must always be subservient to the love of God and of neighbor. Perhaps his most important achievement was to reconnect reform with spirituality. To those who were fixated by externals, he offered a healthy vision of carnality—a sacramental carnality.

Bernard benefited from the emergence of a new interest in nature and in humanity in the twelfth century. Armed with the insights they had gleaned from studying people's behavior and motivations, reformers like Bernard worked to apply these psychological, sociological, and anthropological principles in their work. Bernard knew, for example, that you cannot take an idea, thing, or privilege away from people without offering something to take its place. He sought to shift people's attention away from the carnal desire for gold, beauty, and sex to the carnal desire to be with Christ, to imagine walking with him, to share a meal, to grieve over the passion, to rejoice in the resurrection. Bernard believed that our desire to touch and be touched, to stop and smell a sweet scent, to hear a good word, to taste and see all find their fulfillment in the incarnate Lord.

As a man who had little juridical power in the church, Bernard's strategies and rhetoric became the model for new reform movements that lacked standing in the church. He showed by example that reformers and their movements should be openly self-critical before they criticize others. He eschewed the terms of accusation and denunciation, law and power, in favor of motherly admonitions and exhortations. Mothers correct through words and deeds. As everyone who has a mother knows, they can also be quite impossible, like chimeras in their way. They can be persistent, nagging, and even painfully irritating in their efforts to reform their children; but they are difficult to ignore or to escape. The sincerity of their love can, from time to time, lead to a misguided sense of zeal. Nonetheless, they conceive, birth, and nurture new life.

Bernard's theology conceived of the ways the church can find new life in new expressions, institutions, and ministries. Through his preaching, he gave birth to many children from Francis and Clare of Assisi, to Catherine of Siena and Jean Gerson, and to Luther and Calvin.[57] Bernard has also influenced more recent figures like Popes John XXIII and Paul VI.[58] In the middle of the twentieth century his exhortations on the necessity of progress and of striving to be better induced the labor of a council. His most relevant message for us may be that there is legitimate diversity in the church. He reminds us that the church is neither you nor I alone, it is not the clergy or the laity; but rather it is all of us with our diverse sins, needs, and gifts. Since love and criticism are inextricably tied together in the experience of being human, Bernard showed how love for the church inevitably evokes a desire for reform.

4

Clare of Assisi:
The Clear Mirror of Christ

Favarone was in a foul and dangerous mood. His daughter Clare, who had grown increasingly impossible to control, had decided to follow the mad example of Pietro Bernadone's son, Francis, and take on a life of poverty and manual labor. Favarone had fought against the merchants and guildsmen of Assisi in 1198 and lost. The merchants burned down his house and drove him into exile. In 1201, he had returned with the nobles of Perugia and defeated Assisi's army in order to reclaim his family's property. Favarone was determined that he was not going to lose his daughter to the filthy beggar Francis. It was an insult he could not bear. At the same time, he was concerned about his daughter's welfare. After all, she had escaped the house to join a band of strange men who rejoiced when people threw rocks at them.

As Favarone and his relatives approached the door to the church of San Paolo, where Clare was claiming the right of sanctuary, he must have been wondering why she was so rebellious. Even before she began to associate with Francis, Clare was filled with peculiar ideas about how she was going to live her life. As the family was choosing a husband for her in 1210, two years before she decided to join Francis, Clare had announced she wanted to live a life of virginity and poverty. At seventeen, she sold off her dowry and gave the money to the poor. Worse still, at least to Favarone, she had refused to sell her property back to the family because she claimed that she did not want to defraud the poor.[1] Clare certainly had not appreciated Favarone's efforts to find a good husband who would accept a notoriously willful girl without a dowry.

Favarone probably blamed his wife, Ortulana, for Clare's odd ideas. Ortulana had long been a religious zealot. Maybe he had been too lenient in allowing her to go on a pilgrimage to the Holy Land by herself. Since Ortulana coordinated efforts with the women in the family to provide for the poor, Favarone may have suspected that they had been supporting Francis's restoration efforts at the church of San Damiano.[2] One thing is certain, by the time he arrived at Clare's sanctuary he had decided that he could no longer be indulgent with the rebellious behavior of the women in his family. He had to put an end to the madness before it spread further.

When her family burst through the heavy doors, Clare knew that she was going to have to be strong. Attacking her with violent force, they beat her, kicked her, and tried to drag her away from the church. Clare seized the altar cloths and revealed that she had already professed a religious life by exposing her shorn head. Favarone and the others knew that they could not remove her from the church without incurring a heavy ecclesiastical penalty. For several days they alternated between pleading with her, threatening her, and attacking her; but the opposition simply deepened her resolve. While Clare had been inspired by Francis, she faced this ordeal without him.[3]

At the beginning of her career, Clare had to stand firm against the men in her family who claimed to have her best interests at heart. Francis was not with her as she faced this trial; nor would he be with her when she had to stand firm against two popes and the decrees of a council. Like Favarone, Pope Gregory IX (1227–41) and Pope Innocent IV (1243–54) claimed paternal concern for her welfare to justify their attempts to force her to abandon an apostolic life of poverty. Clare weighed their paternalistic concerns against the portrait of women contained in the New Testament. In the end, she concluded that such patriarchal views of women were less than genuine. Clare set out to teach these men that women were capable of authentically living an apostolic life.

Clare the Franciscan Reformer

St. Clare of Assisi is not an obvious choice as a reformer. Everyone recognizes the importance of reform in Francis's agenda and the various ways the Friars Minor became agents for implementing the pastoral-care reforms of the Fourth Lateran Council in 1215, but Clare's role in creatively implementing the Franciscan vision of reform has been ignored. There are several reasons why Clare the reformer disappeared from our collective consciousness. First, most of the work of recovering medieval theological sources has been done by men who were not particularly interested in the lives and efforts of medieval women. This does not mean that they were trying to foster patriarchy or to silence women's voices. Because they accepted the general critique of medieval European society as extremely sexist, if not misogynistic, many did not see the value of recovering medieval ideas about women. While there is a great deal of truth to this general critique about medieval thought, when we look at particulars a more complex picture emerges.

A second reason why Clare has been overlooked is that scholars have privileged scholastic materials, collections of canon law, and the various chronicles written by educated monks and clerics. When one makes this decision the voices and roles of women in shaping the life, worship, and theological tradition of the church disappear; however, if one admits the lives of the saints written in the Middle Ages as a legitimate source for understanding the development of the tradition, then the efforts of these medieval women represent a great untapped resource for our understanding of the positive role of women in church history.[4] When we come to recognize their contributions more clearly, we will come to a deeper appreciation of the church itself.

One of the most exciting aspects of medieval studies is the recovery of hagiography, which is the study of the lives of the saints. As we learn more from the lives of these medieval women, we are beginning to see various ways they ministered and exercised authority in the medieval church. Not surprisingly, much of the work recovering the stories of medieval women has been done by feminist scholars. This has not helped to bring Clare forward because she does not fit in very well with the language and concerns of feminism. There is even a certain degree of embarrassment over her inspiration by and love for Francis of Assisi.[5]

While Clare of Assisi certainly followed Francis in identifying with the poor and calling people to reform themselves through a life of penance, she also played a critical role in the ongoing process of reforming the problem of sexism. As the first woman to write her own rule for her community, she demonstrated that women could govern themselves in community. By winning the "privilege of poverty," Clare taught a generation of clerics, from popes to friars, that women are full Christians.

Clare's impact on the clergy can be seen in her relationship with Cardinal Hugolino. In 1220 Cardinal Hugolino, who would be elected Pope Gregory IX seven years later, expressed his admiration for Clare this way:

> And although I have always known and have considered myself to be a sinner, yet after having recognized a sure sign of your merits and having observed the rigor of your way of life, I have learned with certainty that I have been weighed down with such a burden of sin and have so offended the Lord of the whole universe, that I am not worthy to be freed from earthly concerns and be associated with the company of the elect, unless your prayers and tears obtain for me pardon for my sins.

He went on to commend and to entrust his soul to Clare, "just as Jesus on the Cross commended his spirit to the Father."[6]

Clare's ability to speak words of wisdom and to perform such powerful deeds as a woman was interpreted in light of Gregory the Great's principle that we are saved by those we despise. The idea that God uses the people we regard as unimportant or as offensive to save us by teaching us humility, which Gregory saw revealed in Christ's life and in the stories of the Old Testament saints, had become quite commonplace. Gregory's theology had experienced a renewal in the Parisian schools in the late twelfth and early thirteenth centuries. Clare seems to have known some of Gregory the Great's theology, but it is virtually impossible to determine whether she was drawing directly from him or from someone who was quoting him. In any case, there was a natural sympathy between Franciscan reform and Gregory's theology.

Francis and Clare's commitment to the idea that we are saved by those we despise, which they found in the gospel, received a ready audience in Rome. Rather than demanding the recognition of rights, Franciscan reform demanded a willingness to be despised in order to save others. This desire to be despised makes Clare largely inaccessible to people who privilege current categories of thought in their historical studies. Ideas such as inherent rights and modern notions of freedom would not begin to appear until roughly five hundred years later. Unfortunately, the idea of equal rights for men and women is far from universally accepted in our country and continues to be absolutely rejected by much of the world.

When it comes to difficult issues, I have followed the advice of Caroline Walker Bynum. Bynum, an expert on medieval women, wrote that we need to pay attention to what these medieval women had to say no matter how distasteful or delightful it is to our sensibilities.[7] For example, Clare's methods of converting people's hearts are deeply rooted in the virtue of humility. The term *humility* presents immediate difficulties. Calling women to humility has often been used as a means to manipulate them into silence and conformity. This was also true in the thirteenth century, but Clare penetrated the misuse of the term to see the liberating power of humility and poverty. It was her humility that allowed her to speak out and to break out of her culturally assigned role, so we cannot expect to appreciate Clare as a reformer without a willingness to be open to her perspective.

Nor should we expect that studying Clare of Assisi will provide us with insight into the essence of women reformers or give us norms for all women reformers. Because Clare was a reformer, we must interpret her in light of thirteenth-century social and cultural concerns, which were frequently different from our issues. As we shall see, her battle for the "privilege of poverty" is just one example of the divide between us. While it is doubtful that her form of enclosed life would be an effective or an appealing reform strategy today, Clare's goal was to reform the people of the thirteenth century.

Although it is clear that Clare wanted to reform the sexist attitudes of the clergy, we must not forget that she promoted her ideas by collaborating with these same men. As Bernard McGinn has explained, "Within the context of the medieval church it was virtually impossible for women to create new ways of living the gospel without the cooperation and approval of men."[8] Clare persuaded the most powerful and respected men of the thirteenth century to promote her agenda. They disseminated her doctrine through the bull of canonization, the creation of a liturgical feast in her honor, and the composition of her official life or legend.

Since the accounts of Clare's legend are colored by the perspectives of the men who wrote them, they should not be used as a means to penetrate the inner life of Clare or of medieval women in general. Still, I do not believe the stories about Clare were simply composed to tell us what men wanted to think about holy women. These stories also reveal what women wanted men to think about holy women. Medieval women like Clare were well aware of male expectations concerning holiness. They were exposed to the various lives of the saints, which often included examples of women preaching, governing, and healing.[9] My working assumption is that Clare of Assisi was deliberate in drawing on a variety of traditional threads of thought about holy women. She wove these strands into a new altar cloth and symbolically demonstrated the central role of women in the living worship of the church.

Clare used these expectations and traditional sources to her advantage. While she wrote little that has survived, she employed symbolic acts to create a type of rhetoric of life. Both Francis and Clare, emulating the symbolic acts of the Old Testament prophets, attempted to preach or teach by means of dramatic events reminiscent of performance art. This strategy was partially the result of prohibitions against laypeople and members of religious orders preaching, but it also grew out of the desire to literally imitate Christ and the disciples in the evangelical form of life. Even the desire to incorporate both men and women into the Franciscan mission was seen as a means of symbolically or sacramentally reenacting the evangelical efforts of the disciples and the church as they are portrayed in Acts.

Clare's reform agenda and strategies bear many similarities to the efforts of other women in the thirteenth century, but it would be a mistake to assume that all or most of the other women working for reform shared her specific message or way of life. She and her sisters were unique. Still, Clare benefited from and tapped into important developments in the thirteenth-century church. As Bernard McGinn has noted, this was a period when women began to take a prominent position in the mystical tradition and marks the beginning of the great age of women's theology and vernacular theology.[10] Before we turn to explore Clare's career, we must briefly consider her historical context and the Franciscan reform agenda.

The Crumbling Church of the Thirteenth Century

The church was extremely corrupt in the thirteenth century, so much so, that Innocent III (1198–1216) believed there was a real danger of its collapse before the Cathars and the Waldensians. As we have seen, the Cathars were anarchic dualists from Eastern Europe who followed a simple form of life and pointed to the incredible corruption of the diocesan clergy. By the early thirteenth century, their simplicity and honesty had gained them a large following with the growing number of people who had good reason to be disenchanted with the church. At the same time the free preachers, who were called the Waldensians, called into question the hierarchical order of the church.[11]

The Waldensians, unlike the Cathars, were Christians. In 1179, at the Third Lateran Council, Pope Alexander III approved their vow of voluntary poverty and gave them the right to preach with the permission of the local bishop. The Waldensians dutifully obtained this permission from the bishop of Lyons and engaged in vernacular preaching, much of which was probably aimed at combating the Cathar heresy. However, the bishop of Lyons died and his successor forbade them to preach. The Waldensians responded by declaring that every Christian has a right to preach.[12] Eventually they denied the importance of the sacraments and the authority of the church, which were inextricably linked realities in the Middle Ages. In response, the bishops reinforced the canons against laypeople or monks preaching doctrinal sermons at the Fourth Lateran Council in 1215.[13]

The popular appeal of these two groups was related to a twofold deficiency of the Catholic Church at the time: The diocesan clergy, particularly the bishops, were largely ignorant and therefore unable to provide proper catechesis and teaching in their sermons; and the diocesan clergy had scandalized the faithful by their lack of morality. Recognizing the problem of the largely immoral and ignorant state of much of the diocesan clergy, the Second and Third Lateran Councils called for bishops to establish cathedral schools, which would offer a free education to those men who were entering the clergy. Unfortunately, this provision of canon law was frequently ignored by the bishops who were loath to spend their own money for educating others.

Because both the Cathars and the Waldensians had denied the validity of the sacraments, the dividing line between orthodoxy and heresy soon came to focus on sacramental concerns. In the early thirteenth century virtually everyone accepted that the church was corrupt, but this does not mean that reformers were welcomed by most bishops. With the birth of the Inquisition at the Fourth Lateran, reform had become a risky venture. The lay reformers who were successful drew upon the popular piety of the day, which was influenced by the idea of following the apostolic life *(vita apostolica)* and marked by a growing interest in the sacraments of penance and Eucharist.

The impact of these popular or lay movements can be seen in the canons of the Fourth Lateran Council, which required people to participate in the sacrament of penance and the reception of the Eucharist at least once a year. The eucharistic devotion of these movements can also be given the credit or blame for the council's definition of the doctrine of transubstantiation. Their influence even extended to the liturgical calendar. For example, Juliana of Mt. Cornillon, who took on an evangelical form of life, was largely responsible for the creation of the liturgical feast of Corpus Christi.[14] One of the most important women behind the success of the new piety and sense of purpose in the church was Mary of Oignies.

Mary of Oignies

In the thirteenth century women like Mary of Oignies initiated an evangelical awakening that spread across Europe. This religious revival helped the church to marginalize and ultimately overcome the popular heretics. These religious mothers *(mulieres sanctae)*, who were often called Beguines, worked to clean up their clerical children and to teach them how to live an evangelical life. They did not preach with words. These women taught people through their deeds. Their service to the sick and the poor and the marginalized shamed the clergy into admitting their own lack of apostolic zeal. Many members of the clergy were converted by their example, but others sought ways to suppress these *mulieres sanctae*.[15]

A common strategy to suppress the Beguines was to claim that they were violating the canons against lay preaching. Even though these women did preach, the more circumspect Beguines limited themselves to offering penitential admonitions or exhortations to holiness. This strategy was intended to keep them from running afoul of the large number of bishops who jealously protected their "rights" to preach to the exclusion of any legitimate Christian witnessing. By restricting themselves to admonitions and exhortations, they hoped to avoid the charge of usurping the bishop's control of doctrinal preaching.

Unfortunately, many bishops and priests were ignorant of the distinction between doctrinal preaching *(articuli Fidei et sacramenta)*, which was restricted to the bishop, and preaching by means of exhortation *(verbum exhortationis)*, which is the Christians' duty to witness their faith and to correct the errors of their neighbors. Ignorance of this distinction was one of the factors that pushed the Waldensians into their radical stance of rejecting ecclesial authority altogether.[16] The Beguines and other lay groups, like the early Franciscan movement, constantly struggled with ecclesial authorities who could not understand how lay people in general and women in particular could be engaged in preaching and in apostolic works.

Nonetheless, women did engage in apostolic works. Mary of Oignies, who is seen by many scholars as one of the first Beguines, helped to pave the way for ecclesial acceptance of groups like the Poor Ladies. Mary was married at the age of fourteen, which was fairly typical, and after a few years of being married she convinced her husband to join her in making a vow of chastity. The couple decided to undertake the apostolic work of helping the disenfranchised and the outcasts of society. Mary was inspired by the gospel message to give up all that she had and to follow the Lord.

Around 1207, Mary's reputation for sanctity drew other women to join her. As she engaged in a ministry of service and healing, she became overwhelmed by the numbers of people who sought her out as an object of devotion. Eventually, she took on a more secluded life at the Augustinian house in Oignies (in modern-day Belgium) where she guided the women who had followed her. In effect, she was a type of "third order" Augustinian, but she never took on the enclosed form of life of a nun.[17] By associating herself with an established order, Mary helped to diffuse the suspicion that she was a heretic.

Mary of Oignies became a point of contact between popular piety and the reform agenda of the clerical establishment through her relationship with Jacques de Vitry. Jacques de Vitry was a member of the "biblical moral school," which included Alan of Lille, Peter the Chanter, and Stephen Langton.[18] While people have questioned whether applying the term *school* to these men is appropriate, they were united by their concern for biblical studies and the application of those studies to the practical tasks of preaching on faith and morals.[19] Their interest in morality and preaching led to a revival of Gregory the Great and Peter Damian's theology, which in turn prepared them to accept a more active role for women in the life of the church.

Jacques de Vitry carried Peter the Chanter's message out into the towns and cities in what is now France and Belgium. He was the most famous preacher of his time. His success was due to the fact that he was very aware of the issues that were of concern for his audience. This awareness was not something that he learned studying theology in Paris; instead, he learned how to adapt his doctrinal training to the people through the advice and guidance of Mary of Oignies. Mary helped Jacques understand how to apply the principles he had learned to vernacular preaching. In fact, he gave Mary all the credit for his homiletical skills, and Mary portrayed him as her mouthpiece on her deathbed.[20]

In 1216, Jacques de Vitry encountered both the Friars Minor and the Poor Ladies in his travels through the Umbrian valley. He wrote about the experience to his friends in Liège:

> I found one consolation in those parts, nevertheless: many men and women, rich and worldly, after renouncing everything for Christ, fled the world. They are called the Lesser Brothers and Lesser Sisters. They are held in great esteem by the lord pope and the cardinals. They do not occupy themselves with temporal affairs, but work each day with great desire and enthusiastic zeal to capture those souls that were perishing from the vanities of the world and to bring them along with them.

He went on to explain how the Poor Ladies, who were also known as the Lesser Sisters of Penance at the time, lived in simple houses and supported themselves by manual labor. Impressed by their humility, he said that these women were offended by the honor both the clergy and the laity bestowed upon them.[21]

Women like Mary of Oignies helped to foster an environment that was friendly to lay expressions of the apostolic life. Mary and the women around her nurtured a spirit of creativity and openness to new forms of ministry. In addition to forming Jacques de Vitry's pastoral skills, Mary had made a deep impression on Archbishop Fulk of Toulouse, who was a pivotal figure in the early formation of the Dominican Order.[22] By helping these men reconnect to the language and concerns of the laity, the Beguines reformed the pastoral formation the priests and bishops had received.

Even though much had been done to prepare the church for women and lay reformers, it was still a dangerous proposition to propose new forms of life and ministry. The crusades against the

Albigensians in southern France in the early thirteenth century, which resulted in genocide, and the abuses of the first Inquisition reveal how courageous Francis and Clare were. Many of the Beguines would find themselves persecuted, suppressed, tortured, and even put to death by their local clergy. At other times, the various reformers would be forced to accept existing forms of life and ministry.[23]

Both the Friars Minor and the Poor Ladies of San Damiano had to struggle to maintain their identity. Since the Fourth Lateran had forbidden the creation of new orders and new rules of religious life, the Franciscan community faced a real challenge to its legitimacy early. The Friars Minor were rapidly clericalized and pressed into the service of *cura animarum*, which has led to endless and pointless debates about whether they remained true to their founder's vision.[24] But no one disputes that the Poor Ladies remained rooted in the initial inspiration of Clare and Francis. Clare did not accomplish this without a fight. At the same time that the popes were transforming the Friars Minor into a preaching order, they were also attempting to change the Poor Ladies into Benedictines. Clare would have none of it and steadfastly defended the form of life she and Francis had created.

Franciscan Reform

Clare believed that the path to peace was poverty. She would not have subscribed to the contemporary idea that there will be no peace until there is justice. Instead, Clare believed it was necessary to give people more than they deserved to establish peace. This idea was central to Francis of Assisi's reform agenda from the outset of his career. Whereas the friars had a great deal of difficulty accepting and acting on Francis's principles, Clare and the Poor Ladies remained deeply committed to this method of reform.[25]

Poverty and penance had long been recognized as forms of renunciation associated with monastic withdrawal from the world. Whereas possessions and privileges were seen as forms of divine chastisement, corporate property and privileges were accepted as a necessary means for fulfilling the church's pilgrimage to perfection. Without denying the necessity of the institutional, the corporate, and the legal aspects of the church, Francis and Clare perceived that it is impossible to overcome the human obsession with status and wealth through accumulating property and privileges.

By calling men and women to actively embrace and to steadfastly love evil people, Franciscan reform went beyond passive resistance. Since many of the bishops were trying to protect their rights and privileges, Francis and Clare understood that claiming privileges would only serve to heighten their fears. Based on the belief that the only way to overcome fear is through love, Francis wrote: "The Gospel teaches us not to dispute, nor strike, nor resist evil—all of which the Rule, before it received the papal seal especially expressed; but now it includes everything in precise and general words."[26] He repeatedly insisted that his spiritual progeny should follow Christ's teaching and example to love their enemies and to do good to those who harm them.[27]

Francis and Clare framed their understanding of reform in terms of penance. Clare wrote, "After the most high heavenly Father saw fit in His mercy and grace to enlighten my heart, that I should do penance according to the teaching and example of our most blessed father Francis...."[28] The brothers and sisters would assume the behavior and appearance of penitents, calling people to fear God and encouraging them to embrace the sacraments. By doing so they took the lowest position in society and revealed their faithfulness to the church. After all, who reveals more fidelity to the church than the penitent? At first, the Franciscans hardly seemed to be a threat to the interests of the unreformed clergy. The popes and many of the bishops realized that attacking the Friars Minor or the Poor Ladies would have been a counterproductive strategy.

Whereas the diocesan clergy had little credibility with the people, the Franciscan brothers and sisters visibly supported the significance of the sacraments regardless of the quality of the clergy. Certainly Francis was not blind to the low quality of the priests and bishops when he gave this admonition in 1220 to the Brothers and Sisters of Penance:

> We must also frequently visit churches and venerate and revere the clergy, not so much for themselves, if they are sinners, but because of their office and administration of the most holy Body and Blood of Christ which they sacrifice on the altar, receive, and administer to others. And let all of us know for certain that no one can be saved except through the holy words and Blood of our Lord Jesus Christ which the clergy pronounce, proclaim, and minister.[29]

Why would Francis have had to make such an exhortation? It seems that some of the brothers and sisters had begun to hold the clergy in contempt. He was so concerned about this attitude that he presented his brothers and sisters with this warning: "We must never desire to be above others, but, instead, we must be servants and subject 'to every human institution for God's sake'" (1 Peter 2:13).[30]

If the brothers and sisters had privileges and power like other human institutions, then they would need to protect them. Francis and Clare discerned that the desire to protect possessions, whether they are physical properties or legal rights, is the source of endless disputes and quarrels. Because it impedes Christian charity, anger was something Francis wanted his followers to avoid absolutely. He gave his brothers and sisters this principle:

> Nothing should displease a servant of God except sin. And no matter how another person may sin, if a servant of God becomes disturbed and angry because of this and not because of charity, he is storing up guilt for himself. The servant of God who does not become angry or disturbed at anyone lives correctly without anything of his own.[31]

Additionally, he forbade the members of the community from reviling anyone, from gossip, from detraction, from judging, and from condemning.

At this point, you might be asking yourself, "Within these parameters, how could the early Franciscans have hoped to achieve meaningful reform?" Many of the bishops were simoniacal, lax with disciplining their clergy, and involved in scandalous behavior from concubinage to embezzlement. Francis's vision of reform fell so far out of the norms of the thirteenth century that Hugh of Digne called his desire to defer to all ecclesiastical persons "marvelous."[32] Clare described his example as wonderful.[33]

In fact, there was something radically subversive about Francis's desires and actions toward the clergy. By desiring to give the bishops the respect they did not deserve, Francis and Clare were imitating the way Christ desires to give to sinners the grace they do not deserve. The early Franciscan men and women saw themselves as taking on the pastoral care of the bishops and their clergy. According to the apologetics of humility, the one who serves also demonstrates his or her Christian authority. Rather than enter into contests over words, the Franciscans set out to reform the clergy through example. By giving these men the respect they did not deserve, they helped the bishops move to a sense of compunction or remorse over their sins.

The Franciscan movement had tapped into one of the most common principles of medieval educational theory, namely, that people learn primarily through imitation. Clare clearly expressed this idea in her Testament: "For the Lord Himself has placed us not only as a form for others in being an example and mirror, but even for our sisters whom the Lord has called to our way of life as well, that they in turn might be an example and a mirror to those living in the world."[34] The Poor Ladies would reform the church through their attempts to provide living examples of Christian life.

Franciscan reform is absolutely nonsensical to those who do not possess the fear of God. It is the fear of God, the recognition that God is just and that people are not, which moves the sinner to seek reconciliation. Grateful for the gift of salvation, the sinner learns to be gracious with others. Fear of God also allows people to let go of their anger and desire for vengeance. In this sense, the fear of God is a mercy for those who have suffered real oppression or evil. Filled with this gift, the only pious or appropriate response to sinners, even clerical sinners, is to feel pity for them. Those who possess the fear of God understand that if anyone stands to be pitied, it is the sinful bishop. This does not mean that they should not be punished, but it means the Franciscan goal is always to save the sinner regardless of rank.

Much of the early history of the Friars Minor was shaped by the fact that most of the brothers had difficulty accepting Francis's reform methods. Speaking for the community concerns in the 1240s and 1250s, the brothers in the *Assisi Compilation* protested to Francis that they needed a privilege to preach because the bishops were impeding the salvation of souls. Francis reportedly responded:

> You, Lesser Brothers, you do not know the will of God, and will not allow me to convert the whole world as God wills. For I want to convert the prelates first by humility and reverence. Then, when they see your holy life and your reverence for them, they will ask you to preach and to convert the people. These will attract the people to you far better than the privileges you want, which would lead you to pride.[35]

The only privilege Francis wanted, according to the story, was not to have any privilege from any human being; instead, he wanted to show reverence to all, and, by obedience to the Rule, to convert everyone more by his example than his word.

By way of contrast, Clare found herself engaged in a fight to win the privilege of poverty. Women were not allowed to have their own religious communities unless they were endowed with income from rents and leases. This meant that women were forced to accept property and privilege because it was assumed that they could not support themselves. This concern was the result of several cases of terrible deprivation and even starvation in some of the poorer communities of religious women; however, Clare recognized that this policy reinforced the sexist attitudes of the age and suggested that women cannot be as Christian as men because of their weakness.

As we shall see, Clare proved that she and her sisters were anything but weak. In the end, the Poor Ladies were able to convert the bishops by their humble example much more effectively than the friars. After some initial setbacks, the bishops invited the Franciscan women to join them in their teaching ministry and efforts to call people to conversion. The impact of these women who imitated Clare's determined humility has reached around the world through their missionary activities, hospitals, and schools. Long before most women held positions of power and authority in any arena Franciscan women were achieving doctorates, running hospitals, establishing colleges, and taking on roles that were traditionally reserved to men.

Clare of Assisi's Understanding of Women and Ministry

Writing to Agnes of Prague in 1234, Clare told her that she was worthy of the greatest respect. Clare did not base her admiration on the fact that Agnes was the daughter of King Premsyl Ottokar of Bohemia. Agnes was worthy of honor because she was "the spouse and the mother and the sister of Jesus Christ" (Matthew 12:50).[36] In a later letter, she explained how Agnes was in the proper sense a "true co-worker of God Himself (1 Corinthians 3:9; Romans 16:3) and a support of the weak members of His ineffable Body."[37] Clare's commendations of Agnes reveal a great deal about her form of life and her reform agenda. Her allusions to these passages from scripture reveal an argument for the ministerial role of women in the church.

Like the reformers who had preceded her, Clare used these letters as a means to disseminate and to preserve her agenda. Both letters come out of a period when Clare was involved in a struggle to maintain the privilege of poverty and the letters' preservation reveals how significant they were to the sisters. In addition to spiritual and communal advice, these letters provided a justification for the ministry of the sisters.

Clare's citation of Matthew 12:50 drew upon St. Francis's "Second Letter to All of the Faithful," in which he wrote:

> We are spouses when the faithful soul is joined to Jesus Christ by the Holy Spirit. We are brothers when we do the will of His Father Who is in heaven. We are mothers when we carry Him in our heart and body through love and a pure and sincere conscience; we give birth to Him through a holy manner of working, which should shine before others as an example.[38]

The Franciscan interpretation of Matthew 12:50 did not rely on the authority of St. Francis alone. Francis's authority was far from certain in the early part of the twelfth century. This portrait of laypeople actively engaged in ministry as the mothers of Christ relied on the authority of Gregory the Great for its legitimacy and was directly related to the issue of preaching.

In a homily on Matthew 12:46–50, Gregory had asked people to consider how they could become mothers of Christ. Answering his own question, Gregory wrote, "We should know that a person who is Christ's brother and sister through belief becomes His mother by preaching." His model was Felicity, whom he described this way:

> By believing she became Christ's servant; by preaching, she became Christ's mother....When caught up in the sufferings of the persecution, she strengthened her sons' hearts in love of their homeland above by preaching. She gave birth in the spirit to those to whom she had given physical birth, so that by preaching she might bring forth to God those whom in the flesh she had brought forth into the world.[39]

It is impossible to say whether or not Francis and Clare knew Gregory's homily as he had written it or through some intermediary source, but they must have known that Matthew 12:50 had been used to advocate the legitimacy of lay preaching. Most significantly, Gregory's interpretation of this passage had been used in the apologetics of men like Jacques de Vitry to justify the Beguine practice of preaching and may even be the source behind calling them *mulieres sanctae*, or holy mothers.

Clare's reference to being a co-worker of God in the sense intended by St. Paul is also significant. Paul uses this phrase in 1 Corinthians 3:9 to describe the apostolic activity of the men and women in the church of Corinth, but he explains what being a co-worker means in Romans. In Roman 16:3, the term *co-workers* specifically refers to Prisca and Aquila, who worked with Paul in his ministry. Further, the passage immediately follows the commendation of Phoebe, who was a minister of the church in Cenchreae. Clare was reminding her sisters and her church that Paul neither presented these women as subordinates nor excluded them from active ministry in the care of souls.

While it is true that Clare and the Poor Ladies took on an enclosed form of life, the picture that emerges out of her official life shows a community that was active in providing a healing ministry, in giving spiritual direction, and in preaching. In addition to preaching to her sisters, Clare even preached to prominent men like Cardinal Hugolino through her "holy conversations."[40] Normally, enclosure would have meant that the sisters would never be allowed outside their house, but Clare redefined its meaning in her Rule. Clare defined the sisters' enclosure this way: "Thereafter, she may not go outside of the monastery except for some useful, reasonable, evident, and approved purpose."[41] While this may seem restrictive to us, it represented a new flexibility for religious women that had not existed since the time of the early church in the Latin West. Clare's form of enclosure meant the sisters could engage in ministerial work such as teaching, helping the poor, and providing care for the sick. The two previous rules that were written by Cardinal Hugolino and Pope Innocent IV would not have allowed the sisters to leave the enclosure for virtually any reason.

Clare's Rule was practical and creative. She freely drew upon Francis's Rule but was not bound by his ideas. Whereas Francis had strictly forbidden the friars from receiving or handling money, Clare allowed the sisters to use and to receive money. In fact, her policy avoided the confusion and difficulties entailed in Francis's prohibition against money. Since the Poor Ladies primarily supported themselves by means of their labor, they had to tap into the new and growing money economy. It was her foresight on this issue that enabled and required subsequent generations of Franciscan women to engage the world and to alleviate some of the inequities of the marketplace.

While Clare did not seem to expect the flowering of her order in her lifetime, it does seem that she envisioned the role her sisters would have in establishing and operating schools, hospitals, and other charitable institutions. Like so many of her male predecessors who had worked for reform, Clare was an institutional reformer in the sense that she built a religious order dedicated to advancing the apostolic role of women in the church. Her fight to maintain her community's ability to define itself and to preserve the privilege of poverty brings forward her qualities of fortitude and determination—qualities normally applied to men.

The Fight for Poverty

Clare had to begin fighting for the privilege of poverty shortly after the Fourth Lateran Council in 1215. Francis had obtained verbal permission for his way of life from Pope Innocent III prior to the Fourth Lateran. While the Friars Minor would have to struggle to defend their legitimacy for almost sixty years, the Poor Ladies' way of life had not been approved before the council forbade the establishment of any new religious orders. Clare had absolutely no legal foundation for the *Form of Life* she had been following at San Damiano from 1212 to 1215.[42] Undeterred, she set out to create a juridical foundation for her vision of apostolic life.

In 1216, Clare wrote to Pope Innocent III and requested formal exemption from the requirement that monastic houses possess sufficient corporate property and goods to support them. She knew such an exemption would mean that the Poor Ladies would not be forced to accept an existing rule. Without corporate property, the sisters would have to support themselves through the same type of labor performed by poor women in the cities and by begging for alms. The privilege of poverty also made strict enclosure impossible. If she won on this issue, she knew that her community could not be pushed out of their ministerial work.

Innocent III also did not want the Poor Ladies to be forced into accepting the strict enclosure followed by the Benedictine communities of women. He responded with a letter that has come to be known as the *Privilege of Poverty*, which stated, "Therefore, we confirm with our apostolic authority, as you requested, your proposal 'of most high poverty' (2 Corinthians 8:2), granting you by the authority of this letter that no one can compel you to receive possessions."[43] He knew enough about canon law to see the implications of this exemption. As Brenda Bolton noted, "It seemed that Innocent has, therefore, helped to create an entirely new form of convent community, which maintained itself on alms and the profits of manual labor in the same way as the Franciscans."[44]

Why was Innocent III so concerned about Clare's mission that he would abrogate one of the provisions of a council? The answer is that he recognized the important role Clare and her sisters were playing in combating heresy. He was deeply concerned by the strength of the Cathars and he knew that they had holy women who spread their faith.[45] Innocent was intent on countering the Cathars with holy women of his own. Since he believed that heresy was the result of the corruption of the Catholic clergy, he also appreciated the role that Clare and her sisters were playing in reforming the lives of clergymen. The Poor Ladies of San Damiano were definitely a bright spot that Innocent could point to as he tried to reaffirm the church's relevancy.

After receiving the *Privilege of Poverty*, Clare came to recognize the importance of her community to the broader church. Over a short period of time, she began to use the power of what we call public relations in her struggle for some degree of autonomy. Still, she faced serious setbacks after the death of Innocent III. In 1219 Cardinal Hugolino imposed a rule based on the *Rule of Benedict* on the sisters. His goals were to exempt the sisters from the jurisdiction of the local bishop and to provide the sisters with some legal cover. Unfortunately, *The Rule of Cardinal Hugolino* also called for a type of strict enclosure that was inconsistent with Clare's charism, but it did not abrogate Innocent III's *Privilege of Poverty* or Francis's *Form of Life*. This legal potpourri made for a confusing mix, but Clare eventually created a new synthesis out of these various components.

When Cardinal Hugolino became Pope Gregory IX, he continued to show an interest in the growing number of women following the evangelical counsels and taking up ministerial work in the church. This interest was a bit of a double-edged sword because his desire to help these women entailed accepting property and strict enclosure. Clare was so concerned that she asked the pope to reconfirm the privilege of poverty in 1228. Though he confirmed the *Privilege of Poverty*, Gregory IX worked to undermine the primitive *Form of Life*. At the request of the Friars Minor, who were tired of serving the Poor Ladies as chaplains, the pope attempted to absolve them of this duty in 1230 with the bull *Quo elongati*. Clare responded by committing her community to a hunger strike. Faced with the scandalous prospect of the starvation of the sisters, Gregory relented and required the Friars Minor to continue to provide pastoral care for the Poor Ladies. This does not mean that he had been fully converted. For example, Gregory IX tried to convince Agnes of Prague that she was not bound by the *Form of Life* eight years later.[46]

With the election of a new pope, Clare had to start the process over again.[47] In 1247 Pope Innocent IV wrote a new rule for the Poor Ladies. One of his goals was to make the Friars Minor assume responsibility for pastoral and economic needs of the sisters. Unfortunately, the new rule also drastically reduced the autonomy of the Poor Ladies and emphasized a stricter observance of monastic enclosure for the sisters. The *Rule of Innocent* spurred Clare into action. She had come to recognize that the various papal interventions were eroding her reform agenda. She knew that she would never reform the problem of sexism by letting men determine the form of life she had been called to follow. Clare concluded she must do something that no woman in the church had ever done: She decided she must write her own rule.

Writing the rule was a process. We know that Clare collaborated with members of the curia and with some of the Friars Minor, but the details of these consultations have been lost to history. Clare also consulted her sisters on a weekly basis for their advice and solicited the opinions of the other abbesses such as Agnes of Prague. The six-year effort must have seemed painfully slow to Clare, but it was a relatively short period for converting the pope and the curia from their paternalistic attitudes. After all, these sexist ideas had been a major part of their personal formation from the cradle to their university training.

Paternalistic ideas were reinforced by the men and women in their families, communities, and the church.

In 1253, it looked like Clare would die before her rule was approved. Moved by her intelligence, determination, and fidelity, Innocent IV finally approved the Rule of Clare. He rushed the document through the curial process so that she would see it. He wanted her to know that she had succeeded in securing the privilege of poverty before she died. When the saint received her rule with the papal seal, her sisters report that she was so excited that she touched and kissed the document many times out of devotion.[48]

In her small quiet way, Clare made one of the most significant advances in the struggle for the equality of the sexes. She challenged the clergy to believe the scriptures they read, to teach what they believed, and to practice what they taught. In the writings that we have, she reminded her sisters that women are co-workers and not subordinates by pointing to the St. Paul's witness to the ministry of women in the early church. In The Testament she wrote, "With what eagerness and fervor of mind and body, therefore, must we keep the commandments of our God and Father, so that, with the help of the Lord, we may return to him an increase of his talent" (cf. Matthew 25:15–23).[49] Her message was that women were also called to trade their talents in the world. In fact, Clare had taught a generation of people to recognize that women represent Christ to the world in a way that men cannot.

The Poor Ladies proved to Francis and his brothers that women could also heroically embrace deprivation, poverty, hard work, trial, and the contempt of the world. By their example, Clare and her sisters taught the people around them that the desire to protect women from hardship and deprivation was a way of limiting their ability to actually join the race and win the prize of salvation. Once Clare converted Francis, who seems to have expected that she and her sisters would flee hardship, the pair worked together to reveal that the very people their society despised were also the ones who carried the key to salvation.[50] From a Franciscan perspective, the conversion of the heart is the result of learning to see Christ in the people we despise. Clare and the noble women who joined her tried to symbolically reflect Christ by hiding the highest nobility in human poverty, strength in weakness, freedom in manual labor, and salvation in shame.

The Bull of Canonization

After Clare's death, Pope Innocent IV moved to have Clare canonized. In the medieval mind, such canonization was considered to be a certain sign of legitimacy not only for the saint but also for her way of life. Innocent saw Clare, the woman who rejected his rule, as another Christ. He proclaimed, "O the ineffable brilliance of blessed Clare! The more eagerly she is sought after for something the more brilliant she is found in everything!" Like the divine Word, Clare can be seen in all of creation. Innocent also recognized Clare's sacramental and christological qualities by highlighting the relationship between the hidden and the visible in Clare's life. The bull states: "Hidden within, she extended herself abroad. In fact, Clare was hidden, yet her life became visible. Clare was silent, yet her reputation became widespread. She was kept hidden in a cell, but was known throughout the world."[51]

Pope Innocent IV also incorporated Clare's position on the apostolic nature of women's ministry and on the ability of women to govern by associating her with the biblical heroine Esther. The bull states:

> This clear spring of the Spoleto Valley furnished a new fountain of living water (cf. Esther 3:13) for the refreshment and comfort of souls (cf. Wisdom 3:13), which, already coming together in many streams in the territory of the church, has irrigated the nursery-gardens of the regions (cf. Esther 11:10). This was a lofty candelabra of sanctity (cf. Esther 15:31; 26:1), strongly burning in the tabernacle of the Lord (cf. Hebrews 9:2), to whose remarkable splendor many have and are hastening, lighting their lamps by its light.[52]

As we have seen, Esther had been used as a justification for women to govern by traditional figures like Peter Damian. Innocent was drawing upon the traditional way the church interpreted the story of Esther to prove the legitimacy of Clare's ability to write her own rule.

What is even more interesting is the way Pope Innocent used images and terms associated with the pastoral office of the bishop to describe Clare's ministry. Clear springs were associated with both the truth of the gospel and with the lives of good pastors. By way of contrast, polluted or muddy waters were associated with bishops who defiled the truth by their wicked lives. Innocent described Clare as water for the comfort of souls, which is strikingly similar to the traditional image of the bishop as the one who is "able to water the dry hearts of others with the streams of instruction imparted."[53]

Pope Innocent emphasized the idea that Clare had the qualities of an excellent bishop by associating her governance with the theology of Gregory the Great. He described Clare this way:

> This woman, the first of the poor, the leader of the humble, the teacher of the continent, the abbess of the penitents, governed her monastery and the family entrusted to her within it with solicitude and prudence, in the fear and service of the Lord, with full observance of the Order: vigilant in care, eager in ministering, intent on exhortation, diligent in reminding, constant in compassion, discreet in silence, mature in speech, and skillful in all things concerning perfect government, wanting to serve rather than to command, to honor rather than to be extolled.[54]

While Innocent clearly recognized her as an abbess in the first half of this statement, the procession of terms following the colon appear to be a paraphrase of the qualities Gregory the Great deemed necessary for a man to be a good bishop. Taken collectively, they also contradict the medieval stereotypes of women as lax, selfish, nagging, gossipy.

The list of Clare's miracles in the *Bull of Canonization* and the official *Legend of St. Clare* highlights her apostolic ministry. During her life she cured those who were mute, deaf, and blind. Clare also healed one of the Friars Minor from insanity, which was an example of her ability to cure souls as well as bodies. After dying, she cast out demons, restored a withered hand, healed a paralyzed leg, and made the lame walk. Of course, these are the miracles performed by Christ and the disciples in the gospels and in Acts. In order to show that women have gifts and abilities that men do not, the friar who wrote *The Legend of St. Clare* included a story of how Clare was able to heal a boy whom Francis could not.[55]

The last two miracles contained in the *Legend* also link St. Clare to apostolic ministry. These miracles show how Clare freed children from wolves, which is the work of the good shepherd who fights for his (or her) flock.[56] By possessing all the virtues and merits that a bishop or pastor was supposed to have, by serving rather than being served, and by her powerful and miraculous deeds, she freed some of the bishops from the twin wolves of sexism and pride. She freed them by humbling them through her example. Clare liberated these men from the worst forms of paternalism by giving them the respect and honor that they did not deserve. Indeed, she gave the men around her the respect and honor she deserved. In this way, Clare was the true mirror of Christ, who lifted up the honor he deserved on the ignominy of the cross.

Epilogue

Clare was one of the few reformers to receive the gift of seeing the fruition of their agenda, but the Franciscan women who followed her faced a significant setback when Urban IV set aside the *Rule of Clare* in favor of his own rule in 1263. All the houses of the Poor Clares, except for those in San Damiano and Prague, were stripped of the privilege of poverty. Further, the Friars Minor were released from their commitment to serve the spiritual needs of the sisters. Clare's Rule, which was buried with her, was lost and forgotten until it was rediscovered in her tomb eight centuries later.[57]

In 1296 the Poor Clares were uniformly pressed into strict enclosure by Pope Boniface VIII. While the *Rule of Clare* was buried and her legislative victory was reversed, Innocent IV's *Bull of Canonization* and *The Legend of St. Clare* continued to witness to her cause. Inspired by their founder's tenacious example, the Poor Clares evolved to meet the challenge by creating extern sisters and new forms of religious life. Franciscan sisters did move out into the world.

After the Protestant Reformation, the church turned its reforming impulse out onto society. Since that time, the Franciscan women have played and continue to play a prominent role in exhorting and admonishing a selfish world to remember that we are saved by those we despise: the poor, the foreigners, the sick, and the imprisoned. Perhaps Clare is more of a saint for our age, as we struggle to find positive and empowering models for Christian women. With the recovery of her rule and the attention being focused on Clare, she has once again become a clear light exposing the sin of sexism in the world and showing the church the way to reform itself.

5

Catherine of Siena: The Insatiable Reformer

Unlike Clare of Assisi and the Franciscan reformers, Catherine of Siena publicly excoriated priests, bishops, cardinals, and popes. She called them "wretches," "idiots," "blind hirelings," and "devils incarnate." Catherine, like Clare, sought to shame the clergy into reform; but Catherine's methods and her inspiration for reform were much more direct and challenging than those of her Franciscan predecessor. Catherine claimed that her reform rhetoric was revealed to her in a series of visions. The legitimacy of these visions was reinforced by Catherine's miracles. From an early point in her career, she was known for her miraculous ability to subsist solely on the Eucharist.[1]

It is not surprising that Catherine struggled with eating disorders for most of her life. Sometime around 1353, at the age of seven or eight, Catherine experienced a vision of Christ that led her to make a vow of virginity. As Catherine reached adolescence, her favorite sister convinced her to make herself more attractive and to consider marriage. Shortly thereafter this sister died in childbirth. Catherine interpreted the death as a form of divine punishment for tempting her to abandon virginity. The following year, 1363, a younger sister died at the age of fourteen. Grief-stricken and filled with guilt, Catherine declared she would never marry and began to eat only bread and raw vegetables.[2]

The tragedy and loss in Catherine's family was minor in comparison to the chaos and death that surrounded her. A year after she was born, the Black Death, or bubonic plague, came to Siena for the first time. When famine struck Siena in 1370, Catherine was no longer able to tolerate bread. As more people died from starvation, she developed anorexia and bulimia. Her Dominican spiritual directors saw these symptoms as a sign of sanctity. Because she vomited up all the food she ate but the Eucharist, she was promoted by the Dominican friars as a woman who lived solely on the Eucharist.

Catherine vacillated between seeing her eating habits as a disorder and as a special grace against the vice of gluttony. The advice she received from her spiritual directors reinforced her inability to eat normal food. Over time, her eating habits became pathological, such as the time when she drank the pus from a woman's infected breast as a penitential food. While we may be inclined to agree with those who saw her eating habits as a sign of delusion, many people in the fourteenth century believed that it was only by the power of God's grace that she could drink pus. Catherine was not alone in this type of behavior. The Catholic imagination began to run through some very dark alleys in the aftermath of the plague.[3]

Just as Catherine was not repulsed by the filth of her neighbors' diseased bodies, she was also not repulsed by the corruption manifested in the body of Christ. For most of her career she tended to the sick, the hungry, and the dying. Her ministry had a strong social dimension and her more palatable miracles involved providing food by multiplying loaves or by refilling empty casks. She was also reported to have restored milk to women's breasts so they could feed their children. The more she worked to provide others with sustenance, the more she denied herself. Her active social ministry led her to become involved in the growing tensions between the Avignon papacy and the Italian republics.

Catherine's approach to the political problems between the papacy and the Italian republics fits Yves Congar's model of reform very closely in two ways. First, her reform rhetoric is restricted to spiritual and moral issues. Second, she was absolutely opposed to any idea that the laity have a duty to punish the clergy when they fail to reform themselves, which is similar to Congar's claim that Catholic reform is never revolutionary in character. Nonetheless, Catherine did believe that God uses disobedient laypeople to punish priests and bishops who were disobedient to God. Though she did not want her followers to punish the clergy, she claimed that God revealed to her that both the impious secular rulers and the unreformed clergy are devils who punish one another in divine justice.[4]

Lacking formal training in theology or canon law, Catherine had no access to Peter Damian's theology or statements in canon law that justify laypeople deposing bad priests and bishops. Still, her Dominican advisors introduced her to the theology of Gregory the Great and St. Thomas Aquinas. Her reform methods have a definite Thomistic and Dominican character. After explaining that anyone who is under the authority of the bishop should not publicly correct him, Thomas offered the following exception: "It must be observed, however, that if the faith were endangered, a subject ought to reprove his or her prelate even publicly."[5] Catherine followed Thomas's advice in her reform work.

Even so, Catherine argued that scandalous clergymen should never be prosecuted or opposed by civil authorities. This meant that the Italian republics could not legitimately oppose the pope's political policies. In the summer of 1375 she wrote to the viscount of Milan saying, "Even if those ministers should take all of our possessions, we ought to be more willing to lose temporal things and bodily life than spiritual goods and the life of grace."[6] She was amazingly consistent on this point. After the Scandal of Cesena in 1377, when papal troops slaughtered at least four thousand innocent civilians to make an example for anyone who would oppose the pope's army, Catherine maintained that any resistance to the pope would result in eternal damnation.[7]

This does not mean Catherine approved of the popes using armies and coercive means to impose their will on others. In response to the Scandal of Cesena, Catherine presented this admonition to Pope Gregory XI (1370–78):

> Oime! It does not seem God wants us paying so much attention to temporal authority and possessions that we lose sight of the great slaughter of souls and dishonor to God that comes from war.... For I don't see how, with these disastrous wars, you can have a single hour of good. What belongs to the poor is being eaten up to pay soldiers, who in turn devour the people as if they were meat![8]

She advised the pope that he would "conquer more people with the staff of kindness, love, and peace, than with the club of war." Catherine believed that the pope was more likely to recover his power in Italy through virtue and good administration than by coercive means.

By 1377 Pope Gregory XI had received several such warnings from St. Catherine. She had squarely laid the blame for the rebellion at the pope's feet in 1376. Having explained that the rebellion was the result of bad pastors and papal administrators, Catherine urged

Gregory XI to attend to spiritual affairs and to return his administration to Rome. Catherine asked the pope to imitate Gregory the Great. The only difference between Gregory the Great and Gregory XI was, she wrote, that the former had virtue and a hunger for the salvation of souls.[9] This was a courageous stance for a fourteenth-century woman to take. It was, after all, a century when the church polluted the air with the smoke of burning women.

Many of the people who lived in Italy believed that the political chaos was the result of the fact that the popes had abandoned Rome and had moved their administration to Avignon. Avignon sat on the border of France in the fourteenth century. The reasons for this move and its effects are complex, but they can be generally traced back to the disastrous pontificate of Boniface VIII (1294–1303). In the fourteenth century, the events were interpreted through the Jewish captivity to the Babylonians as it is described in the Old Testament. In order to understand Catherine's efforts to return the papacy to Rome, we need to briefly consider the causes and the impact of the Babylonian Captivity of the papacy.

The Babylonian Captivity

The claims to absolute spiritual and political power advanced by the popes of the thirteenth century had the unintended effect of making the papacy an irresistible lure for the emerging nation-states in Europe. If a monarch could control the pope, theoretically he could dominate the rest of the Christian world. At the same time, papal claims to possessing the power to establish and to depose rulers created intense antagonism between the European monarchs and the popes of this period. The problem was that the popes had never had the authority to depose secular rulers. With the exception of Innocent III, the popes also lacked the coercive power necessary to overthrow the kings or emperors. By claiming power that they objectively did not have, they undermined their authority.

Pope Boniface VIII, who was placed in hell by the poet Dante, set the stage for the Avignon papacy. By exalting his power, he created his own downfall and damaged the credibility of the papacy for more than a century. Boniface had become involved in a dispute over ecclesiastical taxes with the French king, Philip the Fair. Philip was called fair because he was supposed to be beautiful, but he was not known for being just.

King Philip had decided to tax the clergy in order to raise money for his conflict with England. Catholic apologists have generally portrayed this as a particularly dastardly decision, but the church had grown spectacularly wealthy in the preceding 250 years. Because of the various grants to the church in terms of land and gold, much of the wealth of Europe was in the church's hands and was effectively removed from the economy. So when war broke out in 1294, neither Philip IV of France nor Edward I of England was willing to accept the idea that the clergy could not be taxed without papal permission.[10] In order to provide himself with some political cover, Philip attempted to declare the war a crusade, which had been a legal means for monarchs to tax the clergy prior to the Fourth Lateran Council (1215).

Pope Boniface, on the other hand, was trying to defend the canon of the Fourth Lateran Council forbidding the taxation of the clergy without the consent of the pope. But Boniface had failed to recognize how much the power and the prestige of the papacy had fallen during the preceding eighty years. When he released the bull *Clericis laicos* in February of 1296, which threatened to excommunicate rulers who taxed the clergy without papal consent, excommunication had ceased to be an effective political tool. Boniface failed to see that excommunication had no effect if the monarchs enjoyed both popular support and the consent of most of their clergy. This is not to say that *Clericis laicos* had no impact. The central thesis in the bull, which was that the laity had been opposed to the clergy since antiquity, was readily accepted by subsequent generations of the church's clergy as a matter of doctrine.[11]

King Philip responded to *Clericis laicos* by forbidding the export of gold from France. Suddenly Boniface VIII found himself in a financial crisis because Rome was heavily dependent on revenues generated by ecclesiastical taxes on the French clergy. Though Philip was no longer taxing the French clergy, he had effectively ended papal taxation on these same men. In July 1297, Boniface crumbled and released the bull *Etsi de statu*, which gave the king the right to tax the clergy in an emergency.[12] Further, the bull allowed the king to determine what was an emergency. Recognizing that he had the upper hand, Philip decided to test Boniface by imprisoning the papal legate in France on trumped-up charges of treason.

Boniface, who failed to acknowledge his political weakness, released *Ausculta fili* in December of 1301. This bull stated that "God has set popes over kings" and demanded Philip's submission. Philip ignored the pope and his bull. For some reason, Boniface tried to discipline the king through another bull, *Unam sanctam,* which included the following points:

1. That there is one holy, Catholic and apostolic church we are bound to believe and to hold, our faith urging us, and this we do firmly believe and simply confess: and that outside this church there is no salvation or remission of sins.... Therefore there is one body and one head of this one and only church, not two heads as if it were a monster, namely Christ and Christ's vicar, Peter and Peter's successor.... Hence, if the Greeks or any others say that they were not committed to Peter and his successors, they necessarily admit that they are not of Christ's flock, for the Lord says in John that there is one sheepfold and one shepherd.
2. We are taught by the words of the Gospel that in this church and in her power there are two swords, a spiritual one and the temporal one.... But the one is exercised for the church, the other by the church, the one by the hand of the priest, the other by the hand of the kings and soldiers, though at the will and the sufferance of the priest. One sword ought to be under the other and the temporal authority subject to the spiritual power.
3. For, the truth bearing witness, the spiritual power has to institute the earthly power and to judge it if it has not been good. So is verified the prophecy of Jeremias [1:10] concerning the church and the power of the church, "Lo, I have set you this day over the nations and the kingdoms" etc.
4. Therefore we declare, state, define and pronounce that it is altogether necessary to salvation for every human being to be subject to the Roman Pontiff.[13]

Philip was not amused. Together with a number of cardinals whom Boniface had alienated, Philip called for a council to depose the pope. When that did not work, Philip sent a band of mercenaries to capture or kill Boniface. The French mercenaries captured

Boniface in Anagni on September 7, 1303; however, the citizens of Anagni decided that they hated the French more than Boniface and helped him escape two days later. A few weeks later Boniface died. Now the independence of the papacy was threatened by French policy, and Boniface's successors were unwilling to oppose a king who was clearly prepared to murder a pope for political gain.[14]

Boniface's second successor, Clement V (1305–14), seems to have been elected as a result of French influence. Clement, who was Philip the Fair's cousin, exonerated the mercenaries who had attacked Boniface and permitted Philip to suppress the Knights Templar. This allowed Philip to seize all their assets for his war machine. Then Clement filled the curia with French cardinals and moved his residence to Avignon in 1309. Even so, the popes continued to try to return to Rome through the pontificate of John XXII (1316–34). After John XXII's expenditure of at least 63 percent of papal revenues in an attempt to militarily pacify Italy ended in abject failure, Pope Benedict XII (1334–42) decided to make the papal residence in Avignon permanent.[15]

During this period of the Babylonian Captivity, the popes and the curia were dominated by the French. Italian patriots like the poet and humanist Petrarch certainly believed the Avignon popes were pawns of French interests. Petrarch popularized seeing this period as reflecting the Babylonian Captivity of the Jewish people in the Old Testament. Both the Italians and the English had good reason to suspect the Avignon popes. All of the popes and 112 of the 134 cardinals appointed during this period were French. While it would be going too far to say that these popes were puppets of the French monarchs, people who lived through this period believed that the papacy had been subverted for the aims of French foreign policy. All of these factors greatly diminished the prestige and authority of the papacy. Worse still, the problem seemed intractable.

Because of the centralization of the church's government in the hands of the pope and the cardinals that had taken place in the thirteenth century, the diminishing credibility of the Avignon papacy was reverberating throughout the church. Many members of the clergy and the laity had called for a council to resolve the issues arising from the Avignon papacy, but the popes refused to comply. In the face of international dissent, the Avignon popes came to rely more and more on the support of their cardinals. The cardinals used this situation to assert unconstitutional and illegal powers over the pope. Describing the cardinals and their plans, Walter Ullmann wrote, "The pope, according to their schemes, was to be a ruler governed by the advice of his counsellors."[16]

Without a council to resolve the problems with the papacy, people began to look for other and extralegal or metajuridical means as a solution. On the one hand, people began to revolt against the papacy or manipulated papal weakness to gain illegal concessions; on the other hand, people like Catherine of Siena began to call for reform using traditional categories such as the fear of God. Catherine found a pope, Gregory XI (1370–78), who was willing to listen during a time when the papal campaigns in Italy had made it possible for him to return to Rome. The efforts of Gregory XI and of Urban VI (1378–89) to reform the curia led to the Great Schism when the church was faced with the scandal of multiple popes, which was an event that Catherine seems to have expected.

But now we are getting ahead of our story. How did St. Catherine manage to convince Pope Gregory XI to return to Rome and to work for reform? Catherine had no wealth, political power, or worldly status. Yet this relatively young and somewhat disturbed laywoman was arguably one of the most important forces in ending the Babylonian Captivity and in provoking the Great Schism. The answer seems to lie in Catherine's miracles, which included her experience of the stigmata in 1375. The miracles supported her claims to receiving personal revelations from God concerning the reform of the church.

Even though Catherine's miracles had an enormous impact on the people around her, the revelations she received could have been discredited as tricks of the devil. Like the successful women mystics and reformers who preceded her, her absolute adherence to the authority of the church and her faith in the sacraments did much to protect her from her ecclesiastical opponents. But in many respects Catherine advanced Clare of Assisi's agenda by publicly arguing that women had a duty to involve themselves in both active ministry and the reform of the church. Whether her inspiration came from her revelations or from her knowledge of the Franciscan tradition is impossible to resolve, but it is clear that she framed her understanding of her ministry in terms of penance.

Penitential Reform

Catherine opened her work *The Dialogue* with a description of sin and the need for penance. She synthesized both the apologetics of love and of humility under the rubric of atonement for sin. At the same time, she was able to formulate an unshakable reference point for her disciples when they met with opposition and tribulation. Reformers who are united to Christ through love atone for their sins and for the sins of others. They are truly *alter Christi* (other Christs) who participate in redeeming the world from sin.

Sin and atonement are not radically individual categories for Catherine. Both sin and atonement reach out to infinity in their effects. Since sin is infinite in its effects, Catherine argued that atonement does not demand suffering for satisfaction. Suffering is always finite in its scope and duration. Catherine taught that the only human capacity that reaches out to infinity is desire, so she concluded atonement can only be accomplished through our desire to love God. This desire can also provoke infinite sorrow because of the offenses we commit against God. At the same time, we participate in infinite sorrow when we grieve over the sins of our neighbors. Citing St. Paul's statement that all the gifts are worth nothing without charity (1 Cor 13:1–3), Catherine concluded, "Finite works are not enough either to punish or to atone unless they are seasoned with loving charity."[17]

Catherine understood sin and atonement as communal realities. Reporting her revelation from God, she wrote, "For there is no sin that does not touch others, whether secretly by refusing them what is due to them, or openly by giving birth to the vices of which I have told you."[18] The source of vice and sin is selfish love because it denies people the charity and affection that is due to them. Selfish love reveals that a person does not truly love God and is not willing to help those who are either spiritually or materially in need. Acting on this knowledge entails the work of reform on individual, communal, and universal dimensions. It also entails trials, tribulations, insults, and even martyrdom. Though these sufferings are not able to atone for sin by themselves, Catherine claimed the power of charity transforms these tribulations into sacramental realities that are able to atone for the sins of the reformer and the people in need of reformation.[19]

Certainly Catherine believed that the worst offenders were the clergy. She claimed God had revealed to her that the priests and bishops were disfiguring the bride of Christ. She described the church this way:

> But look how my bride has disfigured her face! She is leprous with impurity and selfishness. Her breasts are swollen because of the pride and avarice of those who feed there: the universal body Christianity and the mystic body of holy church. I am speaking of the ministers who feed at her breasts. They ought not only to feed themselves, but hold to those breasts the whole body of Christianity as well as whoever would rise from the darkness of unbelief and be bound into the body of my church.[20]

Yet even these defects reveal aspects of God's providential plan for the church.

The various problems and defects in the church ground an idea in Catherine's theology that represents a movement toward the recognition of the priesthood of all believers. Just as Christ came to minister or to serve, she taught that all his disciples must be prepared to serve one another. Repeating one of her mystical revelations, she wrote:

> Thus have I given you reason—necessity, in fact—to practice mutual charity. For I could well have supplied each of you with all your needs, both spiritual and material. But I wanted to make you dependent on one another so that each of you would be my minister, dispensing the graces and gifts you have received from me.[21]

In fact, Catherine's belief that God structured the church this way explains why it is necessary to reform the corrupt clergy in the ordained hierarchy. God made their sacramental services necessary in order to prevent the laity from simply abandoning them to their own destruction.

Catherine believed this interdependent relationship served to remind everyone of their own insufficiency. In this way the church recalls the importance of keeping a sense of humility in its members as they struggle to atone for themselves and others. If Christians could remember how their sins have had an incalculable impact on others, she concluded they would see that they must always do service for all people. The service of reform must spring from the infinite desire of love in such a way that the Christian soul must always keep her focus on the concrete needs of her neighbors. Catherine taught her disciples that they needed more than an abstract or generalized desire for the whole world's salvation.[22] Having justified her ministerial role, Catherine proceeded to lay out her strategy.

Strategy

Catherine's strategic advice for her disciples found its center of gravity between the poles of an insatiable desire for reform and an ever-deepening sense of humility. There was no place for self-satisfaction in her understanding of the Christian life. "For as long as you are pilgrims in this life," she concluded, "you are capable of growing and should grow."[23] She warned that those who do not move forward are, in fact, going backward. As her disciples worked to reform themselves and the church, they had to avoid becoming judgmental of others. This was true even if they were given the grace necessary to achieve extreme acts of mortification like her own eating habits, which she described as feeding at the table of penance.

Reformers who lose sight of their own need for humility sin when they set themselves up as judges over others. By insisting that everyone follow their practices and opinions, Catherine decided that such people simply desire to remake everyone in their own image. To her mind this attitude is the result of a spirituality that seeks to mortify the flesh but does not aim at slaying the selfish will. She promised her disciples that people who let go of selfishness will be able to peacefully and calmly seek to save rather than to condemn others. The benefit of such a spirituality, according to Catherine, was that it protects the reformer from scandal, which finds its origin in self-will.[24]

Catherine taught that Christians who had dried up the wellspring of self-centeredness would be able to walk on the waters of tribulation and temptation without sinking. These souls find joy in the diverse paths to holiness and even in the diverse merits of the members of the church. When such a Christian encounters something plainly sinful, Catherine promised they would be moved to compassion rather than judgment. A reformer operating out of this spirituality does not presume to read the intentions of people, to find hidden subtexts, or "to judge the hidden heart."[25] To make sure her disciples understood how to measure themselves, Catherine insisted that the Christian reformer concentrate on discerning God's merciful will in all situations.

Of course reformers do have to contend with sin and corruption, so Catherine presented her disciples with three basic principles to guide them. These principles were: (1) Your judgment should always be qualified; (2) Do not make judgments on appearances alone and leave every judgment to Christ; (3) Never try to force everyone to follow your path.[26] Catherine used these three principles as a means to explain how her disciples should proceed in their efforts while preserving their own sense of faith, hope, and love.

Catherine wanted her followers to recognize that they must qualify their judgments in such a way that they did not alienate the people they were trying to correct. She advised that Christians should not confront people with specific sins as if they could read their intentions. Reformers should not, as a general rule, presume to take on the role of the prosecutor who makes accusations and draws up charges. Catherine recommended correcting bad habits in a general way and attempting to plant virtues in their place.[27] For example, rather than charge a local bishop with greed, Catherine would suggest speaking out against the sin of greed in the clergy. Thus she was advocating the use of admonition and exhortation to move people to reform themselves.

Drawing upon the theology of Gregory the Great, Catherine advised her followers to mix in kindness with their admonitions or warnings about sin. Further, she believed her followers would be better received if they admitted how they struggle with sin and vice. She wrote, "And when you think you discern a vice in others, put it on your own back as well as theirs, acting always with true humility. Then if the vice is truly there, such people will change their ways all the sooner, seeing themselves so gently understood."[28] Catherine promised her disciples that the agreeable correction or word of reproof would be a more effective way to persuade people to change.

Catherine warned her disciples to avoid making judgments on the basis of appearances. This category of appearances extends beyond our normal use of the term because it included the way people might appear to us in our prayers. Catherine believed that when we pray for people, God sometimes reveals that they are struggling in their spiritual lives. Of course we can know people are wrestling with a sense of spiritual aridity by more mundane means such as observation or conversation. Catherine forbade her disciples from assuming the cause of spiritual dryness was some unresolved sin. Instead, she urged them to leave judgment to God alone. Speaking for God, she wrote, "Give up judgment, which belongs to me, and take up compassion with hunger for my honor and the salvation of souls."[29]

Reformers must either drink deeply from the wellspring of compassion and follow the path of reconciliation, or, Catherine believed, they would risk losing their way in the swampy terrain of impatience and bitterness. She taught her disciples that the communal task of reform has deep significance for the individual Christian. The Christian reformer should expect constant temptations to abandon the conciliatory path of peace; but she promised that these temptations offer an opportunity to imitate Christ and participate in his earthly ministry before he returned as judge. Medieval Christians shared the belief that Christ had established the church as an extension of his earthly ministry of salvation, which would end when he returned. Thus it is the judge himself who has revealed the urgent need to save people from being found guilty.

It was the certainty that Christ will return to judge the living and the dead that empowered Catherine to let go of her desire to punish sinners. She perceived that the desire to punish is simply inconsistent with the Christian mission to save souls. When a person believes that they have the standing to act as the judge of another, he or she has forgotten the infinite nature of his or her sins. Catherine wrote, "In this way [leaving judgment to Christ] you will come to me in truth, and you will show that you have remembered and observed the teaching given you by my Truth, that is, to discern my will rather than to judge other people's intentions."[30] Since judgmental people can no longer look at the sins of others with sympathy, they also lose their ability to discern the will of Christ. They forget that Christ gave humanity the church for the mission of salvation.

Catherine's third principle for her disciples was that they should recognize that their way of pursuing reform and holiness should not be imposed on everyone. The idea that reformers should avoid the temptation to remake the church in their own image is one of the saint's deepest insights into Catholic reform, namely, that it must be open to the reality that there are many paths to God within the church. She described how penitential reformers often want to inflict their own disciplines and practices on others. Catherine said that these people become "displeased and scandalized because they think that others are not doing the right thing."[31]

All three of these principles respond to the issue of self-centeredness. The first forces the reformer to recognize the limitations of his or her perceptions. Catherine, in her elliptical way, pointed out how the attempt to read other people's intentions is simply a projection of the self on others. The second principle brings reformers to see the selfishness inherent in the desire to be the judge. When people judge others, they set themselves up as the standard. Finally, the third principle showed Catherine's disciples that the desire to force everyone to follow their path is simply another form of self-centeredness. She described such people this way: "They judge according to their own blindness and lame vision. They carry on like frantic fools and deprive themselves of the goods of earth as well as of heaven. And even in this life they have a foretaste of hell."[32]

While it might seem like Catherine was really restricting her disciples, she also provided one crucial exception to these rules. When the Christian clearly sees something sinful or has an explicit revelation from God concerning sin, she said that the Christian should correct the sinner. If they correct others, she advised them to follow Christ's instructions in Matthew 18:15–17. Catherine believed that correction should be done privately, but if the person refuses to change, the matter should be brought to the attention of two or three others and then to the whole church.[33] While the ability to correct prominent clergy would have been too intimidating for most people, she used this method in her own reform efforts. She was absolutely fearless in confronting both secular and political leaders. When they ignored her, Catherine publicly corrected them by exposing their sins to the world and to history.

As we shall see, even the more general admonitions she offered to the clergy in *The Dialogue* were powerful and hard-hitting. Unlike Clare of Assisi, Catherine advocated the use of public criticism as a means to reform the church and its clergy. Even so, Catherine employed many of the strategies of the thirteenth-century women who worked to reform the clergy, such as prefacing her reform rhetoric with a long statement on the significance of eucharistic ministry.[34] It is the dignity of eucharistic ministry, according to Catherine, that demands priests and bishops be held to a higher standard than others in terms of being more loving and pure of heart.

Reform Rhetoric

As is clear from *The Dialogue*, Catherine primarily understood ecclesial reform in terms of reforming the clergy. The idea that people learn more by means of imitation than by instruction led the reformers of this period to focus their efforts on reforming the heads of ecclesial communities. They reasoned that if the head is reformed, the members will surely follow. Catherine clearly expressed this idea when she wrote, "Once she (the church) is reformed with good shepherds, her subjects will certainly change their ways."[35] Because they neither give their people a good example for imitation nor demonstrate any urgency in their mission to save souls, she concluded that evil ministers abuse themselves and others with their sins.[36] This was especially true since the church and the state had separate legal systems, which formally excluded the clergy from civil prosecution. Given the state of civil law in fourteenth-century Italy, it is not terribly surprising that Catherine strongly advocated the total separation of the ecclesiastical legal system from the civil.

Given the separation of ecclesial and secular legal systems, bishops who refused to enforce church law created an environment where the clergy were virtually unaccountable for their actions. Drawing on a medical analogy, she wrote:

> No rank, whether of civil or divine law, can be held in grace without holy justice. For those who are not corrected and those who do not correct are like members beginning to rot, and if the doctor were to apply ointment without cauterizing the wound, the whole body would become fetid and corrupt.[37]

Catherine believed there were two reasons the bishops refused to cauterize the wounds of sin: They were slaves to the fears generated by self-love and they were unable to correct people who committed the same sins as themselves. In the second case, she said it was a clear example of the blind leading the blind; but in the first, the bishops deceived themselves into believing they could climb in rank through injustice. The saint warned them that their failure to change themselves and their clergy would certainly result in their condemnation to the torment of eternal fire.[38]

Catherine drew from scripture and tradition to portray and to praise the worthy ministers of the past like St. Paul or Pope Sylvester, who was credited with having a part in the conversion of Constantine. In this way, she provided her contemporary bishops with models for imitation and for measuring themselves. According to Catherine, these good pastors in the past did not simply speak about humility; instead, they demonstrated humility by their deeds. These ministers were unashamed by derision, abuse, torture, or death.[39] Catherine praised them, writing:

> O my loved ones! They who were superiors became as subjects. They who were in authority became as servants. Though they were healthy, without the sickness and leprosy of deadly sin, they became as if afflicted. Though they were strong, they became as if weak. With the dull and the simple they showed themselves as simple, and with the lowly as lowly. And so with every sort of person they knew how to deal humbly and with charity, giving to everyone the right food.[40]

She explained that they were empowered in their service by their desire for God and their urgent desire to save souls. Catherine was also making it clear that the pastor's authority is based on service and demonstrated in humility.

Having described how the apostles and saints acted as ministers, Catherine turned to the quality of the clergy and religious in her day. She softened the blow to come by claiming that God was revealing the "wretchedness of their lives" to her so that she and others would see the need to offer up constant prayer for the clergy and the religious. Reporting God's revelation to her, she wrote, "No matter where you turn, to secular or religious, clerics or prelates, lowly or great, young or old, you see nothing but sin. All of them pelt me with the filth of deadly sin."[41]

Just as the virtuous ministers receive a greater reward for their use of the gifts given to them, Catherine concluded that wretched ministers will incur a more cruel punishment. This was why she believed that Christians should truly grieve over them. Having framed her critique in terms of penitential grief rather than judgmental anger, she proceeded to offer one of the most public, most powerful, and most courageous admonitions of the clergy presented by any reformer who remained in the Catholic Church. Many women who had been less inflammatory found themselves either silenced or condemned by the opponents to reform, but Catherine's insistence that it was the duty of the clergy to reform themselves through the use of existing church laws and institutions protected her.

Catherine described the clergy as failing to recognize how they were unworthy of the tremendous mystery they had received from God. Instead, she said they were bloated with pride. These "fancily dressed" clerics took on the appearance of lords or courtiers and thus visibly abandoned the simplicity of the clergy and manifested their pride and presumption. Catherine wrote that this pride led them to desire earthly pleasures and caused the clergy to be greedy.[42]

According to Catherine, God revealed to her that the three pillars of vice are pride, impurity, and greed. Further, she claimed that all of these pillars are founded upon self-centeredness.[43] As a result of greed, she said the ministers were withholding what they should give to the poor. Worse still, they were selling the sacraments. With their money, they found they could afford the luxuries of life. Catherine explained that the clergy's desire for earthly pleasures, which she identified as impurity, led them to be concerned about having "grand horses, many gold and silver vessels, and well-adorned homes." She wrote that the problem with these ministers was that they only loved their people for what they could obtain from them. Out of their feasting and vanity, Catherine concluded it was inevitable that they fall into sexual sins.[44]

Catherine rebuked such ministers. She wrote, "They devour souls who were bought with Christ's blood, eating them up in so many wretched ways, and feeding their own children with what belongs to the poor." In their grasping for wealth, food, and luxury as people were suffering from famine, the plague, and financial collapses of the period, the clergy were devouring precious material resources in a time of want. By the bad example they were setting and the scandal they presented to their people, Catherine concluded they were spiritually devouring people's souls. She called them devils doing the devils' work and wrote, "Indeed, they are the cause of confusion and suffering to the consciences of those they succeed in dragging down from a state of grace and the way of truth, for by leading them into sin they make them walk in the way of falsehood."[45]

By their villainous deeds, Catherine argued that wretched priests and bishops were disgracing the eucharistic ministry. Since the dignity of the priestly and episcopal offices proceeds from their sacramental role, she observed that their sinful behavior leads the laity to lose respect for the office. If people do not respect the priestly and episcopal offices, she concluded that they would lose reverence for the whole sacramental nature of the church. While Catherine did not allow that people could ever be excused from respecting the offices of the ordained clergy, she felt free to criticize and correct the men who held those offices. Catherine called them "wretches who had become mirrors of wickedness" when their offices demanded them to be "mirrors of virtue."[46]

After an equally devastating assessment of the religious orders as being filled with wolves in sheep's clothing, Catherine boldly aimed her criticisms directly at the papacy. She reminded the pope of his duties and warned him about participating in the sin of simony. In one of her visionary experiences, God gave her this message to deliver:

> But if my Son's vicar becomes aware of their sin he ought to punish them. He should relieve those of office who will not repent and change their evil way of living. As for those who do the bribing, they would do well to receive imprisonment for their bargaining, both to change their sinful ways and that others may see an example and be afraid to do the same thing any more. If Christ on Earth does this, he is doing his duty. If he does not, his sin will not go unpunished when it is his turn to give me an account of his little sheep.[47]

In this case she also claimed that God had revealed that the pope was not punishing the members of the clergy who were involved in simony and other sins, which was the cause of all the other abominations in the church.

The pope and his ministers were also responsible for the rebellions in Italy that had killed so many people. The clergy's hunger for riches and temporal possessions such as the papal state caused them to forget their concern for spiritual things. Switching to a direct address from God to these clerics, she wrote, "You have become like a ferocious beast without any fear of me. You devour your neighbors and thrive on dissension."[48] By showing preferences to the powerful and the wealthy, Catherine said, a minister is like a shameless whore boasting about her highly placed courtesans and brigade of children. "Unless they change their ways," she warned, "they will be swept on to eternal damnation with such reproach that your tongue could never describe it."[49] After such strong words, she reminded her audience that her purpose was to give people a sense of compassion for the clergy, who will suffer more for their sins than the laity.

The problem was that the clergy were blind to their own sinfulness. They did not see that a death-bearing tsunami was rushing down upon them. Catherine explained that the consequences for the clergy, especially those in positions of authority, were so terrible that the only Christian response was to try to save them. Since the way to forgiveness is through penance, she argued that Christians have a duty to call their clergy to account before they face the moment when the demons appear to accuse them of their sins.[50]

While Catherine would not say that hell is other people, she certainly believed that penance is other people. The infinite desire and charity associated with penance compel Christians to try to save sinners, even clerical sinners. Thus all Christians are reformers. Catherine claimed that God had revealed these sins of the clergy and the religious to stir up compassion rather than vengeance. In the height of ecstatic experience, she proclaimed, "Immeasurable Love! By revealing this you have given me a bitter-sweet medicine so that I might rise up once and for all from the sickness of foolish indifference and run to you with concern and eager longing."[51] She closed her discussion of reform with a prayer for the clergy and for the church.

Conclusion

Catherine successfully navigated her way through numerous dangers with her reform rhetoric. As she laid out her exposé on the church and the clergy, she followed her own advice and modeled how to employ the strategies she had presented to her disciples. While she identified many sins, she treated them in a general way without actually accusing the people she was trying to reform of personal sin. She mixed in kindness with her admonitions by proclaiming her deep concern for the welfare of the clergy and the religious. Her repeated statements that secular rulers should not assert authority over the church or judge members of the clergy was also a form of consoling the fears of the fourteenth-century clergy. She left judgment to God, which was her second principle. Finally, she resisted the temptation to remake the church in her image.

When Catherine corrected the pope, she provided an example of the exception to her general strategies. The fact that the pope was involved in the sin of simony and was involved in sinful behavior in his attempts to preserve his territory through war was something that was clear to everyone. Before writing *The Dialogue*, Catherine had privately confronted Pope Gregory XI on these issues. She had also taken the matter to a few others and urged them to confront the pope. So even the direct and public nature of her charges over simony and injustice manifested her reform strategies. Catherine's demonstrated loyalty and concern made this medicine of correction more palatable for the pope.

The rhetoric Catherine employed in *The Dialogue* is an excellent model for understanding how powerful and passionate and public criticism can be absolutely consistent with deep love and loyalty for the church. However, we must be careful to remember that she did not understand the church as an abstract entity or as simply an institution. For Catherine, loving the church meant loving people; and thus reforming the church begins by reforming the selfishness that prevents us from loving others. Perhaps as a reward for her commitment to charity, she stands out as one of the few reformers who saw their initiatives come to fruition in their lifetimes. Of course, Catherine also lived long enough to see the beginning of the next great crisis of the church, the Great Schism.

6

When Reformers Collide: Jean Gerson and Jan Hus

Wearing a paper crown painted with three horrible devils about to greedily tear a soul to pieces and inscribed with the words, "This is a heresiarch," the rector of the University of Prague was led to the stake on July 6, 1415. During his time as rector, Jan Hus had spearheaded the Czech reform movement. As he was stripped of his clothes and chained, Hus reportedly said, "The Lord Jesus Christ, my redeemer and savior, was bound by a harder and heavier chain. And I, a miserable wretch, am not ashamed to bear being bound by this one."[1] After they had piled the wood up to his chin and lit the fire, Hus proclaimed that he had always been a faithful Catholic adhering to scripture and tradition. As we shall see, his claims of innocence were certain evidence of his guilt under the peculiar logic employed by the Inquisition.

Having affirmed his faithfulness, Hus began to sing, "Christ, you are the Son of the living God, have mercy on us; Christ, you are the Son of God, have mercy on me..." until the flames blew into his face. Peter of Mladoňovice, an eyewitness to the event and a supporter of Hus, reported that Hus continued to move his lips in prayer though he could produce no sound. After the fire died down, the soldiers broke his bones and found his heart, which had not been fully consumed. They skewered his heart with a spit, rebuilt the fire, and reduced Hus's heart and bones to ash. In this way the story of what happens when reformers collide comes to an end. We do not know whether Jean Gerson, who was the chancellor of the University of Paris, was present for this atrocity, but it is certain that he played a pivotal role in the martyrdom of Jan Hus.

Jan Hus and Jean Gerson present us with a cautionary tale or something of a medieval morality play. Both men were committed to reform. Both held similar ideas on many issues of law and morality. Both came from poor families, rose through the ranks of the church by hard work, held positions of honor in universities, and were determined to restore church order and Christian morals. Whereas Hus's career was cut short, Gerson continued to work for reform after successfully resolving the Great Schism, which refers to a period from 1378 to 1417 when the church had multiple popes. Gerson's understanding of the use of councils for the governance of the church was, nonetheless, undermined by the followers of Hus and their negotiations with the Council of Basle (1431–37). While there are many ways to explain why the relationship between Hus and Gerson came to a violent conclusion, it was the Great Schism itself that put these two deeply committed Christian men on a collision course.

The Great Schism

The Great Schism brought issues of authority and power to the forefront of reform thought. It raised doubts concerning the very nature of the church's ordained hierarchy and the manner of church governance. The breakdown in church discipline began to erode the morals of the clergy, which as we have seen were not terribly high going into the Great Schism. This erosion also undermined one of the fundamental assumptions behind having ordained clergy, namely, the idea that clerics were both set apart and bound to lead lives worthy of imitation. With the spectacle of multiple popes before them, theologians began to question the edifice of papal authority as it had been built up over two centuries by the canon lawyers. Naturally, these questions had an impact on their understanding of ecclesiastical law itself.

During the Avignon papacy the canon lawyers had been extolling papal power and privileges to the point of undermining the authority of scripture and tradition in favor of seeing the pope as almost a living oracle of an ongoing revelation from God. One of the master canonists of the first half of the fourteenth century wrote, "The pope is wonderful, for he holds the power of God on earth: he is the vicar of him to whom the earth and the fullness of the universe belongs."[2] A medieval textbook of canon law, the *Speculum judiciale*, taught that the pope may say and do anything he pleases and that he has creative power in the field of moral obligations. Since the pope was seen by many of the canonists as the supreme legislator, they concluded that popes were above the law.

These rather extreme statements reflect the political struggles between the popes and the dynastic ambitions of European rulers. They are more the product of political interests than legitimate religious doctrines. Such behavior reflects a pattern in church history that George Tavard, a leading Catholic theologian and *peritus* at Vatican II, said should not surprise us, namely: "In times of social unrest political interests may force canon lawyers to run amock."[3] The Great Schism also reveals another dynamic that had been in play since the thirteenth century, the struggle between the popes and their cardinals. This latter struggle is arguably the most direct cause for the schism.

During the Avignon period the cardinals gradually gained new and unconstitutional powers. They saw the pope as a monarch who was to be governed by the advice of his counselors. It was the election of the archbishop of Bari, Bartolomeo Prignano, as Pope Urban VI (1378–89) that brought all the building tensions over law and authority to the surface with explosive force.[4]

It is safe to assume the cardinals did not know they were electing a man with a volcanic temper and irrational behavior. Urban supported reform and thought it should begin with the cardinals and the bishops, but his methods alienated potential supporters and embittered his opponents. In the sermon he preached on the day after his coronation, Urban charged the bishops and abbots living in Rome with being traitors because they left their sees vacant in order to be in the curia. Two weeks later in another sermon, he denounced the lives the cardinals and bishops were leading.[5] At one point he even kicked an aging cardinal who had irritated him. The cardinal of Geneva, who would become the Avignon Pope Clement VII (1378–94), warned Urban VI: "Unlike your predecessors, Holy Father, you do not treat the cardinals with the honor you owe them. You are diminishing our authority, but truly I tell you that we will do our best to diminish yours."[6]

The French cardinals sent a letter to the Italian cardinals declaring the Holy See vacant on July 20, 1378. In a document called the *Declaratio*, which was issued less than three weeks later, the rebelling cardinals claimed that they had voted under duress and that the election was null and void. By September 20, Cardinal Robert of Geneva was elected pope. In October he was crowned as Pope Clement VII and took up residence in Avignon. Each pope had advocates who were morally upright, versed in theology, and experts in canon law. European leaders were almost equally divided between the two popes, which made a military solution practically impossible. Even the saints at the time were divided. Catherine of Siena supported Urban VI, and St. Vincent Ferrer (1350–1414) supported Clement VII.

Hus and Gerson were both concerned with the disorder. Hus was fighting to preserve order in his local church, which was being solicited for indulgences, manipulated by the king, riddled with simony, and threatened by interdict. Gerson was primarily interested in restoring order on a universal scale by ending the papal schism. The idea that reforming the head would lead to the reform of the body was absolutely commonplace in Gerson's French milieu and fit in quite naturally with his understanding of the church's hierarchy. After looking at the positive contributions of Gerson in reforming the church as an international institution, we will turn to examine Hus's efforts at reforming the church in Bohemia before we consider the Council of Constance and Hus's trial.

Jean Gerson: Conciliarist

Jean Gerson is known as a conciliarist. The conciliarist theologians of the fourteenth and fifteenth centuries began to see councils as the best or even the only way to reform the problems resulting from the Great Schism. Gerson was late in coming to the conciliarist camp. As chancellor of the University of Paris, Gerson was a powerful supporter of the *via cessionis*, or mutual abdications of the two popes, which he framed in terms of personal penance rather than in legal categories.[7] However, after serving on a French commission from 1407 to 1408, he lost hope in persuading the popes by moral arguments. Only then did he begin to advocate a conciliar solution.

Gerson was very much an institutional reformer working within established structures of authority. Perhaps his upbringing in a pious family of farmers living near Rheims contributed to his basic trust in the church's institutions and his conservative tendencies.[8] It is likely that he did his initial studies in Rheims, but it is certain that he had visited the cathedral as a boy. Rheims, like most medieval cathedrals, visibly reflects the church's hierarchical structure in the art; but unlike most, the figures of authority such as the angels, apostles, and saints smile down benevolently at the faithful. The beautiful order of the Gothic cathedral may have helped to mold his vision of church as ordered hierarchy.[9]

Though Gerson was fifteen when the Great Schism broke out, the French church experienced minimal disruptions on a local level because of strong national leadership. The church in France afforded him an opportunity to study in Paris, where he became associated with some of the most powerful men in Europe. Eventually his mentor, Pierre d'Ailly, chose him to be his successor as chancellor of the University of Paris. Gerson, who held multiple benefices in places as remote as Bruges and Paris, basically saw the benefice system and structures of church governance as generally satisfactory early in his career. For the chancellor, there were essentially three problems with the church: schism, heresy, and the morality of the clergy.[10] Each problem impacted the ordered working of the ecclesiastical hierarchy.

From late 1408 through early 1410, Gerson formulated lines of thought that justified conciliar action in response to the Great Schism. The positions he developed in this short period of time would eventually be incorporated into the decrees of the Council of Pisa (1409) and the Council of Constance (1414–18). Though his work during this time is not indicative of every aspect of his reform agenda, it does reveal why he came into conflict with Jan Hus as he struggled to reform the ecclesiastical hierarchy.

Gerson began by considering the goal of the ecclesiastical hierarchy, which he restricted to the clergy. The goal of the ecclesiastical hierarchy is, he claimed, to establish internal peace and union. It does so by modeling its order and activity on the angelic hierarchies and the heavenly Jerusalem. Just as the angelic hierarchy is under one head, so also the church should have one visible head. Just as the angels hold offices for the purpose of ministering or serving those below them, so too the officeholders in the church must recognize that their authority was given to them for service. Gerson's reform agenda was founded upon restoring the links between office and duty or between ecclesiastical rank and service. He formulated his principle this way: "God has given no status, no degree of dignity, no ministry of any kind except in order to serve the common benefit of all."[11]

By recalling the connection between service and authority, Gerson was able to formulate a principle for reforming the various problems with canon law that were preventing a resolution of the schism. Unfortunately, his works about hierarchy were colored by the ongoing struggle between the mendicant orders and the diocesan or secular clergy.[12] Gerson was opposed to anything that would infringe upon the rights of the diocesan clergy. Out of his arguments against the mendicants, he came to the position that the ordained diocesan clergy essentially constitute the church. He also wrote that the laity, especially laywomen, are less a part of the church because they do not possess hierarchical power.[13] Gerson's understanding of hierarchy did not have room for the laity or religious correcting or even publicly criticizing the clergy.

This does not mean that Gerson had ruled out all criticism of the behavior of the pope, bishops, priests, and deacons. He believed that the model of fraternal correction in Matthew 18:15–17 extended to all members of the ecclesiastical hierarchy, but here again he was thinking of the ordained. So a deacon could correct his bishop or even the pope privately, and if that did not work he could publicly correct the offender in an ecclesiastical synod or council; however, since laypeople are not members of the ecclesiastical hierarchy, Gerson held that they should honor and respect every member of the hierarchy regardless of the cleric's immoral behavior. Even more significantly, he maintained that the laity were bound to tithe even if their clergy were corrupt.[14]

While a priest might privately confront another priest or even a bishop over some sin or injustice, Gerson was particularly opposed to any member of the clergy who would expose these problems to the laity. Even though a member of the clergy is a terrible sinner, he should be treated with respect as an intrinsic member of the hierarchy. Because Gerson believed that the rights of the parish priests are so central to the church's immutable hierarchy, he argued that even the pope cannot deprive them of their pastoral functions of preaching and performing sacramental ministry.[15]

This defense of the immutability of clerical rights built up support for Gerson's agenda among the bishops. Of course Gerson was not denying the ability of the pope or of a bishop to depose a wicked member of the clergy. He was certain that the Great Schism and turmoil in the church were the result of a failure to distinguish between different types of law and their respective levels of authority. Gerson identified three types of law: divine, natural, and positive.[16] Divine law, which obviously has the highest authority, is revealed in scripture. He described divine law as aiming at love, peace, and unity. Natural law is revealed through nature and is accessible to reason. It also aims at love and cannot be contradicted, though it is subordinate to divine law. Positive law, however, is by its nature imperfect because it is written to address particular circumstances and thus can never provide for all possible situations. Gerson was essentially arguing that canon law should not be identified with tradition, which was a position that would eventually find formal ratification in the canons of the Council of Trent (1545–63).

All the impediments to removing the rival popes were various decretals or statements in canon law. Since the popes refused to voluntarily resign or to submit to arbitration between them, the only way to legally depose these popes was for heresy. The relevant canon stated:

> If the pope, neglectful of his own and his brother's and sister's salvation, is proved useless and remiss in his duties and moreover drags innumerable people down with him horde-like, away from the good, he will suffer many afflictions in the slavery of hell for all eternity. [Still] let no mortal presume to argue his guilt since, though he judges all, he is not to be judged by anyone, unless he deviates from the faith.[17]

This was a well-established legal tradition by the fifteenth century. Pope Honorius I (625–38), one of Gregory the Great's disciples, had been posthumously condemned on the charge of heresy at the Council of Constantinople (681). Even Innocent III (1198–1216), who certainly had a high conception of papal power, incorporated this idea into a sermon he published on the consecration of pontiffs.[18]

Finding a way to charge the rival popes with heresy was not terribly difficult. Simony was considered to be a form of heresy. According to some schools of thought in canon law, popes could also be charged with notorious crimes and scandalous behavior; however, the problem was that canon law also stated that the pope could be judged by no one. Gerson and the conciliarists had to find a legal means to charge the popes with heresy and other notorious crimes, but the only precedent was the case of Honorius. While a council could judge a pope on charges of heresy, it was unclear whether it could depose a pope for other crimes. Even if a council could judge a pope on issues other than heresy, canon law established in the twelfth century stated that only the pope had the jurisdiction to call a council. Of course neither pontiff was willing to call a council for the purpose of charging him with crimes and heresy.

Gerson argued that the laws stating that only the pope can call a council and that the pope cannot be judged by anyone were both aspects of positive law, which meant that both legal claims had to be subordinated to divine and natural law. One aspect of the divine law, according to Gerson, was that Christ established the office of the supreme pontiff when he instituted the ecclesiastical hierarchy. Since Deuteronomy 32:4 teaches that all God's works are perfect, including conservation and consummation, he argued that the church or the hierarchy's structures must be permanent and stable. Thus Gerson concluded that it was impossible for the church to operate without one visible head of the hierarchy.[19]

Insofar as Christ established various offices for building up the body, Gerson maintained that the proper operation of these offices is necessary for Christians to grow into the fullness of Christ. Thus the schism was impeding the mission of the church, which is to build up the body. In this way, Gerson developed a mission-driven imperative for reform.[20] If the office of the papacy is aimed at building unity, then papal prerogatives in positive law cannot obstruct ending the schism. Further, he argued that if the church was perfectly instituted by Christ, then it must have the capacity to resolve issues like the Great Schism.[21]

This capacity to restore order can be imagined to be like a seed (semen) that penetrates the whole body and guarantees the body's ability to propagate and to heal itself through many generations. Gerson's seed was, in essence, a microcosm of the church as a whole. He associated this seed of reform with the idea of God forming a remnant as prophesied by Isaiah 1:9. Because a general council represents the entire hierarchy, he saw the council as the only institutional manifestation of this remnant, microcosm, or seed. Thus Gerson concluded a general council was the only institution that had the necessary power to restore order to the church.[22]

Finally, Gerson argued that a council could be called against the will of the pope. Whereas it was not normally legal for a council to be convoked without the consent of the pope and for it to judge a pope, these were only provisions of canon law or positive law. In this case, the letter of the law did not apply because it had not foreseen an event like the Great Schism. "Because of these exceptions," Gerson wrote, "a superior law has been ordained to interpret the law. This is what

Aristotle called equity *[epikeia]*."[23] He also found support for his appeal to *epikeia* in Acts 5:27–30, when Peter told the high priest he must obey God rather than people. Gerson argued that the church must prefer the commands of God to human laws.[24]

The arguments put forward by Gerson in 1409–10 persuaded many people to advocate a conciliar solution. His various treatises and sermons helped to justify the Council of Pisa. From 1410 until he arrived at Constance in 1415, Gerson promoted his principles and worked to build consensus for settling the Great Schism. Before we turn to consider the case of Hus, it will be helpful to review the key events and personages from the Council of Pisa to the convocation of Constance.

From the Council of Pisa to Constance

Drawing upon Gerson's arguments and rhetoric as well as the efforts of some of the other conciliarists, in 1409 the cardinals claimed that they had the right, by means of *epikeia*, to call a council since they had the power to judge papal elections. Cardinals from both popes met with bishops and secular rulers in 1408 and with their consent summoned a general council. This council opened at Pisa on March 28, 1409. On June 5, 1409, the council deposed both popes on the charges of heresy and of being schismatics. Their sentence was signed by twenty-four cardinals.[25] During the proceedings, they elected the archbishop of Milan to be Pope Alexander V (1409–10).

Even though the Avignon and Roman popes refused to accept the legality of their depositions, the Great Schism would have probably ended except for the fact that Alexander V only lived ten months. The cardinals associated with the Pisan papacy then elected Cardinal Baldassare Cossa as Pope John XXIII (1410–15). By all accounts, John XXIII was an unsavory character with an incredible lust for power. Many of the European leaders decided to abandon their commitments to the Pisan papacy. In the end, the Council of Pisa simply added one more pope to the schism.

Seeing his support wither away, Pope John XXIII was prepared to end the Great Schism by means of force. By 1412 he had captured Rome and was able to call a council for church reform. The council did little more than pass a resolution to call another council the following year. Shortly thereafter John XXIII was driven out of Rome by

King Ladislas of Naples (r. 1386–1414). Under pressure from the recently elected Emperor Sigismund (r. 1411–37), John sent two cardinals to plan the promised council. Sigismund was worried about political instability in Europe and civil unrest in Bohemia. The negotiations between Sigismund and John XXIII resulted in the Council of Constance. It was the first council called by an emperor or empress since the eighth century, but it also had a bull of convocation from John XXIII. Unlike Pisa, Constance met the twofold historical test of being called for by an emperor according to the will of a pope.

The events surrounding the Council of Pisa and leading up to Constance created the conditions for the downfall of Jan Hus. The story of Jan Hus offers us insight into concrete ways that the Great Schism touched people's lives on a local level. It was the failure of Pope John XXIII that necessitated the Council of Constance, and more than anything else it was Jan Hus's opposition to John XXIII's misguided attempt to finance his war against Ladislas of Naples by selling indulgences that brought Hus to stand trial on charges of heresy in Constance.

Jan Hus

Whereas Gerson was the supreme diplomat, Hus had all the charm and tact of an outraged goose. Since Hus means goose in Czech, his enemies made sport of him as the "Bohemian Goose." Regardless of his lack of political acumen, Hus was a good theologian who was deeply committed to reform on a local level. He was not the type of man who would try to solve an international crisis like the Great Schism, though he did consider the implications of schism in his more academic writings.

Hus was five years old when the Great Schism began. He decided early on to pursue a clerical career because it afforded him an opportunity to escape poverty, which was a motivation that he was ashamed of later in life. The clerical establishment in Prague was already undergoing reform prior to the Great Schism. The struggles between the reformers and their opponents were formative for the young cleric.

Emperor Charles IV (1316–78), who was also king of the Bohemians, brought reformers to Prague to address the deplorable conditions in the 1360s. Charles had studied under Pierre Roger, who became Pope Clement VI (1342–52). He was a pious and knowledgeable ruler who cared about the spiritual lives of his subjects. Conrad Waldhauser, a famous Augustinian Canon, was recruited to clean up the situation. Waldhauser started a preaching campaign that brought the people back to Masses and he insisted on the moral reform of the people and the clergy. Almost immediately the Dominicans brought charges against the reformer for exposing the faults of the clergy among other things, but Waldhauser was able to clear himself in Rome.[26]

What were the conditions in Bohemia at the time? Most of the priests who held the best offices were Germans. The Czech clergy, who were systemically excluded from the better schools, largely held rural benefices and tended to have substandard educations. Many Czech priests were keeping concubines, had problems with alcohol, and were using their positions to extort and swindle people out of their property. Prostitution, alcoholism, gambling, and violence were major problems facing the people of Bohemia.

The reformers began a series of initiatives to turn things around. More Czechs like Jan Hus were afforded an opportunity to study at the University of Prague. There was an effort to see to it that the Czech clergy would receive some of the better positions in the Prague diocese. As one might imagine, the policy embittered the German clergy in Bohemia. Finally, there were innovations in the liturgy that helped to spark a religious revival in Bohemia. The clergy began to preach in the language of the people, to incorporate folk songs that people could sing into the liturgy, and to provide people with vernacular Bibles. Special chapels, like the Bethlehem Chapel in Prague, were set up for vernacular preaching.

One of Charles's last acts was to see to it that he had a reformer, Jan of Jenstejn, installed as archbishop of Prague. Archbishop Jan (1378–96) ordained Hus. When Hus was twenty, Archbishop Jan came into conflict with the emperor of the Holy Roman Empire, Wenceslas IV (r. 1378–1419), who was Charles IV's son. Unlike his father, Wenceslas was neither pious nor particularly knowledgeable. Wenceslas became emperor and king of Bohemia at the age of seventeen. His reputation was that of a vain and impulsive playboy. He was so disliked that there was an attempt to assassinate him in 1393. This was also the period when he decided to wage war on Archbishop Jan.

When one of Wenceslas's administrators was excommunicated by Archbishop Jan in 1393, the emperor retaliated by dividing the archdiocese from a territory that was going to have both a new monastery and bishopric. By claiming these benefices, Wenceslas could sell them to the highest bidder and keep the money for himself; but the archbishop refused to recognize the legitimacy of the move and installed a new prior in the monastery before the emperor could act. Wenceslas was furious and had four principal officials of the archdiocese tortured in response. One official died from the torture.

Shocked by the audacity of Wenceslas, Archbishop Jan appealed to the Roman pope, Boniface IX (1389–1404). Boniface refused to hear the charges against the emperor. The Roman pope was afraid that he might drive the emperor to change his allegiance to the Avignon pope by disciplining him. Disillusioned by the pope's refusal to protect the clergy of Bohemia from a tyrant, Archbishop Jan resigned his office in protest in 1396, which was the same year that Hus received his MA degree. Archbishop Zbyněk, who succeeded Jan of Jenstejn, was much less scrupulous from the outset. He scandalized his clergy by buying his office.

The reformers had challenges within the University of Prague as well. The university was dominated by the German faculty. The Germans were solidly in the philosophical camp of nominalism, so the Bohemians chose to adhere to a strict realist philosophy. Due to the moral rigorism and realist commitments of the Bohemian clergy, they came to appreciate the works of the English reformer John Wyclif (1324–84). As the works of Wyclif came under attack, the Czechs found themselves defending his writings against the German theologians. Wyclif had gained symbolic value for the Czech reformers, and Hus can be seen as trying to salvage as much as he could from the English theologian as part of his polemics with the antireformers. This was, to say the least, something of a strategic and rhetorical blunder.

Before the controversy over Wyclif broke out, Hus grew famous as a fiery preacher. By 1402 he had been named as the rector and preacher of the Bethlehem Chapel, which was seen as the center of the reform movement. He preached some three thousand sermons in the course of his career. One of the favorite themes in his early sermons was that only faith formed in love, or faith expressed in works of charity, is saving faith.[27] In 1405 and again in 1407, Hus was invited to preach to the clergy. On both occasions he emphasized the duties of the clergy and denounced clerical impurity.[28] While he used very strong language on these occasions, he was not denouncing the clergy to the laity. Even so, his enemies remembered these sermons and used them against him.

Since 1403 the German masters at the university had been attacking the Czech masters by charging them with the heresy of Wyclifism, which was a vague accusation because it associated the Czech clergy with a series of disparate statements extracted from the writings of John Wyclif. The charges presented against the reformers did not have much effect initially. One reason was that the teachings of Wyclif had not ever been condemned by a council. Twenty-four of Wyclif's propositions had been condemned by a synod in London in 1382, but this does not mean that he had the status of a heretic. It was common for a theologian to have some points that were seen as erroneous and still be seen as a valuable source on other issues. When the German masters at the University of Prague expanded the suspect propositions to forty-five, it still only represented forty-five statements out of volumes of work.

The antireformers at the university focused the debate on eucharistic theology. Hus's opponents knew that Wyclif's denial of the doctrine of transubstantiation was in clear opposition to defined doctrine. The German masters wove several propositions important to the Czech reform movement into a list that included Wyclif's most clearly heretical statements. The strategy worked. Though Hus would eventually defend only five of Wyclif's articles as having an orthodox meaning, his opponents were able to convince people that he had denied transubstantiation. Events in 1408 pushed this dispute out of the university and onto the stage of international affairs.

After several years of efforts, the German masters at the University of Prague had convinced the Roman pope, Gregory XII (1406–15), that there were problems with heresy in Bohemia. King Wenceslas, who had been deposed as emperor in 1400, was anxious to satisfy Gregory XII that he had purged the land of any heresy. Under pressure from the king, Archbishop Zbyněk decided to move against the reformers. Hus was incensed and began to preach more publicly about heresy, simony, and the moral faults of the unreformed clergy. By September 1409, a group of clergy led by the German Dominicans charged Hus with making severe and critical statements about simony and the lives of the clergy. Hus easily defended himself and wrote a treatise explaining why it is permissible to speak charitably against the vices of the clergy, *De arguendo clero pro concione*.[29]

After the Council of Pisa elected Pope Alexander V in June 1409, the archbishop was under increasing pressure to withdraw his obedience from Pope Gregory XII. When Alexander V started proceedings against Zbyněk, the archbishop crumbled and switched his allegiance. As a concession, Archbishop Zbyněk managed to obtain a bull from Alexander in December that condemned the forty-five articles and that forbade all preaching outside of diocesan and monastic churches. This last provision was aimed at Hus and the Bethlehem Chapel. Hus defied the bull and continued to preach. Alexander V died before he could act against Hus.

Once again, international affairs would intrude upon the work of the Czech reformers. After King Ladislas of Naples drove the Pisan Pope John XXIII out of Rome in 1411, Pope John XXIII issued a bull authorizing the sale of indulgences to support a crusade against Ladislas. The bull stated:

> And also by apostolic authority granted me, I absolve you from all sins, if you are truly contrite and confess them to God and me. If you cannot personally take up the project [of joining the crusade], but wish to bring a contribution according to your ability in compliance with my and the commissioner's terms in defense and aid of the above-named project I grant and concede you the fullest remission of all your sins, including punishment and guilt.[30]

In order to bring in the support of secular rulers who were already wavering in their commitments to the Pisan papacy, John XXIII also had a provision that would give them a percentage of the revenues.

When Hus decided to oppose the bull authorizing the sale of indulgences, he must have suspected he would alienate his last powerful supporter, King Wenceslas. Hus's zeal impelled him to throw caution to the wind and to publicly oppose the bull. He preached against the indulgences and held public disputations. Hus argued that it was improper for Christians to give money for the purpose of killing other Christians and that the pope and the clergy should not be fighting with the material sword or engaging in warfare. He also opposed the way the bull seemed to imply that no repentance was necessary for forgiveness. His critiques were perfectly orthodox on these points.[31]

Wenceslas was furious and enlisted the aid of Hus's opponents at the University of Prague to draft a series of articles that forbade preaching against the indulgences. Hus defended his opposition to the indulgences by citing the provision in canon law that whatever is contrary to the law of Christ is heretical and should not be obeyed.[32] In a letter written in May 1412, Hus explained his actions:

> As to my not obeying the wrong commands of my superi-
> ors, while offering no resistance to power which is of the
> Lord God, that I have been taught by the scriptures, and
> above all by the word and deed of the apostles who, against
> the will of the chief priests preached our Lord Jesus Christ'
> saying that "we ought to obey God rather than people."[33]

Like Gerson, Hus cited Acts 5:29 to show that the commands of superiors must be subjected to God's law as expressed in scripture. To save the people of Prague from an impending papal interdict, which would have suspended all sacramental ministry as long as the people supported Hus, he voluntarily went into exile.

While Hus was in exile from Prague, he began to write a small tract called *The Six Errors*. He said he wanted it to be a shield for the people from the errors that the unreformed clergy were teaching in order to deny any accountability for their crimes. Some of the clergy were arguing that since a priest creates God's body at the Eucharist, then a priest is the Father of God. As such, even a priest in mortal sin, which would include actions like simony or murder, cannot be called a servant of the devil. The antireformers used the eucharistic service of the priesthood to claim that the worst priest is better than the most virtuous member of the laity. According to Hus, these insane priests went so far as to exalt themselves over the Virgin Mary because she only bore Christ once whereas they create God repeatedly during the Masses they celebrate.[34]

The second error had to do with the teaching that one must believe or have faith in Mary, the saints, and the pope. Hus argued that one must only believe in God and in what has been revealed in scriptures. The focus of his argument was on the claim that people had to believe in the pope. After discussing the high devotion that is due to Mary, he explained that we do not have faith in Mary. If we do not have faith in Mary, he reasoned, then it does not seem appropriate to have faith in the pope. Hus pointed to two scriptural passages to justify his position. The first was Peter's denial of Christ (Matt 26:69–75), which was both apostasy and perjury; and the second was Paul's exhortation to the Corinthians to identify themselves as belonging to Jesus Christ rather than to Peter, Paul, or Apollos (1 Cor 1:11–17). The first example proved that Peter can be wrong and the second demonstrated we should only believe in Christ. To shore up his argument, Hus cited statements from both the Venerable Bede and Augustine to demonstrate his continuity with the church's tradition.[35]

The third, fourth, and fifth errors all had to do with the authority of the clergy. The third error was that a priest forgives sins by his own will rather than acting as a minister proclaiming God's forgiveness. This teaching would mean that a priest would have almost absolute power over his people's eternal salvation as a matter of his own whims. The fourth error naturally flows from the third: One should always obey his or her ecclesiastical superiors. Hus responded by teaching the Czech people that they must evaluate the commands of their clergy in light of the teaching of the scriptures, which Hus used in a sense that would include traditional materials like Augustine or creeds. If a command violates the teaching of scripture, he advised people to disobey. The claim that the church can excommunicate people for any reason the authorities might give was the fifth error. Hus argued that the church could only excommunicate people for mortal sin.[36]

The sixth error was at the heart of the various problems in the Bohemian clergy. Hus claimed that priests and bishops were preaching that they could legitimately buy and sell offices in the church. Others justified the idea that ecclesiastical offices could be granted or received for political purposes. Hus argued that the only reason for anyone to be admitted into holy orders was to serve the common good.[37] In each case, he cited scriptural authorities and traditional theologians like Augustine and Gregory the Great. To provide a permanent shield against these errors for the laity, Hus inscribed *The Six Errors* in Czech on the walls of the Bethlehem Chapel.

The Six Errors represents the heart of Hus's reform agenda. He was retrieving a reform theme that runs through the writings of Gregory the Great, Peter Damian, and Pope Gregory VII: The clergy are accountable to their neighbors as well as to God. The test was whether or not the clergy were following the law of Christ and serving the common good. Gerson's reform agenda was fundamentally similar to Hus's, but Hus was teaching laypeople to be discerning when it came to the lives and demands of the clergy. Hus's denial that the clergy are more a part of the church than the laity, his rejection of the claim that priests and bishops should be regarded as holy simply because of their offices, his argument that tithes should be freewill offerings, and his defense of the idea that civil authorities may legitimately deprive bishops and priests of their possessions certainly set men like Jean Gerson against him.[38]

Other aspects of Hus's theology were even more provocative for Gerson's ecclesiastical colleagues. For example, they were offended by his argument that the church should not put heretics to death because Christ did not execute people. Instead, Hus advocated following the rule laid down in Matthew 18:15–17, which advised shunning those who sin against the community as publicans or Gentiles. He also cited the examples of Augustine and the fathers who willingly entered into discourse with heretics and schismatics in order to persuade them to reconcile themselves to the church. Gerson's colleagues at the Council of Constance were also more than a little upset to find that Hus had compared the guilt of the clergymen who turned innocent people over to the secular arm for execution to the guilt of the priests, scribes, and Pharisees who turned Christ over to Pilate.[39]

In the end, the council members were not moved by Hus's arguments, and the trial of Jan Hus was a foregone conclusion from the outset. Hus found himself inextricably caught in the peculiarities of inquisitorial logic. Even so, he could have saved himself but refused to do so. By all accounts, the council members were hoping Hus would recant so that they would not have to execute him. Perhaps Hus was naïve, but he failed to see that the bishops and lower clergy were not willing to reform their behavior. The problems associated with the bishops and lower clergy, including their accountability to the laity, would only begin to be addressed after the cataclysmic events of the Protestant Reformation. The focus at Constance was resolving the Great Schism and preventing new schisms in the future, and anyone who stood in the way would be sacrificed for restoring unity.

Council of Constance

The Council of Constance is one of the most intriguing events in the history of the Roman Catholic Church. Convened in November 1414, the council's agenda was shaped in terms of Gerson's rhetoric, though he was not the only voice calling for the types of reforms passed by the council. Constance aimed at ending the schism, extirpating heresy, and reforming the church in its head and members. It included almost three-dozen cardinals from the three curias at the time as well as hundreds of other representatives, including archbishops, bishops, theologians, canon lawyers, abbots, delegates from the mendicant orders, and envoys from the emperor and other civil rulers. The various members were divided into five basic nations, each of which received one vote regardless of their size, and the college of cardinals, which also had one vote. Because the representatives of the universities, of the secular rulers, of the monastic and mendicant orders were able to vote within the nations, the Council of Constance was truly representative of the whole church: lay, religious, and clerical.[40]

Almost immediately the Council of Constance faced a crisis. Pope John XXIII fled from Constance during the night on March 20, 1415. John XXIII had promised to abdicate at the council, but he had hoped that the council would then reelect him. When he realized that they were not going to reelect him, he decided to desert the council in an attempt to call its validity into question.

If it had not been for the efforts of Jean Gerson, John XXIII's plan might have been successful. Two days after the pope's flight, Gerson gave a sermon that stiffened the resolve of the council members to continue. He took his theme from the Gospel reading, John 12:35, "Walk while you have the light, so that the darkness may not overtake you" (NRSV). To underscore the significance of the passage, he told them that Christ had decreed that his followers should walk when they have the light with them, not in some Roman fable inscribed in air, but in the book of life. The light, he explained, is none other than the light of the world, Jesus Christ, who said, "Those who follow me do not walk in darkness but will have the light of life" (John 8:12). This light, this sun of justice, he continued, is described by the Psalmist as "great and terrible above all that are around Him" (Psalm 88:8 [89:8]). Gerson assured the assembly that the infallible promise of this great and terrible light, "whenever two or three come together in my name, I am in their midst" (Matthew 18:20), was being fulfilled.[41]

Returning to the Psalms, which say that the works of the Lord are great in the council of the just (Ps 111:1), Gerson told the council members that they had already seen great works of God in the short time since the council had begun. He did not elaborate as to what those great works were, which left open the possibility that the flight of John XXIII was an act of providence. If the assembly believed in Christ's promise, Gerson concluded, they must recognize that the light was with them. The reading from John clearly indicated, according to Gerson, that the council members must move forward while they had the light with them. The Holy Spirit, he preached, was actively working in their presence to liberate the people of God from the darkness of schism, heresy, and the horrible sins of the clergy. Gerson exhorted them to walk while they had the light, to act while the truth was in their midst, to believe Christ's promise to remain with his church, to recognize that the God who is above, beneath, and beyond every earthly power was with them.[42]

Having inspired courage in his audience, Gerson reiterated the conciliar principles that justified the council's existence and recalled the problems with heresy in Bohemia, England, and France. His sermon was so effective that parts of it were incorporated word for word into the most controversial and most significant decree of the council, *Haec sancta*, which was approved in the fourth session of the council. The decree stated:

> First, that this synod, legitimately assembled in the Holy Spirit, constituting a general council, representing the catholic church militant, has power immediately from Christ, and that everyone of whatever state or dignity, even papal, is bound to obey it in those matters which pertain to the faith and the eradication of the said schism.[43]

According to *Haec sancta*, the council had authority over the pope because its power came from Christ immediately. The significance, authority, and applicability of this decree has been debated by Catholic theologians ever since.

Regardless of later assessments of whether councils can legitimately assert authority and jurisdictional power over the pope, the

Council of Constance did assert its superiority and almost immediately moved to depose John XXIII as an "unworthy, useless, and damnable person."[44] The charges against him were numerous, but they began with his flight from Constance in indecent dress (a reference to the claim that he disguised himself as a woman), moved to his failure to fulfill his oath to abdicate, paused to consider his poor administrative skills, and concluded with a description of his basic immorality. The council forbade all Christians from that point on to recognize him as pope, to call him pope, and to adhere to him as pope in any way.

At the same time, the council moved to prevent the proliferation of more popes before they could end the schism. First, they forbade the election of any new pontiff by the cardinals without the consent of the council. Further, any new election had to be confirmed by the council. Finally, they decreed that none of the men who held the papal office during the Great Schism could be reelected. With these measures, the council gave itself time to work out the final resolution to the schism and to address the problems associated with heresy.

Earlier that May, the council had condemned forty-five of John Wyclif's articles, all of Wyclif's books, and 260 more of his articles. There was broad support among the secular rulers as well as the clergy because Wyclif had taught that no one in mortal sin is a lord, prelate, or bishop. Then they condemned him as an obstinate heretic even though he had been dead for decades. Normally one has to be alive to be obstinate, which is why a person was supposed to be alive to be charged with heresy. Regardless of their legal reasoning, these actions provided a strong basis for condemning Hus.

Hus had been in Constance since November 1414. On his journey to the council one of the Czech bishops, John of Borsnicz, preceded him and spread the rumor that he was a mind reader.[45] It was a sign of things to come. Hus had been lured to Constance by the promise of safe conduct from Emperor Sigismund, but almost as soon as he arrived in the city he was arrested. He spent the period from November 29, 1414, until the opening of the trial on May 5, 1415, in prison and in chains.

By the time the trial began, Hus's enemies had been very successful in turning opinion against him. They had sent a list of articles that were supposed to be Hus's to the faculty at the University of Paris during the late summer or early fall of 1414. Gerson read these articles and concluded that Hus was a dangerous heretic. Two months before Hus arrived in Constance, Gerson wrote the archbishop of Prague condemning twenty of the articles he had received and he gave this warning: "The government of the world cannot be based on predestination or love, things which remain insecure and uncertain in this life, but must rest on established ecclesiastical and civil laws." Gerson identified Hus's statement that those in mortal sin cannot exercise jurisdiction or dominion over the Christian community as his most pernicious error. Given the daring and obstinacy of Hus, Gerson recommended that he should be dealt with by a summary judicial condemnation rather than by attempting to reason with him.[46] The problem was that Hus never made the statement in question. Gerson simply accepted the articles as they were proposed by Hus's enemies.

When Hus was granted a hearing on June 5, he was given copies of his writings that had not been tampered with by anyone. He acknowledged the works as his and declared his willingness to be corrected and to amend anything that was shown to be erroneous; but the articles that were read to the council were the ones produced by Hus's enemies. Hus tried to respond to the articles, to distinguish between what was his work and what was not, and to provide the context for the articles that had not been tampered with, but the council members shouted him down, saying, "Leave off your sophistry and just say yes or no." When Hus gave up and was silent, his enemies shouted that his silence was a sign of his consent to the condemned articles.[47]

Hus was a victim of the inquisitorial method. On one level, a heretic was one who denied the authority of the church. So when the church charged a person with heresy, the only way someone could demonstrate that he or she was obedient was to accept the charge. Any attempt to defend oneself against the charge of heresy was seen as proof of heresy. This type of reasoning also prevented Hus from having the advocate he had requested. His request was denied because it was even illegal to defend someone suspected of heresy.[48]

Heretics were also forbidden to call witnesses in their defense. So when the official inquisitor for Prague arrived in Constance to testify that Hus had never been charged or found guilty of any heresy, he was arrested and forced to recant the statements clearing Hus in his written deposition. When the Czech inquisitor was released, he fled Constance and did not testify at the trial.[49]

Witnesses for the prosecution, on the other hand, were allowed to testify. The witnesses against the suspected heretic were presumed to be truthful. The reasoning for this presumption was based in scripture, as can be seen from Cardinal Zabarella's question to Hus at his trial:

> Master Jan, you know that it is written that "in the mouth of two or three witnesses stands every word" (Deuteronomy 19:15). And look! Here are well-nigh twenty witnesses against you—prelates, doctors, and other great and noble men, some of whom depose from hearsay, others from knowledge, adducing reasonable proofs of their knowledge. What then, do you still oppose them all?[50]

Hus responded that if he knew in good conscience that he did not teach the condemned articles, then he could not admit to them regardless of the number or quality of witnesses. Cardinal d'Ailly responded that the judges could not base their decisions on Hus's conscience but on the testimony of the witnesses, which included Gerson, whom d'Ailly credited with being the most renowned doctor in all of Christendom.[51]

At the end of the first hearing, Cardinal d'Ailly urged Hus to submit to the council's judgment and promised merciful treatment. During the second hearing, an exasperated d'Ailly tried to persuade Hus, saying:

> Master John! Behold, two ways are placed before you, of which choose one! Either you throw yourself entirely and totally on the grace and into the hands of the council, that whatever the council shall dictate you, therewith you shall be content. And the council, out of reverence for the lord king of the Romans here and his brother, the king of Bohemia, and for your own good, will deal kindly and humanely with you. Or if you still wish to hold and defend some articles of the aforementioned, and if you desire still another hearing, it shall be granted you. But consider that there are here great and enlightened men—doctors and masters—who have such strong reasons against your articles, that it is to be feared lest you become involved in greater errors, if you wish to defend and hold those articles. I counsel you—I do not speak as judge.[52]

All Hus had to do was to abjure or recant the articles the council attributed to him, but he refused to do so.

Hus was caught in the trap of his own scrupulosity over morals. He argued that he could not abjure something he had never taught because that would be a lie, which he believed would be a snare of damnation for him. Cardinal Zabarella advised Hus to recognize that he would be denouncing the articles as they were formulated by the council instead of arguing about their meaning or whether he taught them or not. King Wenceslas warned Hus that if he refused to follow d'Ailly's advice that "the doctors have their rules as to what they ought finally to do with you."[53] As the day drew on it became evident that Hus would not, depending on your perspective, either recant or perjure himself, which amounted to the same thing in this case.

Over the following weeks, a council member tried to convince Hus that he would not be culpable if he perjured himself under duress. This council member, whom we only know as "the Father," advised Hus to consider the example of St. Paul, who was lowered down in a basket (Acts 9:23–25) in order to escape death so that he could continue his ministry. If Hus would only take this example from the apostles, the Father promised that Jesus would grant Hus even greater struggles for the faith in the future.[54] It was to no avail. Hus respectfully responded that if he recanted he would scandalize his people. He believed it would be better for him to have a millstone hung around his neck and to be thrown into the sea than to give a public example of consent to sin.[55] Given the methods of the Inquisition, Hus's refusal to admit and to recant his heresy proved his guilt and ended with his execution.

On July 4, 1415, the Roman pope, Gregory XII, reconvened the council under his authority and abdicated his office. Two days later the council burned Hus at the stake. Then the council turned its attention to the Avignon pope, who absolutely refused to resign. After a series of diplomatic efforts, the council deposed Benedict XIII on July 26, 1417. It then passed a decree known as *Frequens*, which was based in large part on the theology of Jean Gerson. *Frequens* required that after Constance a council should be called in five years, then another in seven, and thereafter every ten years for the express purpose of reform. Finally the council members set up provisions to guard against future schism and to explicitly tie the pope's authority to the traditions of the apostles, to the decisions of ecumenical councils, and to the writings of the fathers.

Having prepared the way for a new election, the Council of Constance elected Cardinal Oddo Colonna as Pope Martin V on November 11, 1417. The Great Schism was over and the Catholic Church has not suffered from another persistent papal schism since the closing of Constance.[56] More than anyone else, Gerson can be seen behind the major documents and decisions produced by the council. The Catholic Church came to the very brink of destruction; and, faced with the potential of an ever-expanding number of papacies, the church opted for unity. Should an insane, heretical, or depraved pope be elected to office, the canonists and theologians will refer to Constance for precedents. Thus the Council of Constance not only reformed the fifteenth-century church, but it serves as a permanent bulwark against the corruptions resulting from severing rights and duties in the papal office.

Even with such impressive accomplishments, the Council of Constance also reminds us that conciliar government of the church was not perfect. The council proved to be unjust to Jan Hus. Although there were provisions aimed at reforming the papal office, Gerson was one of the few council members who had an interest in episcopal reform. Without progress on reforming the bishops, the worst and most scandalous problems facing Catholics on a concrete level were allowed to continue. The impact of the failures of Constance was far-reaching. A century later another reformer, Martin Luther, was reminded of the fate of Hus by an advisor when he was planning to obey a summons to Rome.

Conclusion

Both Jean Gerson and Jan Hus deserve to be recognized as great Catholic reformers who sought to help the church fulfill its mission of saving souls, but both men also have tarnished reputations. Gerson's reputation as a reformer diminished as Catholic theologians became increasingly distrustful of conciliarism in general. While there has been a renewal of interest in Gerson's theology since Vatican II, his antipathy toward Jan Hus and the lay reform movements of his age continues to hurt his standing. Jan Hus, whose reputation has been improving, still tends to be seen as either a sympathetic heretic or as an orthodox reformer suffering from excessive zeal. Actually, there is something excessive about both of these reformers and the environment that produced them.

In the late Middle Ages theology took on an axiomatic quality, which tended to push theology to extreme positions. On the one hand, this tendency can be seen in Gerson and the council's willingness to judge Hus based on a list of abstracted articles without consideration of intended audience, occasion, context, or qualification. On the other hand, Hus demonstrated a type of moral absolutism whereby he thought it better to die than to admit to an error he did not make. Gerson's emphasis on the clergy and their legal rights in service to the mission of the church was so absolute that he could not see how the laity could even legitimately criticize the clergy. Hus's insistence on the link between holiness and authority was so absolute as to make it virtually impossible for anyone to legitimately assume roles of leadership in either the ecclesiastical or secular spheres without becoming martyrs. Neither man was able to see how the clergy and the laity have to constantly maintain mutual accountability, mutual patience, and mutual mercy in a balanced way.

Perhaps the unbalanced character of their respective theologies resulted from their understandable preoccupation with legal questions. One would have thought that Gerson, who affirmed that all Christian authority is based on service, could have found much common ground with Hus, who taught that Christian authority is based on holiness defined as imitating the example of Christ and the apostles. These ideas are absolutely compatible. After all, Christ came as a servant. The difficulty comes from trying to express these ideas in legal and jurisdictional terms, which is the primary way that both men framed their reform agendas in the period leading up to Constance. If they had recalled Bernard of Clairvaux and Catherine of Siena's advice to their disciples to humbly recognize that their way of approaching reform is not the only way, then Gerson and Hus might have accomplished more.

Jean Gerson recognized the lost opportunities resulting from the condemnation of Jan Hus. In a poetic treatise aimed at reforming the study of theology, Gerson wrote these lines:

> For zeal, since it cherishes and loves something,
> Does not stand for harm to [what it loves] but is roused at once,

Is seized with just rage and does not inquire,
Feels hatred, goes in pursuit, takes no rest,
Feigns justice and attempts the difficult,
Is fierce beyond its strength—breaks, tumbles,
Drags with it much that perishes as well.[57]

Gerson saw these lines as referring to Hus; but he failed to see how they also applied to his own actions. Out of his love for the ecclesiastical hierarchy and order, he failed to seriously inquire into the details of Hus's case. His inquisitorial methods only feigned justice and were ultimately not strong enough to end the Czech reform movement. Gerson's zeal helped to drag Hus to the stake.

The condemnation of Hus planted one of the seeds of destruction for the conciliar movement. The Czech people rose up after Hus's condemnation and formed a group known as the Hussites. The Hussites formed armies and became a serious military threat to Bavaria, Saxony, Austria, and Brandenburg. They were influential enough to force the council members to negotiate with them on theological matters. After the Council of Basle approved the Hussite demands for communion in both kinds, the punishment of criminal members of the clergy by secular authorities, and the right of priests to preach freely, Pope Eugenius IV (1431–49) moved to dissolve the council in 1437. This set into motion an ongoing struggle between the pope and Council of Basle that ended in defeat for the council.

For all their failings, Gerson and Hus remain pivotal figures in the history of reform. Gerson and his conciliarist allies saved the Catholic Church from endless schisms and chaos by linking authority and service, arguing that canon law did not carry the force of tradition, and emphasizing educational reform for the clergy. These ideas resurfaced in the reforms of Trent. Hus addressed the inequities between the Czech clergy and their German counterparts, stopped the sale of indulgences, and helped to revitalize the faith of the Czech people. Most of the liturgical reforms advocated by Hus, such as vernacular Masses, the use of folk music that ordinary people could sing, and allowing the laity to drink from the chalice, would be enacted at Vatican II some 550 years after his death.

Their most valuable legacy may be the cautionary tale they left for subsequent generations. In a medieval morality play Gerson could have been cast as theological absolutism or clericalism and Hus as moral absolutism or scrupulosity. Both men could have been cast as examples of inordinate zeal. For the medieval playwright, their story would serve to edify those who do not keep spirituality at the center of their reform efforts. This is not to say that they did not preach and write about spiritual matters such as humility and charity, but they failed to see that these virtues demand acceptance of legitimate diversity within the church in terms of theological ideas on the one hand and in terms of the moral qualities of church members on the other. In the end, the story of the collision between these men recalls Christ's answer to those who wish to reform the church by ripping up the weeds: "No; for in gathering the weeds you would uproot the wheat among them. Let both of them grow together until the harvest; and at harvest time I will tell the reapers, Collect the weeds first and bind them in bundles to be burned, but gather the wheat into my barn" (Matt 13:29–30 NRSV).

7

Gasparo Contarini: Christ's Diplomat

As the Venetian ambassador, Gasparo Contarini, looked over the large hall crowded with Emperor Charles V's court, diplomats from the powers outside the empire, and prominent members of the clergy, he probably wondered whether the young Augustinian friar accused of heresy would defend himself. The previous day, April 17, 1521, Friar Martin Luther had been unable to speak before the majesty of the emperor and the other members of the imperial diet at Worms. There was a great deal of speculation that he would recant. Many hoped that he would not, but some of Luther's sympathizers would be alienated at the end of the day. This was by far the most significant event the young ambassador from Venice had witnessed.

Luther would not disappoint those who were looking forward to a theological showdown. He was ready to fight. After being accused of following the heresies of John Wyclif and Jan Hus, of emboldening the Turks by questioning the legitimacy of the faith, and of denying the authority of the popes and councils, Luther declared:

> Unless I am convinced by the testimony of scripture or by clear reason, for I do not trust either in the pope or in the councils alone, since it is well known that they have often erred and contradicted themselves, I am bound by the scriptures I have quoted and my conscience is captive to the Word of God. I cannot and will not retract anything, for it is neither safe nor right to go against conscience. I cannot do otherwise, here I stand, may God help me, Amen.[1]

Luther exited to hisses from the Spanish delegation. Even his most ardent supporters were stunned by his bold and revolutionary proclamation. Although Contarini had little to say about the event in his writings, Luther made a deep impression on him.

Six years before Luther had his "tower experience," which led him to the idea of a gracious and merciful God, Contarini had had a similar experience. Struggling with the question of whether or not to take on a life of penance as a monk, he sought advice from his confessor on Holy Saturday 1511. Although we do not know the specific content of the advice he received, Contarini concluded, "And, in truth, I understood that even if I did all the penance I could, and more, it would not suffice in the least to merit happiness or even to render satisfaction for past sins."[2] He came to recognize that Christ's passion was enough to render satisfaction for our sins, but he still affirmed that God demands an effort from Christians to unite themselves with Christ in faith, hope, and love.

Since Contarini believed that the faithful unite themselves to Christ through the sacramental ministry of the church, his experience of God's merciful and justifying grace led him to embrace the institutional church even as he decided to work for its reform. Rather than take up a life of penance or of sacramental ministry, he concluded that he could work for reform as a layman involved in the affairs of the world. The experience and contacts he generated over a twenty-four year period as a businessman, diplomat, and officeholder in the Republic of Venice served him well when he was ordained a priest and elevated to the ecclesiastical rank of cardinal at the age of fifty-one.

Becoming a cardinal had never been one of Contarini's goals and accepting the post meant relinquishing his position as a leader in the Republic of Venice. Because he was not a career cleric, he was detached enough to speak his mind without fear of losing his ecclesiastical standing. When Pope Paul III (1534–49) tried to manipulate Contarini to change his position on a matter of policy by reminding him who had given him the honor of being a cardinal, he responded, "I do not consider that the [red] hat is the greatest honor that has ever been bestowed on me."[3] By looking at problems from the perspective of a theologically educated layman, Contarini was able to penetrate through the patronage system that was paralyzing the church.

On the other hand, Contarini was also an experienced diplomat. He was skilled at knowing when to speak and when to remain silent. His willingness to work for peaceful reconciliation between people helped him bring together a coalition of reformers with different aims, temperaments, and theologies. Contarini also introduced a new type of reform movement that has come to be known as ecumenism. Ecumenism, which is a reform movement aimed at healing the divisions between Christians, was a failure at the time; but it is now seen as essential for the church's mission to evangelize the world.

Recognizing the impediments to unity inherent in ecclesiastical corruption, Contarini worked assiduously for the reform of the abuses. Starting with the reform of the head, he called for a more spiritualized papacy without armies and political power. In addition, he identified a host of financial abuses associated with ecclesiastical offices, which ranged in nature from outright simony to simple veniality. Contarini did not limit his agenda to the reform of the papacy and the curia, but he also pushed for reform of the episcopacy and of the monastic houses. His wide interests were the result of years of contacts with leading reformers among the scholars, clergy, and religious orders in Italy, Spain, and the Holy Roman Empire.

In order to understand the various Catholic reformers who influenced Contarini either directly or indirectly, one must first appreciate the state of the church at the end of the fifteenth century and the beginning of the sixteenth. While this period of time was certainly the absolute low point of the church's moral credibility and authority on matters of faith, it was also a time when the Catholic Church was at the height of its history in terms of its patronage of the arts and its commitment to aesthetics. Perhaps there is a correlation between these two factors. The great building popes of the Renaissance were also the most corrupt popes in history, and it was the Dominican John Tetzel's indulgence preaching for the building of St. Peter's in Rome that sparked Luther's Reformation.

Abuses in the Early Renaissance Church (1475–1512)

Scandal, abuse, and corruption were widespread but not universal problems during the Renaissance. The church was reasonably healthy in England on a diocesan level. Additionally, there were areas in the Low Countries where new and vibrant forms of spirituality were emerging. Nonetheless, concubinage was so common in Paris that the clergy debated whether or not fornication is a mortal sin. In the

Diocese of Constance the clergy were said to be sexually active enough to produce some fifteen hundred illegitimate children a year.[4] The church was strong in some ways in Spain, but the office of the Inquisition had been co-opted into a repressive arm of the monarchy. Most scandalous of all, Rome had become synonymous with corruption and decadence throughout Europe.

The battered state of the church was clearly identified by the theologians of the period. Edgidio da Viterbo, minister general of the Augustinian Order, posed these questions in an address to the Fifth Lateran Council (1512): "When has ambition been more unrestrained, greed more burning? When has the license to sin been more shameless?"[5] While Edgidio was convinced that the lack of regular councils was the primary source of ecclesial corruption, many others focused their critiques on papal abuses.

Pope Adrian VI (1522–23) famously identified the Holy See as the source of the ecclesial abuses and scandals spreading throughout the Catholic Church. In 1522 he wrote:

> Scripture proclaims that the sins of the people are a consequence of the sins of the priests, and therefore (as Chrysostom says) our Savior, about to cure the ailing city of Jerusalem, first entered the Temple to chastise first the sins of the priests, like the good doctor who cures a sickness at its source. We know that for many years many abominable things have occurred in this Holy See, abuses on spiritual matters, transgressions of the commandments, and finally in everything a change for the worse. No wonder that the illness has spread from the head to the members, from the Supreme Pontiffs to the prelates below them.[6]

To fully appreciate Pope Adrian's statement, we need consider only three examples of his predecessors: Sixtus IV, Innocent VIII, and Alexander VI.

Pope Sixtus IV (1471–84) had been a Franciscan theologian before his election to the papacy, but his pontificate reflected nothing of Francis's commitment to simplicity and poverty. He spent a third of the papacy's annual income just for his coronation tiara. He also commissioned the building of some of the most famous structures in Rome, including Ponte Sisto, Santa Maria Popolo, and the Sistine

Chapel. Sixtus employed the best artists to reinforce papal claims to both temporal and spiritual authority, such as Perugino, who painted "Christ Consigns the Keys to Peter," and Botticelli, who painted "The Challenge to Moses," both of which adorn the Sistine Chapel. Unfortunately, his pursuit of beautiful propaganda threatened to bankrupt the Catholic Church.

While Sixtus IV's spending on art was profligate, it was not the most scandalous aspect of his papacy. He involved himself in a series of unseemly wars against the Italian city-states of Florence, Ferrara, and Venice. Further, his administration was known for its nepotism. Sixtus made six of his nephews cardinals, including Giuliano della Rovere, who would become Pope Julius II (1503–13). He enriched these nephews by heaping benefices upon them. For example, Giuliano simultaneously held the following positions before he became pope: archbishop of Avignon, archbishop of Bologna, bishop of Lausanne, bishop of Coutances, bishop of Viviers, bishop of Mende, bishop of Ostia, bishop of Velletri, abbot of Nonatola, abbot of Grottaferrata, and more than twenty other benefices. For devout Catholics, Sixtus IV's greatest impiety was his attempt to have Lorenzo and Giuliano de Medici murdered during Mass in Florence's Duomo.

Pope Innocent VIII (1484–92), Sixtus's immediate successor, bribed his way into the papacy. This fact was not so scandalous at the time, but his penchant for openly inviting his illegitimate children into the papal palace did provoke people to question Innocent's authority. Innocent even arranged for his children's marriages to take place in the papal palace. To secure one of these dynastic marriages to the Medici family in Florence, Innocent agreed to dispense with canon law and to make a thirteen-year-old Medici boy a cardinal. This boy would later become Pope Leo X (1513–21). Perhaps Innocent's most notable act was publishing the papal bull *Summis desiderantes*, which initiated the witch hunts in Europe. Even worse from the perspective of his contemporaries was the pope's treacherous collaboration with the successor to the Turkish sultan who had defeated Constantinople. However, Innocent's involvement in nepotism, power politics, and sexual misbehavior paled in comparison to the pontificate of Alexander VI (1492–1503).[7]

The most notorious papacy in history was that of Alexander VI. Like Innocent VIII, he bribed his way into office and he was known for having illegitimate children. Alexander was infamous for stealing church property to enrich his children. He also openly conducted an adulterous affair during his papacy with a married fifteen-year-old girl named Giulia Farnese. Giulia was the last and the youngest of a number of open mistresses he had kept throughout his career. She can still be seen in St. Peter's because she was immortalized in marble as the statue of Justice before the tomb of Pope Paul III. In addition to his sexual sins, Alexander was known for being violent and even treacherous. He involved himself in several small wars and had a reputation for poisoning his elderly cardinals so that he could exercise the papal right to seize their property.

The popes of this period, with the exception of Adrian VI's short pontificate, were lavish in their spending on their relatives, art, building projects, mistresses, or wars. To support these activities, they had to find ways to raise money. One way that the popes raised funds was by selling ecclesiastical benefices to the highest bidder. Because holding a benefice entitled a person to the ecclesiastical revenues associated with it, people began to speculatively invest in them. By the beginning of the sixteenth century, taking out loans to buy benefices became commonplace. These practices had the effect of making ecclesiastical officeholders extremely resistant to reforming the church if it diminished the return on what they saw as their "legitimate" investments.

Since most of the bishops had bought their benefices, they also tended to sell offices to people within their own jurisdictions. To pay the ever-increasing fees associated with their offices, not to mention the interest on the loans they took out to buy them, the bishops also devised new fees for their clergy. The lower clergy, in turn, found new ways to take money and goods from the laity. By the time Luther began his reform, the church had become economically oppressive in many places.[8] Even with a host of fees and ecclesiastical taxes, the system was unable to keep up with the expenses of the popes and the bishops. To make up for the shortfalls, the clergy resorted to the selling of indulgences, charging fees for reserved sins, and peddling dispensations as a voluntary way to raise funds.

The selling of indulgences was a particularly profitable and politically painless way for a pope to raise funds. In many ways, the practice was similar to the policy employed by governments that use lotteries to pay for their expenses without raising taxes. According to Luther, the indulgence preachers in Saxony were claiming that they could absolve even someone from the sin of raping Mary, the Mother of God.[9] As scandalous as the sale of indulgences was for a handful of theologians and reformers of the period, the penitential system's practice of associating certain monetary fines with specific sins that were reserved to either the bishop or the pope was much more damaging to the church's reputation and authority.

How did this system work? Certain sins and dispensations were reserved to the pope, others to the bishops, and the remainder went to the priests. One of the most lucrative sources of revenues for many dioceses was what came to be called the "concubinage tax." By paying a penitential fee to his bishop, a priest could keep a concubine. Moreover, the priest could also have children without facing ecclesiastical sanctions by paying another fine. To have the child born out of such a union baptized required yet another payment to the bishop. Allowing priests to have concubines and children became such a stable source of income that many bishops had no interest in ending the practice among the clergy.[10]

Reserved sins and the fees associated with them also applied to the laity. For example, a layperson who had divorced and remarried without an annulment could simply pay a fee to the bishop and have the matter absolved. Because sins such as infanticide, homicide, incest, and sodomy were reserved to the bishop and had various fees associated with their absolution, many people began to doubt the legitimacy of the whole penitential system. These problems were reflected in the preoccupation of late medieval and early Renaissance theologians with questions over justification, grace, free will, and merit.

Whereas some Catholic reformers concentrated on the theological issues and their relationship to church discipline and practice, others focused on systemic institutional abuses of the popes' and bishops' power to offer dispensations from canon law. Despite being profitable for the popes and bishops, this policy was disastrous for pastoral care. Bishops could and did pay the popes of this period for dispensations from residing in their dioceses; and, in turn, priests sought and obtained dispensations from residing in their parishes from their bishops. Other types of dispensations freed men from canonical barriers to ordination. While there were plenty of priests and bishops, many left their posts vacant as they pursued their personal interests elsewhere.

Given the scope of the problems facing the church on the eve of the Protestant Reformation, it is not terribly surprising that there were many people who were calling for reform. Prior to Luther, there was a diverse but coherent reform movement in the church. What held this movement together was the commitment to work for reform within the traditional framework, structures, and institutions of the church. Its purpose was to correct the corrupt practices and to reinvigorate a sense of mission.[11]

The success of the Protestant reformers made it very difficult for Catholic reformers to continue their work without being accused of disloyalty. As a result, there was a shift in the methods and rhetoric of the Catholic reform movement after 1517. By the time Contarini attended the Diet of Worms, Catholic reformers had learned to become circumspect and diplomatic. Contarini brought the political acumen necessary to help the reformers navigate their way through the treacherous waters churned up as the Catholic Church turned to confront the Protestants.

Contarini and the Catholic Reformers before 1517

There were at least three major types or groups of reformers active throughout Contarini's lifetime. The first type sought to reform the church on a grassroots level by reforming individuals. They hoped for a spontaneous reform of the members of the church, which they believed would lead to institutional change in the future. Their approach was to concentrate on issues of education, spirituality, and devotion. The second aimed at institutional reform through the use of canon law, the abolition of corrupt practices, the establishment of new institutions, or the restructuring of old ones. Some sought to reform the papacy while others concentrated on the episcopacy. This group was most marked by the humanist theologians of the period, who based their proposals and rhetoric on the practices of the church fathers. Finally, there were apocalyptic reformers, who sought to persuade individuals in positions of power to end ecclesial abuses by employing fiery prophecies of doom and destruction. Contarini came to know these different approaches to reform and to embrace aspects of all three.

What held these groups together was that they were marked by a twofold concern for reinvigorating the mission of pastoral care and for the reform of the individual.[12] Another feature common to the Catholic reformers of this period was their use of a new apologetic for reform. Whereas medieval reformers tended to employ the apologetics of humility, which held that the church has been flawed from the beginning because it is adapted to our imperfect condition, the Renaissance reformers employed the apologetics of decline and rebirth, which posited a virtually perfect early church that fell into decline over time. Such decline was seen as inevitable and required periodic moments of rebirth and renewal.[13] This rhetoric allowed the reformers to extol the church in its ancient purity as they excoriated the corruptions they faced, but it also tended to reinforce the idea that the church can achieve a nearly perfect state within the confines of history.

One important source for this new apologetic was the recovery of classical Greek and Latin sources on the nature of history. The ancient idea of history as a decline from a glorious antiquity came to seize the European imagination during the Renaissance. While this vision of a virtually perfect early church can also be seen in the theology of Jean Gerson, it came to full bloom during the second half of the fifteenth century. The majority of Catholic reformers in this period assumed that the church had fallen from its pure or nearly pure state in the age of the apostles, or of the martyrs, or of the early fathers.[14] Such an idea allowed reformers to identify corruption or decline with specific events or periods. It also provided a blueprint for their vision of a renewed church. Depending on the reformer's agenda he or she could identify corruption with Constantine's decision to support the church, the rise of the papal monarchy, the establishment of the mendicant orders, the Babylonian Captivity, the Great Schism, or the acts of some specific council such as the Fourth Lateran or Constance.

Contarini was first exposed to classical ideas about history and humanist reform rhetoric when he studied under the humanist scholar Giorgio Valla. Valla was famous as an orator, for his translation of Aristotle's *Poetics* from Greek into Latin, and for his encyclopedia. After what must have been a thorough education in the Greek and Roman classics, Contarini entered the University of Padua where he continued his study of Aristotle and Greek. During this period he became increasingly interested in the theology of Thomas Aquinas and Duns Scotus.

While in Padua, Contarini was deeply impressed by the local bishop, Pietro Barozzi (d. 1507), and became associated with a group of devout scholars from aristocratic families. These relationships served as "living books" that taught Contarini more than he received through formal instruction.[15] Bishop Barozzi, who had reformed the administration of his diocese by drawing upon patristic sources, became the model for Contarini's reform treatise on the office of the bishop. Two of Contarini's closest friends, Tommaso Giustiniani and Vincenzo Quirini, began their careers as humanists but became significant reformers as Camaldolese monks.

As Giustiniani and Quirini moved into the more eremetical and monastic reform movement, they became more interested in the ideas of Peter Damian and of apocalyptic reformers. Giustiniani and Quirini published the *Libellus ad Leonem X* in 1513, which exhorted the newly elected Pope Leo X to implement the reforms of the Fifth Lateran Council (1512–13). The *Libellus* stressed the pope's authority to restructure the Catholic Church's administration and urged him to act on that authority. Their proposals were extensive and included the following: Cardinals would become assistants supported by salaries instead of benefices, bishops would be subject to close supervision and accountability, general councils would be held every five years, canon law would be revised and simplified, and the Bible would be translated into the vernacular.[16]

Evidently Pope Leo X was impressed enough by the *Libellus* to select Giustiniani in 1516 to examine whether or not Savonarola had been legitimately condemned as a heretic. Savonarola was a Dominican preacher who had prophesied that the church would be scourged and chastised by God if it failed to reform ecclesiastical corruption and moral decadence. When Pope Alexander VI attempted to silence Savonarola in 1495, the Dominican refused to stop his preaching and his prophetic calls for reform. Three years later, Savonarola was seized, tried, and burned to death. The primary questions being considered were whether or not his claims to the gift of prophecy or his disobedience to the pope were legitimate grounds for the charge of heresy. Giustiniani turned to his old friend Contarini for advice on the matter.

After examining Savonarola's writings and the case against him, Contarini wrote a short report on September 18, 1516. This report is the earliest literary evidence of Contarini's ideas about reform. Citing Thomas Aquinas as his source, Contarini argued that one must distinguish between divine, natural, and positive law when considering Savonarola's disobedience to Pope Alexander VI. Since divine law or charity is the highest law, Contarini asserted that positive law must be subordinated to charity. In the case of Savonarola, Contarini claimed that the pope had used his power in terms of positive law against the demands of charity and in pursuit of political purposes. When popes act against the principle of charity, Contarini concluded that they do not have to be obeyed. Thus he argued that Savonarola's disobedience was insufficient grounds for calling the Dominican a heretic. Although Contarini refused to comment on the specific nature of Savonarola's visions, he did not see them as grounds for heresy either. Indeed, he wrote that Savonarola's prophecies that the church needed renewal were clearly true because they accorded with both natural and divine reason.[17]

Whereas the treatise on Savonarola highlighted the limits of papal and institutional authority, Contarini's treatise on reforming the office of the bishop widened the significance and scope of episcopal activity. He divided the work into two parts. The first part outlined the virtues the bishop should possess, and the second presented a specific daily routine that included some general rules of conduct for bishops. While some scholars have criticized the work as being too general and lacking any detailed program for reforming the episcopacy, others have described De officio episcopi as representing the highest reform ideals of humanists prior to the controversy with Luther.[18] These two perspectives can be easily reconciled. Contarini wrote this work as a layman who was trained in Christian humanism but who had little experience with the concrete operations and administration of ecclesiastical affairs. His proposals became much more specific as he learned more about ecclesial administration, but De officio episcopi reveals the sentiments of the growing number of scholarly laymen who were calling for the reform of the church.[19]

The occasion for Contarini's composition of De officio episcopi was the elevation of Pietro Lippomano to the bishopric of Bergamo in 1516. Because Lippomano was a teenager, his installation as bishop was a scandalous dispensation from the statute of canon law that required bishops to be at least thirty years old. Rather than bring attention to the dispensation Lippomano had already received, Contarini framed his work as providing advice for a man who had been made bishop without much preparation for the office. He began by citing a common scientific principle that every educated sixteenth-century aristocrat could be expected to know, namely, that every efficient cause brings forth an effect that resembles itself.[20] This was a principle of physics, but it was also a principle that served as a foundation for the idea of aristocracy. When Contarini explained that this law of nature demonstrated how the good ruler causes his or her people to be good, he knew that the young bishop would recognize this idea. Contarini extended the principle to help the aristocrat to understand why the bishop must have virtues in order to instill virtues in others.

Perhaps fearing that Bishop Lippomano was tempted to abandon his see, Contarini raised the issue of episcopal absenteeism. He denounced the practice writing:

> At this point I cannot fail to deplore with all my heart the calamity of our age, when you will find very few guardians of the Christian people who spend their time in the cities under their care. In truth they think they have done enough with respect to their duty if they have handed over the administration of the city to a deputy, though they themselves retain the revenues. And indeed they join the retinue of some great personage in the Roman Curia and busy themselves with the affairs of kingdoms and wars. But concerning the people over whom they are placed, they do not even receive news as to whether or not they are making progress in the Christian religion or whether they are forsaking it and they completely neglect and disregard the poor of their flock. Is this the conduct of a bishop? Is this the imitation of the disciples of Christ? Is this the observance of the Gospel precepts?[21]

Because Contarini assumed that the bishop was supposed to be a visible model for the community to imitate, absenteeism represented to him a total breakdown of the church's sacramental ministry for the care of souls.

Presuming that Bishop Lippomano would not contribute to this calamity, Contarini explained the various virtues the bishop should possess and should exhibit by his life. First and foremost, a bishop should understand all his duties in terms of the chief virtue of both his office and of all Christian life, the virtue of love or charity. Love should guide the way the bishop performs his duties in the liturgical life of the church, in the care of his flock, in assisting the poor, and in the administration of diocesan finances. To maintain this virtue's centrality in their lives, Contarini advised that a bishop should pray the Divine Office throughout the day, should celebrate Mass daily, and should spend the better part of his morning and afternoon hours receiving, hearing, and helping all those who needed him.

Lest the bishop become too grim, Contarini also advised him to spend some leisure time after lunch, a meal that should not be meager but should be sparing. He deemed it unseemly for bishops to squander the revenues that the laity had donated to alleviate the needs of the poor and to advance divine worship on great dinners and gluttonous feasting. Still, he allowed the bishop to enjoy some music, to take some time for relaxation, and to engage in some jesting and humor to refresh his spirits. Contarini advised Bishop Lippomano that he needed to balance affability with dignity if he wished to earn love and respect rather than contempt and hostility. While the bishop may have formal and institutional authority, Contarini believed it meant little or nothing on a pastoral level if his people did not respect his authority. In short, he was trying to help the young bishop to see that he would have to work to earn people's respect.

While Contarini believed following this type of schedule would help a bishop earn respect, in part, by making him respectable, he suggested that bishops need to be flexible. Because it is impossible for any sphere of human activity to be bound by a fixed rule, he advised bishops to employ a rule that is flexible and can be bent according to the circumstances of the time and the persons involved. Since pastoral care begins with accepting that people are different and that circumstances vary, Contarini tried to show the young bishop that he could not afford to be rigid.

Beyond schedules, rules, and routines there were issues that Contarini believed required firmness and consistency on the part of the bishop. For example, he argued that a bishop should not allow anyone into his household who either has or could justly be suspected of having bad morals. He wrote, "Thus the bishop, and all the more because his life has been set before others as an example, ought to be free not only from the stain but also from every, even the slightest, suspicion of stain." He was also firm in his insistence that the practice of admitting men to holy orders without any discrimination of their wicked lives and ignorance must end. Only men with good morals and outstanding learning should be ordained. While it may seem incredible that Contarini would need to raise this issue, he also warned against the practice of admitting criminals seeking immunity from civil prosecution to the priesthood.

De officio episcopi closed with a call to educate the people of the diocese, which was typical of the humanist reformers. Contarini asserted that it was the bishop's duty to teach people to avoid superstition, which he saw as an excess of religion, and to avoid impiety and unbelief, which he saw as a lack of religion. Finally, he urged the bishop to establish schools for the education of the young in order to prevent them from falling into ignorance and vice. In the final analysis, Contarini's model bishop was a perfectly balanced Renaissance man guided by the patristic ideals associated with pastoral care.

While there is much to be admired in this Renaissance vision of a bishop as dignified and affable, one must concede that there were serious deficiencies in the humanist efforts at reform that are reflected in *De officio episcopi* as well. The most glaring weakness was, as we have seen, that it did not address the myriad problems related to the benefice system and its attendant ecclesiastical taxes and fees. Prior to 1517, most of the humanist reformers did not seem to recognize that many of the problems faced by the church were systemic in nature. Instead, they sought to reform individuals through education and formation in virtue.

The early humanists were excellent diagnosticians for the ailments of the church such as episcopal absenteeism and clerical ignorance, but they lacked the expertise to do the surgical bypass around the arteries blocked by systemic abuse. If their prescriptions were followed by bishops, their advice would ease the pain and could even temporarily restore some semblance of health on a local level; but because the ecclesiastical revenue system associated with benefices, indulgences, and dispensations tended to promote men motivated by financial or political gain, reform efforts on a diocesan level frequently died when the reforming bishop died. Increasingly, reform looked like a Sisyphean task because all progress seemed to be fleeting, which is one of the reasons Luther lost patience with the reform efforts taking place within the Catholic Church.

After Luther and the other early Protestant reformers began to underscore both systemic institutional abuses and the corrupt theologies supporting them, most of the Catholic reformers became more interested in correcting systems and institutions. From 1517 until the Council of Trent, Contarini and the other Catholic humanists began to consider how to reframe their agenda to account for both systemic problems and theological confusion. As Contarini became more knowledgeable about the state of the Catholic Church in different countries, how ecclesiastical and secular politics intersected, and the theological questions posed by the Protestants, he began to develop much more concrete reform proposals that accounted for how the levers of power operated in the church.

Ambassador and Statesman

Gasparo Contarini came to appreciate and understand the mechanics of secular and ecclesiastical government during his career as an ambassador and as a senator of the Republic of Venice. After writing *De officio episcopi*, he spent several years holding minor posts in the Venetian government before being elected the ambassador to Emperor Charles V from 1520 to 1525 and as ambassador to Pope Clement VII from 1528 to 1530. When he returned to Venice in 1530, he was elected a senator and over the next several years came to hold several of the highest posts in the government. Each of these periods played a role in bringing Contarini to Rome as a cardinal.

As ambassador to the emperor, Contarini honed his diplomatic skills and built contacts with reformers, Protestant and Catholic. He grew skilled in the art of listening to others and in observing how their words corresponded to their behavior. These skills granted him an acute ability to understand the intentions and motivations of other people.[22] As a result, Contarini had the rare gift of being able to see and to appreciate disputed issues from other points of view. A major influence that helped him to develop this openness to others was his study of theology.

By reading Thomas Aquinas and Dionysius the Areopagite, Contarini learned that Truth, or God, absolutely transcends our minds. Since he was suspicious of seeing theological propositions as adequate for expressing the mysteries of faith or as legitimate grounds for Christian divisions, he became suspicious of the tendency try to make any one point of view absolute.[23] He was not, however, a relativist. Contarini simply exhibited a virtue that receives little attention today, intellectual humility or the ability to recognize the limited nature of one's own ideas and beliefs.

When some Venetian ships were seized by the Spanish Inquisition on the charge of selling Lutheran books, Contarini came to see how the lack of intellectual humility could be quite insidious and dangerous within the church. Since Spain was part of the emperor's dominion, Contarini went to Spain to personally argue for the release of the Venetian citizens and ships from the Inquisition. He charged the council of the Inquisition with having departed from the Catholic tradition by trying to suppress books. He reminded the council that the whole church had tolerated the works of infidels like Averroes and others whose teachings contradicted the faith. Further, he claimed that the Inquisition should not prevent Catholics from learning about the position of the church's critics. After resolving the matter, he wrote to his government that the inquisition in Spain was "a most terrible thing." He described the Spanish Inquisition in his dispatch this way: "As far as the New Christians are concerned, what appears to us as insignificant seems serious to the Inquisition."[24]

After five years as ambassador to Charles V, Contarini resigned his post and returned to Venice in 1525. In 1527 Emperor Charles V's troops invaded Rome because Pope Clement VII had allied himself with England, France, Florence, Milan, and Venice in the League of Cognac, which had attacked the empire. Pope Clement was worried that Charles had too much power in Italy and spent much of his pontificate warring with the emperor, which was one of the reasons the emperor was unable to move against Luther. The emperor's troops, who had not been paid, decided to pillage the city. Imperial forces slaughtered civilians, raped nuns, looted churches, and took the pope prisoner. Charles allowed Clement to be restored to power on the condition that the pope would call a council to settle the religious revolt in Germany. Clement agreed to call a council, but as soon as he was free he refused.

Many of the refugees from the sack of Rome came to Venice, including members of the Roman Oratory of Divine Love and fourteen members of the Theatines. The Roman Oratory was based on the Genoese Oratory, founded by a prominent layman, Ettore Vernazza, in 1497. Vernazza was inspired to form this group by St. Catherine of Genoa, a mystic who ran hospices to care for the sick and the dying. The Oratories of Divine Love were predominantly lay associations of men who wanted to deepen their spiritual lives through prayer and through service to the poor and the sick. Their charter stated: "Our fraternity is not instituted for any other purpose than to root and to implant in our hearts divine love, that is to say, charity."[25]

While they were in Venice, Contarini became involved with members of the Roman Oratory and built a close relationship with the superior of the Theatines, Gian Pietro Carafa. Inspired by the ideals of the Oratories of Divine Love, several priests, including Carafa, founded the Theatines, who were dedicated to pastoral care and charitable work.[26] Later, Contarini would recommend Carafa's appointment as a cardinal. Thirteen years after Contarini died, Carafa was elected Pope Paul IV (1555–59). The exiles also introduced Contarini to a nearby bishop, Giberti of Verona, who had been associated with the Roman Oratory and who was a leading bishop in the Catholic reform movement.

Bishop Giberti addressed one of the most pressing issues of the sixteenth century, episcopal accountability for the pastoral care of their people. He worked to reform his diocese by selecting only worthy candidates for the priesthood, by insisting priests preach the gospel and instruct the young, by establishing a society for the relief of the poor, and by founding an academy for scholars and poets. Contarini learned much about the administrative and economic issues facing bishops from Giberti. Giberti's diocesan regulations would eventually be published and served as a pattern for many of the disciplinary reforms of Trent.[27]

After spending two years in minor offices and conversing with the displaced reformers, Contarini was elected to be the Venetian ambassador to Pope Clement VII (1523–34) in 1527. Having begun to appreciate some of the systemic and institutional problems associated with the episcopacy, he now had the opportunity to learn about the problems and abuses associated with the papacy. He found Pope Clement to be weak, fearful, and indecisive; but he managed nonetheless to build a close enough relationship to exhort the pontiff to pick up the cause of reform. In a private audience with Clement, Contarini used the opportunity to give this short lecture about priorities:

> Your Holiness should not think that the welfare of Christ's church is comprised in this little temporal state she has acquired. Even before this state existed there was a church, and a most excellent one. The church is the community of all Christians. This state is like the state of an Italian

prince, joined to the church. But Your Holiness should above all be concerned with the welfare of the true church, which consists in peace and tranquility among all Christians, and for the present relegate to second place the interests of this temporal state.

The pope responded with a rather petulant question: "Don't you see that the world has reached a point where it is the most cunning schemer who reaps the most praise, is esteemed and extolled as an admirable man, whereas he who acts in an opposite fashion is thought of as good but worthless, and is only left with the name of a 'good man'?" Contarini simply reminded the pope that scripture teaches that nothing is more powerful than truth, virtue, goodness, and right intention.[28]

While Contarini failed to change Clement's mind as to how he should exercise his papacy, he made an impression on the members of the papal court. In particular, Contarini impressed Cardinal Alessandro Farnese, who as Pope Paul III would make him a cardinal. When Contarini returned to Venice in 1530 and took his senatorial seat, he completed a treatise calling for a more spiritualized papacy without a papal state, a military, and a host of dubious financial transactions. Even as he called for an end to the papal state, he affirmed the pope's absolute authority and plenitude of power in judging, binding, and loosing. Christ instituted the papacy, according to Contarini, so the church would have a supreme shepherd with the ability to make final decisions on matters of faith and dogma.[29]

Perhaps it was Contarini's firm adherence to papal authority that led Clement VII and Paul III to overlook his conciliatory stance toward the Protestants. While he was in Venice, Contarini wrote a response to sixteen of Luther's articles presented in the Augsburg Confession. After discussing the various points, Contarini explained how Catholics should respond to Luther and his followers in order to restore unity:

No councils, battles of words, syllogisms, or biblical citations are needed to quiet the unrest of the Lutherans, but good will, love of God and one's neighbor, humility of soul in order to do away with avarice, luxury, large households, and courts; and to limit oneself to that which the Gospel's prescribe. This is what is needed to overcome the tumults of the Lutherans. Let us not move against them with masses of books, Ciceronian orations, subtle arguments but with an exemplary life, humble mind, without luxury, only desiring Christ and the good of our neighbor.[30]

If Catholics followed this course of action, Contarini promised that not only the Lutherans but the whole world would be converted. He firmly believed that presenting theological arguments would be useless in reconciling Catholics and Protestants.

Both the treatise on reforming the papacy and the response to Luther's Augsburg Confession won Contarini admirers across the political and theological spectrum. By 1535 he had earned a reputation as one of the leading reformers within the Catholic Church, which is why Pope Paul III decided to bring Contarini to Rome. Paul III wanted to send a signal to the different types of Catholic reformers that he was aware of the crisis he was facing and of the need for reform. Contarini spent a lonely year as a reformer in Rome until Paul III appointed three members of his reform circle to the curia: Jacopo Sadoleto, Gian Pietro Carafa, and Reginald Pole. Sadoleto, a bishop, and Pole, a layman, were both humanists who sought reconciliation with the Protestants. Carafa, on the other hand, believed the best way to respond to the Protestants was through the use of the Inquisition.

The movement of Contarini and his friends into the highest circles of power in Rome marks the beginning of the twofold thrust of what scholars call the Counter-Reformation. The first aspect of the Counter-Reformation was to end the abuses and to clarify the theological issues that began the Protestant Reformation; the second was to bring Protestants back to the Catholic Church by persuasion, if possible, and by coercion if more gentle means failed. In the early days of the Counter-Reformation the reformers were united in their desire to clean house in the Catholic Church, but as the reformers turned their attention to either dialoguing with or confronting the Protestants their unity was gradually eroded by mutual suspicion.

One of the best examples of the unity and collaboration between disparate Catholic reformers was the drafting of the *Consilium de emendanda ecclesia* in late 1536 and early 1537. The *Consilium* was a report drawn up by a reform commission established by Pope Paul III. Contarini was the president of the commission and he was responsible for choosing the members, who included the following: Cardinal

Carafa, Cardinal Sadoleto, Cardinal Pole, Archbishop Federigo Fregoso of Salerno, Archbishop Jerome Aleander of Brindisi, Bishop Giberti of Verona, Abbot Gregorio Cortese of Venice, and Friar Tommaso Badia. The report they produced is credited with providing the Catholic Church with an authoritative analysis of ecclesial problems and a program for reform; however, it would not be until 1547 that the Council of Trent would begin to put the report's recommendations in place.[31]

The *Consilium*

Contarini brought together the most outspoken and talented advocates for reform to write this pivotal report. The document was produced by committee though most scholars would see Contarini and Carafa as its principal editors. Even though it was a committee report, it was the product of men skilled in Renaissance rhetoric and schooled in the history of reform. Contarini and his committee had the delicate task of highlighting the systemic corruptions in ecclesial government without alienating their patron and pope.

However, the *Consilium* did not spare the papacy from its critiques. Instead, the report distinguished between Pope Paul III, whom God chose to rebuild and to restore the collapsed church of Christ to its pristine beauty, and some of his predecessors, who "having itching ears heaped up to themselves teachers according to their own lusts (2 Timothy 4:3)." In other words, they laid much of the blame for systemic corruption on the various Renaissance popes and the canon lawyers who served them.

The report described the growing trend in canon law to see the pope as completely unaccountable, which was fostered by canon lawyers serving papal interests. These deceitful lawyers taught the popes that the only rule governing them was their own wills. As the lord of all benefices, these lawyers also claimed, the pope could sell appointments to ecclesiastical offices without committing the sin of simony. The *Consilium* lamented:

> From this source as from a Trojan horse so many abuses and such grave diseases have rushed in upon the Church of God that we now see her afflicted almost to the despair of salvation and the news of these things spread even to the

infidels (let your Holiness believe those who know), who for this reason especially deride the Christian religion, so that through us—through us, we say—the name of Christ is blasphemed among the heathens.[32]

But Contarini and the commission praised Pope Paul III for having rightly seen that the cure for the Catholic Church must start where the disease began, that is, in the office of the papacy.

Whereas Paul III's predecessors sought out teachers according to their lusts, the commission praised him for seeking people to give him the truth concerning all of the abuses in the Catholic Church. The document obliquely reminded the pope that all Christian authority comes from service this way:

> ...and having followed the teaching of the Apostle Paul you wish to be a steward, not a master, and to be found trustworthy by the Lord, having indeed imitated that servant in the Gospel whom the master set over his household to give them a ration of grain in due time (Luke 12:42); and on that account you have resolved to turn from what is unlawful; nor do you wish to do what you should not.

Contarini and the other reformers softened their theological position that the pope was accountable to canon law and to Christ by presenting the idea as if it were the pope's and praising him for it.

The starting point for reform, according to the commission, would be to observe the laws and to refrain from offering dispensations from the law except for an urgent and pressing reason. Just as failure to observe and enforce the laws is the most dangerous threat to the stability of any secular government, the same holds true for ecclesiastical government. Underlying their argument was the recognition that if the church is a visible and organic society on earth, then it is also governed by the laws and constants of what we would call political science. Additionally, the commission stated that the church and the papacy are also under the divine law. The precept most germane to the abuses surrounding dispensations from the law and the general breakdown of ecclesiastical government, according to Contarini and his commission, was Christ's command: "Freely you have received, freely give" (Matthew 10:8). This was a gentle way to say that the

Catholic Church was riddled with simony and veniality from the papacy down to the rest of the members.

The most significant problem associated with simony had to do with the quality of the men ordained to the priesthood. The *Consilium's* rhetoric is quite direct and incisive:

> The first abuse in this respect is the ordination of clerics and especially priests in which no care is taken, no diligence employed, so that indiscriminately the most unskilled, men of the vilest stock and evil morals, adolescents, are admitted to Holy Orders and to the priesthood, to the [indelible] mark, we stress, which above all denotes Christ. From this have come innumerable scandals and a contempt for the ecclesiastical order, and reverence for divine worship not only has been diminished but has almost by now been destroyed.

The commission indicated that bishops should set up tribunals to investigate and to examine potential candidates to the priesthood. Further, bishops should observe the ecclesiastical laws and establish free schools for clerics in minor orders. These ideas would coalesce into the establishment of the seminary system at the Council of Trent, which was arguably one of the most effective and significant reforms of the council.

This brought the commission to the problems associated with the benefice system as a whole. First, bishoprics were being given to men who were completely unsuited for the position. In some cases they were unsuited because they lacked education or moral virtue and in others they were unlikely to reside in their diocese because they were foreigners. "A benefice in Spain or in Britain," they concluded, "then must not be conferred on an Italian, or vice versa." Ultimately Contarini and his associates believed that bishops should be local men who wish to remain with their people.

The second major abuse of this system was that many people who held benefices to either a parish or a diocese reserved some or all of the revenues it generated for themselves for some period of time. While the popes were the worst offenders, the *Consilium* tactfully left that unpleasant reality unstated. The committee declared that the only justification for reserving any income generated by a parish or diocese should be either for poor relief or for pious purposes such as paying for expenses associated with divine worship. This abuse was closely related to the third corruption stemming from a failure to follow the law "to freely give," namely the various simoniacal arrangements used to sell church offices with no consideration other than profit.

After briefly noting problems with clergymen who were naming heirs to their benefices, which converted the common property of the church to private property and generated tremendous ill will against the clergy, the *Consilium* exposed several problems with the practice of holding multiple and incompatible benefices or positions. Obviously it was impossible for someone to effectively exercise the offices of an archbishop in Bologna, a bishop in Vivier, and an abbot of a monastery in Grottaferrata all at the same time. The commission laid the blame for this state of affairs squarely on the papal practice of granting dispensations from the laws banning men from multiple and incompatible positions. They asked Paul III, "What about the lifelong unions of benefices in one man, so that such a plurality of benefices is no obstacle to holding benefices that are 'incompatible'? Is that not a pure betrayal of the law?"

The report identified the cardinals as the worst offenders, which was certainly the case. Cardinals were being granted multiple bishoprics, which Contarini and the others believed to be an abuse of great importance for two reasons. First, they declared that the offices of cardinal and bishop are incompatible: "For the cardinals are to assist your Holiness in governing the universal church; the bishop's duty, however, is to tend his own flock, which he cannot do well and as he should unless he lives with his sheep as a shepherd with his flock." Even if a bishop lived with his people, the critique would still hold because the cardinal bishop must divide his attention between his diocese and Rome, as an adulterer would divide his attention between his mistress and his bride.

The second problem with the cardinals' multiple benefices was the example they were setting. The *Consilium* asserted that the behavior of the cardinals would undermine the credibility of any papal initiatives toward reforming the other members of the church. The report offered this withering assessment of curial abuse:

> Nor do we think that because they are cardinals they have
> a greater license to transgress the law; on the contrary, they

have far less. For the life of these men ought to be a law for others; nor should they imitate the Pharisees who speak and do not act, but Christ our Savior who began to act and afterward to teach. This practice [of cardinals holding bishoprics] is more harmful in the deliberations of the church, for this license nurtures greed. Besides the cardinals solicit bishoprics from kings and princes, on whom they are afterward dependent and about whom they cannot freely pass judgment.

Picking up on one of the reform recommendations Contarini's friends Giustiniani and Quirini published in the *Libellus ad Leonem X*, the commission suggested that the cardinals should receive equal salaries and should not hold other positions in the church. "We believe that this can easily be done," they concluded, "if we wish to abandon the servitude to Mammon and to serve only Christ."

After returning to the problems associated with absenteeism on the part of cardinals, bishops, and priests, the *Consilium* attacked the corruptions associated with the Roman penitentiary and the datary. One corruption involved reserved sins. Certain sinful acts could only be forgiven by bishops and others could only be pardoned by the papacy. The Roman penitentiary absolved people from reserved sins for a fee and involved itself in indulgence sales, and the datary was the institution that provided exemptions and dispensations from church law. According to the commission, the result was that wicked clergymen were being protected from any punishment by Rome. They claimed this was so great a scandal to the people that words could not express how much it angered them. Having recalled the principle that no human government could survive such systemic erosion of its laws, the commission offered specific recommendations, including: the abolishment of indulgence preachers, of concubinage taxes, of dispensations with marriages for a fee, and of monetary payments for exemptions. In particular, the commission felt that people should not be allowed to buy absolution from the sin of simony.

Finally, the *Consilium* pointed to the glaring problems with the Roman diocese. Everyone who visited Rome, according to the commission, was scandalized by the vile and ignorant priests celebrating Mass in St. Peter's Basilica. "Also in this city harlots walk about like matrons or ride on mules," they continued, "attended in broad daylight by noble members of the cardinals' households and by clerics." The commission urged the pope to properly attend to the poor, orphans, and widows in Rome and to conciliate the feuds and hatreds among the Roman people. Having outlined the various abuses in the church, Contarini and his commission ended on a note that was simultaneously apocalyptic and hopeful:

> Indeed, we hope that you [Paul III] have been chosen to restore in our hearts and in our works the name of Christ now forgotten by the nations and by us clerics, to heal the ills, to lead back the sheep of Christ into one fold, to turn away from us the wrath of God and that vengeance which we deserve, already prepared and looming over our heads.

Given the bluntness of the *Consilium* and its conciliatory position toward the Protestants, it is hardly surprising that the document was not well received. One cardinal remarked that the suggested reforms would be seen as a concession to the Lutherans that their criticisms of corruption were justified. Carafa defended the report, saying that the church could not omit doing good out of fear that evil would result from it.[33] Soon thereafter, one of the cardinals leaked the confidential study to some printers who quickly distributed it all over Europe. Luther printed a version with a running commentary lampooning its contents and denounced the members of the committee as scoundrels and liars.[34] With all of the curial opposition and public furor, the *Consilium*'s recommendations were put on hold. This was the first in a series of apparent setbacks for Contarini.

Contarini's Legacy

After the controversy over the *Consilum* died down, Contarini continued to work for reform. From 1536 until 1540 he participated in several commissions that aimed at reforming the datary, the office responsible for the sale of dispensations, benefices, and so on. His recommendations would have cut the revenues generated by the datary almost in half. They were rejected. Contarini's absolute opposition to simony led the pope to add members to the commission so it would be less influenced by the cardinal from Venice. During this time he was successful, however, at protecting a young Spanish reformer,

Ignatius of Loyola, from the Inquisition. Contarini helped to win papal approval for the Jesuits, which certainly had a tremendous impact on the life of the Catholic Church. Unfortunately, his most significant curial assignment, to serve as the papal legate to the Regensburg Colloquy, ended in his most disappointing failure.

The Regensburg Colloquy was the last serious attempt to reconcile the Protestants and Catholics prior to the twentieth century. The emperor had hoped to use the meeting to restore Christian unity in his empire as he faced threats from both the Turks and the French. Pope Paul III was also hopeful that reunion could be accomplished, which is why he chose Contarini as his legate. Paul III knew that the polemical and partisan positions of some of the Catholic delegates needed to be reigned in if the talks were to succeed.[35] When Contarini arrived in Regensburg in March 1541, the Protestants greeted him with enthusiasm. For the next several weeks things proceeded well. The theologians reached agreement on the following points: the human condition before the fall, free will, original sin, and justification. Unfortunately, they could not agree on the teaching authority of the church, the necessity of confession, and on the doctrine of the Eucharist.[36]

Contarini refused to compromise on these points. When someone suggested that the members could agree to a statement that affirmed Christ's real presence without specifying transubstantiation, he refused to consider the possibility. Contarini firmly held transubstantiation to be a defined doctrine that could not be abrogated or obscured even in the pursuit of unity. Such unity would be based, he felt, on a counterfeit agreement.[37] Even if the conference had been able to move forward, both the pope and Luther had rejected the agreement on justification as obscure. In the end, the Regensburg Colloquy served to clarify the depth and significance of the disagreements between the Catholics and Protestants.

With Contarini's failure to win back the Protestants through ecumenical efforts at dialogue, the Catholic Church took up the more coercive approach of Carafa. Carafa had come to suspect Contarini as a crypto-Lutheran and might have moved against his former friend except for the fact that Contarini died shortly after Regensburg. When he died, it looked as if his whole career had been a failure. The church had not implemented the ecclesial reforms he called for in the *Consilium* and Christian unity seemed to be hopelessly shattered;

however, just four years after Contarini's death, the Council of Trent opened in 1545. Trent would implement many of Contarini's reform proposals over the course of eighteen years.

Ecumenism, on the other hand, took much longer to gain acceptance in the Catholic Church. The Second Vatican Council adopted ecumenism as part of its mission in the *Decree on Ecumenism (Unitatis redintegratio)*. Like the *Consilium*, the Second Vatican admitted that there was blame and responsibility on both Catholics and Protestants for the divisions between them. It also recognized ecumenism as a form of renewal of the church that "essentially consists in an increase of fidelity to her own calling."[38] This commitment to unity has been reaffirmed by the popes who followed the Second Vatican and led to the *Joint Declaration on Justification by Faith*, which was signed on October 31, 1999. It was 482 years after Luther posted his ninety-five theses on the cathedral door that Catholics and Lutherans stated: "Together we confess: By grace alone, in faith in Christ's saving work and not because of any merit on our part we are accepted by God and receive the Holy Spirit, who renews our hearts while equipping us and calling us to good works."[39] As Lutheran and Catholic theologians looked into the issue of justification, Contarini's efforts at Regensburg helped to provide them with a model for behavior and with clues as to how to move forward.

Like so many Catholic reformers, Contarini did not live to see the reforms he fought for implemented. He spent his last year under a cloud of suspicion as he watched the Catholic Church take an increasingly hostile position toward the Protestants. Yet he never defected. Perhaps he believed that a prophet is never recognized in his own country. It is possible that his faithfulness to the Catholic Church was simply the result of his firm belief in God's providence. Maybe Contarini expected that the winds would turn in his favor. While we will never know what sustained him, Gasparo Contarini's career shows us that men and women who are active in the world have insights and gifts to bring to the church, can be as loyal or more loyal than the clergy, and should be included in responding to ecclesial abuses.

8

The Most Dangerous Man in England: The Convert Cardinal Newman

John Henry Cardinal Newman has become something of a hero to many English-speaking Catholics despite the fact that he spent most of his career in the Catholic Church under a cloud of suspicion. Newman, who had been an Anglican priest, attempted to reform the Church of England before his conversion to the Catholic Church. Unlike many of his fellow converts such as Henry Edward Manning, who became archbishop of Westminster in 1865, Newman understood that the Catholic Church needed to balance its claims to institutional authority with an appreciation for the individual believer's freedom of conscience. For this reason Manning and others believed he lacked an appropriate sense of loyalty to the Roman See. At the same time Catholics who wanted the church to adopt a more open stance to modern developments such as democracy and who were distrustful of the church's claim to infallibility perceived him to be less than honest. Lord Acton, a leading liberal spokesman for the nineteenth-century Catholic Church in England, described Newman as a sophist who manipulated rather than served the truth.[1]

For his part, Newman felt that Acton's efforts at reform were not properly suited to the position of the Catholic Church in England and that figures like Manning suffered from small-mindedness. If Acton's goal was to rehabilitate Catholic intellectual life by pushing for critical scholarship and by teaching the laity to be discerning about magisterial

claims, then Newman advised him to do so in a less pugnacious manner. Newman explained to Acton that publishing criticisms of the hierarchy's authority in the deeply anti-Catholic context of England in the
nineteenth century was "to court inevitable disaster." Instead, Newman
suggested Acton should use his journal "to praise as many people as it
can, to gain friends in neutral quarters, and become the organ of
others by the interest it has made them take in its proceeding." In that
way, he concluded, "it will be able to plant a good blow at a fitting time
with great effect."[2]

Whereas Newman had a great deal of sympathy with Catholics
like Acton, he was repelled by the autocratic and intellectually fearful
positions espoused by Manning and by many members of the episcopacy. He complained that the bishops "fancy that, as justice does not
exist between the Creator and His creatures, between man and the
brute creation, so there is none between them and their subjects...."[3]
Some of Newman's harshest words were reserved for the Ultramontane
Catholics who made extravagant claims concerning papal authority,
denounced the secular world, and refused to recognize Catholics who
disagreed with them as members of the church. He described the character of the Ultramontane movement this way:

> Instead of aiming at being a world-wide power, we are
> shrinking into ourselves, narrowing the lines of commun-
> ion, trembling at freedom of thought, and using the lan-
> guage of dismay and despair at the prospect before us,
> instead of, with the high spirit of the warrior, going out con-
> quering and to conquer.[4]

By balancing his critiques on the respective positions of these two parties on the question of authority, Newman was able to pass through the
factions without being destroyed. Of course, he was not loved by either
side.

How did Newman manage to have an impact on the church if
he was almost universally distrusted? Further, how could he push for
reform when the official stance of the Catholic hierarchy was that the
church was impervious to defect and thus could not be reformed or
renewed? Newman presented his reform agenda as an apologetic
against the attacks of Protestants. Without ever using words such as
reform or *renewal*, he crafted an apologetic for the church that forced

people to rethink the doctrinal and theological positions promoted by the popes and bishops since the early eighteenth century. His efforts to champion the causes of doctrinal development, intellectual freedom, freedom of conscience, and the active role of the laity in the church were all framed using history, which had been the primary weapon of those who wished to deny the infallibility and even the credibility of the Catholic Church.

Rather than identifying the perfection of the church with a particular set of propositions or institutions, Newman located this perfection in the church as a whole as it moves to an ever-deeper understanding of the revelation it has received. Perhaps his most valuable insight was that history, which reveals both the triumphs and the failures of the church, was not something that Catholics should fear. By framing his agenda in terms of the teachings of the fathers and doctors of the church, he was able to demonstrate his loyalty to the church, even as he criticized some of the doctrinal stances promulgated by the magisterial hierarchy. To understand the significance of his recovery of the place of history in Catholic theology, we must first understand how the church came to fear history, reform, and development.

Reform after the Protestant Reformation

Following the Council of Trent, the Catholic Church became increasingly suspicious of the very idea of reform. As the leaders of the church turned their attention to implementing the reform decrees of the council, they suffered from what can be called a collective corruption of memory. This corruption began with the apologetic efforts of church historians in the sixteenth and seventeenth centuries like Cesare Baronius (1538–1607), who attempted to eradicate all evidence of scandal from the church's history. Because Baronius's text became the standard source for the textbooks employed by the new seminary programs established at the Council of Trent, generations of clergymen were taught what can only be described as a dishonest form of history. By a sleight of hand, the imperfect church militant or pilgrim church became the spotless bride. The net effect of this apologetic was to see the church as the fully realized kingdom of God on earth.

During the pivotal years following Trent, the papacy became the primary force in implementing the reforms of the council. This was the result of the collapse or abdication of other agents for reform such as the secular rulers and the religious orders.[5] The unintended consequence was that people began to identify the Catholic Church with Rome. In the late sixteenth century the goal of the popes was to combat the Protestants by reconverting them. The church came to understand itself as standing counter to the Reformation, which led Catholics to interpret the term *reform* as indicating a Protestant idea.

Whereas reforming a religious order or the government of a missionary diocese still took place under the aegis of the papacy, it was seen as seditious to suggest that the church as a whole or that the papacy stood in need of reform and correction. As Galileo found out, to question the authority of the pope on any matter, including issues of astronomy, was grounds for condemnation. In 1632 Pope Gregory XIII described Galileo's defiance of the Inquisition's warning to stop teaching that the earth went around the sun as "an injury to religion as grievous as ever there was and of a perverseness as bad as could be encountered."[6]

The link between sedition and reform was cemented in the minds of the popes and in the opinions of most of the members of the Catholic hierarchy by events that took place during the French Revolution. At the outset of the French Revolution in July 1789, the church had taken a cautious but open stance to the idea of democracy. The clergy in France had initially supported the revolution, but as the nobles were required to forfeit their feudal dues and privileges the clergy began to worry about the security of their tithes. Tithing was still involuntary in France and the clergy were opposed to anything that might change this system. When they began to backslide on the validity of the revolution over the issue of tithing, the revolution turned on them and anticlerical factions among the revolutionaries gained the upper hand.[7]

The deputies of the revolution decided to reform the church under their own authority without consulting the clergy. Since the church owned 10 percent of the land in France and the higher clergy was dominated by men from aristocratic families, it was easy for the anticlerical revolutionaries to stir up distrust of the clergy. On July 12, 1790, the French government passed legislation on the Civil Constitution of the Clergy. The government declared that bishops and pastors were to be elected by the people, clergy were to be subject to the disciplinary control of the government, and all jurisdictional links to the pope were to be severed. Later that year the French

Assembly passed a law requiring all priests and bishops holding ecclesiastical offices to take an oath of loyalty to the constitution, but half the priests and all but seven bishops refused. Pope Pius VI responded in March 1791 by condemning the principles of the revolution and its constitution.

By 1792 the situation of the church in France had seriously deteriorated. In August a group of revolutionaries massacred over two hundred priests in Paris. From that point forward, many of the revolutionaries decided to try to destroy the Catholic Church. With the rise of Napoleon in 1795, the French exported their revolution and their anticlerical policies across Europe. All across the continent the church had been stripped of its property, monasteries and seminaries were closed, and clergymen had been imprisoned, exiled, or executed. By the time Napoleon was defeated, the church had been decimated and most of Italy lay in the hands of foreign powers.

When the Italian people began to desire political liberty and the unification of Italy in the 1830s, Pope Gregory XVI opposed them. In 1831 Italian rebels stirred up protests and revolts in cities within the Papal States. Sensing a threat to his monarchical power, Gregory called in Austrian forces to pacify the population. The pope had committed himself and the papacy to opposing the forces of democracy by the most repressive means. Stretching papal revenues to their limits, he armed his supporters, filled the papal prisons, and exiled democrats. His paranoia about democracy, which he saw as inextricably linked to modernity, led him to reject everything that could be seen as an innovation, including helpful inventions such as railroads and streetlights.

In August 1832, just thirteen years before Newman's conversion to Catholicism, Pope Gregory released the encyclical *Mirari vos*. In this encyclical, he exhorted Catholic bishops to act "against imposters and propagators of new ideas." He condemned the idea that freedom of conscience should be defended. According to this encyclical, freedom of conscience is a "poisonous spring of indifferentism." Since the church had been instituted by Jesus Christ and is guided by the Holy Spirit, he concluded that it is absurd and insulting "to suggest that the church stands in need of restoration and regeneration." For Gregory XVI the church could never stand in need of reform because it was, as he stated in his encyclical, impervious "to exhaustion, degradation or other defects of this kind."[8]

Newman must have been aware of the pope's position when he joined the Catholic Church in 1845. Yet even as he contemplated his conversion, he was busily writing a treatise that identified the perfection of the church with development. Though he handled the matter quite delicately, he also affirmed that corrupt doctrinal positions can find at least a temporary foothold in the church. These claims implied that the church was periodically in need of renewal and reform. In short, Newman's career as a Catholic had a rocky start.

Development of Doctrine

Long before his conversion, Newman had been thinking about the question of development. It had been a component of his reform agenda within the Church of England. Newman had hoped to reassert the Catholic identity of the Church of England and to purge it of some of its Protestant elements. As early as 1836, he had recognized that polemical charges against the Catholic Church of having departed from primitive Christianity could be seen as developments of gospel truth. Further, he admitted that such developments could also be identified in Anglicanism. He began to wonder why doctrines bearing on Trinity and Christology, which Anglicans shared with Catholics, were not also seen as departures from primitive Christianity. This led him to distrust the Anglican grounds for dismissing later doctrines, such as transubstantiation, on the basis that they were not primitive. Ultimately, these questions led Newman to convert to Catholicism.

As Newman was preparing to enter the Catholic Church, he was also writing *An Essay on the Development of Christian Doctrine.* Generally this work has been seen both as a justification for his decision to become Catholic and as an attempt to persuade other Anglicans to follow him. Both of these claims are certainly true, but this essay was also aimed at reforming doctrinal positions espoused by the Catholic hierarchy. In fact, his apologetic stance vis-à-vis the Protestants provided him with rhetorical cover for attempting to change Catholic positions on history and doctrine.

Newman's apologetic for Catholicism was grounded in historical arguments, but the magisterium of his day was deeply suspicious of historical inquiry. For this reason, Newman's essay opened with an apologetic for the value of history. He wrote:

> Christianity has been long enough in the world to justify us in dealing with it as a fact in the world's history. Its genius and character, its doctrines, precepts, and objects cannot be treated as matters of private opinion or deduction, unless we may reasonably so regard the Spartan institutions or the religion of Mahomet. It may indeed legitimately be made the subject-matter of theories.... It has from the first had an objective existence and has thrown itself upon the great concourse of men. Its home is in the world; and to know what it is, we must seek it in the world, and hear the world's witness of it.[9]

By placing history as a medium between two extremes, private opinion and deduction, he was attempting to show how history was an antidote to two movements that generated concern in the Catholic Church. The first, corresponding to private opinion, was liberalism. Liberalism in Newman's context was the tendency to reduce Christianity to an individual's personal and subjective experience or feelings. The second, corresponding to deduction, was typical of various forms of rationalism that sought to omit all elements of Christianity that were deemed to be irrational. An example of this second tendency would be the deistic movements of the Enlightenment era.

To highlight the importance of history for defending Christianity, Newman drew out the implications of rejecting the proposition that Christianity does not fall within the province of history. Beyond reducing Christianity to a matter of private opinion, he warned that the denial of history suggested that *Christianity* only refers to a "cluster or family of rival religions" that merely claim the same name even though they share neither the same doctrine nor the same foundation. Worse, some of those who denied the historicity of Christianity concluded that "all existing denominations of Christianity are wrong, none representing it as taught by Christ and His Apostles" and that they inherited, at best, some fragments of Christ's teachings. Others who denied the historical nature of the faith, according to Newman, concluded that Christianity is "nothing more than a mere assemblage of doctrines and practices" derived from Eastern religions, Platonic philosophies, and polytheistic sources. Finally, he drew the conclusion that rejecting the historicity of Christianity would lead to a type of relativism.[10]

Newman's list of consequences for rejecting the historical nature of the Christian faith could have just as well have been a list of why Pope Gregory XVI feared history. Thus he was trying to demonstrate why Catholic fears about history were inappropriate and self-defeating. Historical science could demonstrate, he assured his audience, that the Christianity of the intermediate centuries "is in its substance the very religion which Christ and His Apostles taught in the first [century], whatever may be the modifications for good or for evil which the lapse of years, or the vicissitudes of human affairs, have impressed upon it."[11] There remained the problem of Protestant polemics that relied on history to attack the validity of Catholicism, which Newman immediately addressed.

To win the church over to an appreciation of history, Newman had to demonstrate that it was not a threat to the infallibility of defined doctrine and that it could be used in an effective way against Protestants. To show that history was not a threat to the church's defined doctrines, he wrote:

> History is not a creed or a catechism, it gives lessons rather than rules; still no one can mistake its general teaching in this matter, whether he accept it or stumble at it. Bold outlines and broad masses of colour rise out of the records of the past. They may be dim, they may be incomplete; but they are definite. And this one thing at least is certain; whatever history teaches, whatever it omits, whatever it exaggerates or extenuates, whatever it says and unsays, at least the Christianity of history is not Protestantism. If ever there were a safe truth, it is this.[12]

By claiming that history was on the side of the Catholic Church, Newman was trying to reform the Catholic stance towards history. While many Catholic apologists today lionize Newman for his claim that to be immersed in history is to cease to be Protestant, they tend to ignore the fact that he was challenging the validity of the doctrinal stance adopted by the magisterium of his day.

Newman then turned to attack various Protestant claims concerning the corruptions they saw as arising out of the Catholic Church's history. For the purposes of this study, his polemic against his Protestant contemporaries are a distraction. In any event, Newman's anti-Protestant polemics were largely ineffective. Nonetheless, they do reveal his strategy. To borrow a phrase from a classic children's movie, he cleverly gave the bishops of his day "a spoonful of sugar to make the medicine go down."

Rather than identifying the perfection of Christian ideas with unchanging doctrines, Newman claimed the perfection lies in their ability to arrest and possess the mind. They take on life in the mind of those who receive them. Even though they have an objective truth, he stressed that they are also subjective insofar as they are apprehended by different people in different ways. He maintained that the more powerful the idea, the more multifaceted it is. Further, truly great ideas extend to many different aspects of life such as social, political, and moral concerns. Because such ideas influence and are influenced by the realities they touch, they draw criticisms from their enemies and defenses from their advocates. As social, political, and even scientific systems change, great ideas must be reexamined and even modified to account for these external factors. Some ideas are shattered by the development of some original fault with them, but Newman certainly did not perceive this to be a real possibility with Christian ideas.

Newman argued that Christianity's strength and perfection was revealed in its ability to adapt to new contexts without losing its identity. He described the nature of a perfect idea this way:

> In time it enters upon strange territory; points of controversy alter their bearing; parties rise and fall around it; dangers and hopes appear in new relations; and old principles reappear under new forms. It changes with them in order to remain the same. In a higher world it is otherwise, but here below to live is to change, and to be perfect is to have changed often.[13]

Thus the vitality and adaptability of the Christian faith was, for Newman, the very indication of its perfection.

All this change did imply, Newman admitted, that some developments might be unfaithful to the original idea from which it sprang. He outlined the following seven tests or notes to determine whether a development was legitimate or not: preservation of type, continuity of principles, power of assimilation, logical sequence, anticipation of its future, conservative action upon its past, and chronic vigor. These tests really amounted to asking whether a doctrine fit into the analogy of faith and the life of the church over time. While his treatment of these notes or tests was designed to show how Catholic doctrines on the sacraments, ecclesiology, and devotions were legitimate, the very idea called all Catholics to think critically about doctrine.[14]

When Newman went to Rome to study for ordination to the Catholic priesthood in 1846, he also had to defend his orthodoxy as a result of the *Essay on the Development of Doctrine*. The main objection was that he seemed to concede that the orthodox doctrine of the Trinity was not held in the earliest centuries of the church. Though he had good reason to fear that his book would be placed on the Index of Forbidden Books, he managed to avoid such an outright condemnation. From 1847 until 1858 Newman was able to recover from his initial difficulties and enjoyed some popularity as a lecturer and apologist for the church.[15] He even served as rector of the newly founded Catholic University of Ireland from 1854 to 1858. Shortly after his resignation as rector in 1858, he wrote his most provocative and prophetic work: *On Consulting the Faithful in Matters of Doctrine*.

On Consulting the Faithful

When Newman returned to England, he was asked to become the editor of a journal called *The Rambler*. The journal was aimed at educating lay Catholics and had recently run afoul of church authorities. This was not surprising considering that it employed high standards of scholarship in order to criticize some of the positions promulgated by ecclesiastical authorities. In 1858, the coeditors, Sir John Acton and Richard Simpson, managed to offend the English hierarchy to the point that they threatened to officially censure the journal. Newman tried to intercede and to mediate the conflict. The end result of his efforts was that he was asked to take over as the editor. Newman reluctantly accepted the position, which he described as "a bitter penance." Little did he know how bitter the penance would turn out to be.

In the first issue produced under Newman in May 1859, the enemies of the journal found grounds to raise new grievances. In a column discussing issues concerning Catholic schools in England, Newman asserted that he believed the bishops desired to know the opinions of the laity on subjects that particularly concerned them. He explained: "If even in the preparation of a dogmatic definition the faithful are consulted, as lately in the instance of the Immaculate Conception, it is at least as natural to anticipate such an act of kind feeling and sympathy in great practical questions."[16] A professor of theology at Ushaw College, Dr. Gillow, reported this statement to the English bishops as suspect and offensive.

Before the month of May had ended, Newman was called in to meet with Bishop Ullathorne. The bishop informed Newman that the journal remained too disturbing for Catholic sensibilities. When Newman tried to convince Ullathorne to consider the issue of education from the standpoint of the laity, the bishop reportedly asked in a dismissive manner, "Who are the laity?" Newman responded that the church would look foolish without the laity. Failing to agree on the lay concerns or even competence over matters involving the education of their children, they agreed that Newman would resign as editor of *The Rambler* after the July issue.[17]

Feeling stung by Ullathorne's criticism of his work as editor of *The Rambler*, Newman decided to use the final issue to defend his claim that the laity should be consulted in matters of doctrine. With this one essay Newman earned Pope Pius IX's (1846–78) personal displeasure and was designated "the most dangerous man in England" by one of the pope's closest advisors, Monsignor George Talbot. Newman's spirit, Talbot declared, "must be crushed."[18] Newman must have known that his defense would simply provoke church authorities, but he decided to publish *On Consulting the Faithful in Matters of Doctrine* regardless of the consequences.

What was so offensive about his claim that the laity should be consulted in matters pertaining to their faith and their lives? The short answer: everything. The essay began with the initial objection raised about his use of the term *consult* and its meaning. Newman defined the word as expressive of trust and deference, but not of submission. In this way, he attempted to dispel any fears that he was suggesting that the magisterium should be made subject to the laity. Further, he explained that *to consult* includes the idea of inquiring into a matter of fact, as well as asking a judgment. He clarified that the laity do not define doctrine, but their belief is sought as a witness to the apostolic tradition.[19]

Just as a weatherman consults a barometer when predicting the weather, Newman concluded that the bishops should consult the laity when formulating church doctrine. A weatherman is not under the power of a barometer, but he would be foolish to make a forecast without knowing whether barometric pressure was rising or falling. Barometers do not make judgments about the weather, they simply reveal matters of fact. Using this analogy between meteorology and theology, Newman was reminding both the laity and the bishops that the consensus of the faithful is a mark of the church's infallibility.[20]

Starting with the consideration of the church under the mark of its unity, Newman argued that the oneness of the church implied the importance of the perspective of the laity. He wrote:

> I think I am right in saying that the tradition of the apostles, committed to the whole church in its various constituents and functions *per modus unius*, manifests itself variously at various times: sometimes by the mouth of the episcopacy, sometimes by the doctors, sometimes by the people, sometimes by liturgies, rites, ceremonies, and customs, by events, disputes, movements, and all those other phenomena which are comprised under the name of history.[21]

He concluded that none of these channels of tradition should be treated with disrespect even though he readily admitted that defining dogma was the sole prerogative of the magisterial hierarchy. While some might legitimately want to lay stress on one or another of these channels, Newman boldly stated his preference was to stress the *consensus fidelium*, or the consensus of the faithful.

Newman knew he was going to generate a great deal of controversy, so he took rhetorical cover under the arguments that had been used to justify the doctrine of the Immaculate Conception. He pointed out that there is little to no evidence that this doctrine was held by the bishops and doctors of the early or even of the medieval church. Instead, the doctrine was justified by the consensus of the faithful in accord with their pastors as revealed in the historical record by the liturgies of the feast of the Immaculate Conception, public devotions, and prayers. He described these historical witnesses to the Immaculate Conception as instruments that provided evidence in favor of the doctrine and that these witnesses could make up for the deficiency of the church fathers on the matter. Finally he appealed to the papal bull of 1854 that defined the doctrine to support his emphasis on the sense of the faithful as a witness to the infallibility of the church's teaching.[22]

If Newman had ended his essay at this point, he might have escaped the worst attacks on his character and orthodoxy; instead, he pressed on to take the offensive. In addition to providing evidence that a doctrine is apostolic, he claimed that the consensus of the faithful was also a type of instinct in the bosom of the mystical body of Christ, a direction given by the Holy Spirit, an answer to prayer, and a jealousy of error manifested by a feeling of scandal. His discussion of the final quality of the consensus of the laity, a jealousy of error, was absolutely incendiary at the time. Newman wrote:

> It is not a little remarkable, that, though, historically speaking, the fourth century is the age of doctors, illustrated, as it was, by the saints Athanasius, Hilary, the two Gregories, Basil, Chrysostom, Ambrose, Jerome, and Augustine, and all of these saints bishops also, except one, nevertheless in that very day the divine tradition committed to the infallible church was proclaimed and maintained far more by the faithful than by the episcopate.[23]

He went on to explain that at various times during the Arian controversy, which was a debate over whether the Son was truly divine, popes, patriarchs, bishops, and even councils either taught errors or obscured and compromised revealed truths.

Newman argued that the Nicene dogma of the divinity of the Son was not maintained by the unswerving firmness of the magisterium. Instead, he asserted that it was the laity who supported the various doctors and confessors of the faith, such as Athanasius and others, in opposition to the majority of the episcopacy. Though subsequent historical research shows that Newman overstated the fidelity of the laity to what would become the orthodox position, he was certainly correct in his assessment that the laity played a pivotal role in the formulation and reception of the Nicene Creed at the Council of Constantinople.

After spending considerable time outlining the historical record over the Arian controversy and later developments when the laity were more faithful to orthodox doctrine than the magisterium, such as the doctrine of transubstantiation, Newman returned to his main point, namely, that the laity should be respected and served by the clergy. The benefit to the clergy, he promised, was that they would be happier if they were surrounded by informed and enthusiastic members of the laity. On the other hand, if the clergy cut off the laity from doctrinal study and required simple obedience, Newman warned that the clergy would create a situation where the wealthy and educated people would become indifferent to faith and the poor and illiterate would fall into superstition.[24]

Unlike his earlier efforts at reform, Newman's essay on the significance of the laity and its role in the church was almost universally condemned by Catholics in England and in Europe. Instead of presenting his agenda in the form of apologetics for the church, he had simply presented a defense of his own position. Without his normal rhetorical cover, Newman was totally exposed to his enemies. The bishop of Newport wrote that Newman's article was "the most alarming phenomenon of our times" and claimed that it undermined the confidence of the old Catholics.[25] The article was referred to Rome by the bishop. Shortly thereafter Newman was informed that his article was seen as suspect, though no one would identify exactly the statements that were seen as being erroneous.

Newman's position on the laity had little effect in Rome. A little over a decade later, Monsignor Talbot, his chief adversary, described the laity as "beginning to show their cloven hoof" under the influence of Newman's writings. After linking Newman and the laity to the satanic symbol of the cloven hoof, Talbot wrote, "What is the province of the laity? To hunt, to shoot, to entertain." When it came to ecclesiastical matters, Talbot smugly pronounced that the laity had no competence at all.[26]

For his part, Newman withdrew from the public arena for five years. Effectively silenced by his ecclesiastical enemies, Newman took on a more monastic form of life. He never doubted the validity of his mission to recover the proper and active role of the laity in the church, but he recognized that "it may be God's will that it should be done a hundred years later."[27] In light of the Second Vatican Council's statements of the apostolate of the laity, Newman's assessment seems to have been prophetic. After his five years of silence, he was given more opportunities to take up his mission. As with his earlier efforts, he again donned the garb of the Catholic apologist even as he advanced the idea that being Catholic meant affirming freedom of thought and freedom of conscience.

Freedom and Infallibility

Protestant polemics against the Catholic Church were reinvigorated in England in the 1860s and 1870s as Catholic claims about the infallibility of the church and of the pope became more strident. In 1864, an Anglican controversialist named Charles Kingsley, wrote a scathing attack on Newman and on Catholic priests as lacking intellectual integrity. A decade later a former prime minister of England, William Gladstone, the Duke of Norfolk, wrote an article claiming that no one can be a Catholic without renouncing his or her moral and mental freedom. Both of these attacks presented Newman with an opportunity to return to the public arena and to redeem himself in the eyes of most of the Catholic community.

The *Apologia pro Vita Sua* was written in response to Kingsley in 1864. While the final chapter was ostensibly written as a defense of the Catholic faith, its primary aim was to respond to both Ultramontane and liberal Catholics. Newman began with a defense of the infallibility of the church. Essentially he argued that the intellect and reason, which are good in themselves, had been severely damaged by original sin. Newman described the state of affairs this way:

> I have no intention at all of denying, that truth is the real object of our reason, and that, if it does not attain to truth, either the premiss or the process is in fault; but I am not speaking here of right reason, but of reason as it acts in fact and concretely in fallen man. I know that even the unaided reason, when correctly exercised, leads to a belief in God, in the immortality of the soul, and in a future retribution; but I am considering the faculty of reason actually and historically; and in this point of view, I do not think I am wrong in saying that its tendency is towards a simple unbelief in matters of religion.[28]

He concluded that reason alone, in this anarchic state of affairs, was rapidly moving the world toward atheism.

To counter this movement toward atheism, Newman held that people need an authority to restrain the impulsive recklessness of fallen reason. Further, he argued that scripture was not intended to serve this purpose. While scripture could serve as the means of conversion for some people, he wrote that a book could never "make a stand against the wild living intellect of man." If God wished to make provisions for retaining a knowledge of himself in the world that could withstand human skepticism, Newman concluded that it should not be surprising to believe God would introduce a power into the world with the prerogative of infallibility in religious matters. Such an instrument, he concluded, was suited to the need of preserving the knowledge of God. Thus when Newman considered the claims of the Catholic Church to infallibility, he wrote that he felt no difficulty in admitting the idea.[29]

Because of the suspicions over his orthodoxy and fidelity to the church, Newman had to make it clear that he had submitted absolutely to the church's claim to infallibility in its teaching authority before he could take up a defense of private judgment or intellectual freedom. He argued that these two realities, authority and private judgment, were held together in a type of dynamic tension in the Catholic Church. In a particularly stirring passage, he wrote:

> It is necessary for the very life of religion, viewed in its large operations and history, that the warfare [between authority and private judgment] should be incessantly carried on. Every exercise of infallibility is brought out into act by an intense and varied operation of the reason, both as its ally and as its opponent, and provokes again, when it has done its work, a re-action of reason against it; and, as in a civil polity the state exists and endures by means of rivalry and collision, the encroachments and defeats of its constituent parts, so in like manner Catholic Christendom is no simple exhibition of religious absolutism, but presents a continuous picture of authority and private judgment alternately advancing and retreating as the ebb and flow of the tide....[30]

Though Newman had difficulty in setting limits to the length of his sentences, he had no difficulty in prescribing limits to the church's infallibility. He gave what may be identified as both moral and theological limits to infallibility. Concerning the former, he cited St. Paul as indicating that apostolic power is given solely for the purpose of building up and not for the purpose of destruction (2 Cor 10:8, 13:10). Thus he claimed that infallibility should only be invoked in cases where there is a need and that it should not be used "to enfeeble the freedom and vigor of human thought in religious speculation."[31] Infallibility should only be used, he argued, to restrain and control the extravagance of the human intellect such as those of the great heretics like Arius, who denied the Son was God, or Pelagius, who denied the necessity of the continual aid of grace for salvation.

The theological limits to infallibility were even more certain for Newman. He wrote, "First, infallibility cannot act outside of a definite circle of thought, and it must in all its decisions, or definitions, as they are called, profess to be keeping within it. The great truths of the moral law, of natural religion, and of apostolical faith, are both its boundary and its foundation."[32] Infallibility could not, he assured his readers, ever go beyond these limits and it must always be guided by both scripture and tradition. Further, he claimed that all acts of infallible teaching must refer to some particular truth from the apostolic era that is being defended or lifted up.

Nonetheless, Newman admitted that the church does render judgments on secular matters that have an impact on religion, such as philosophy, science, and literature. The church censures books, silences authors, and forbids discussions. In these matters, Newman claimed the church is not speaking doctrinally but is acting in a disciplinary manner. He asserted that just because the church is infallible in matters of doctrine does not mean it is infallible in all its acts, policies, and disciplinary measures. Recalling that history supplies ample evidence where the church has harshly used its power, he alluded to the fact that St. Paul had taught that the divine treasure is held "in earthen vessels" (2 Corinthians 4:7).[33]

After recounting some of the church's misguided decisions, Newman explained that he did not see these errors as a justification for dissent. He claimed that some people correctly recognize a truth, desire to reform an abuse, or advocate for a change in policy, but fail to consider whether the time is right to pursue their agenda. These people, according to Newman, ought to be restrained because they spoil a good work in their own time and set up impediments to future reformers.[34] While his position may seem exceedingly restrictive, Newman did allow for reformers to oppose the magisterium when it came to matters of conscience.

Newman took up his defense of conscience in *A Letter to His Grace the Duke of Norfolk*, which was written in 1874. Again the key issues revolved around authority and infallibility, but this time

Newman had to contend with the fallout from the First Vatican Council's definition of papal infallibility. His defense of conscience was certainly generated as a response to the Duke of Norfolk, the former prime minister William Gladstone, but it also represents a development of his own thought. He declared that conscience is "the aboriginal vicar of Christ" and that papal infallibility could never speak out against conscience without committing a "suicidal act."[35]

Conscience had a very specific meaning for Newman. He chose to take an ecumenical approach and defined the term this way:

> When Anglicans, Wesleyans, the various Protestant sects in Scotland, and other denominations among us, speak of conscience, they mean what we mean, the voice of God in the nature and heart of man, as distinct from the voice of revelation. They speak of a principle planted within us, before we have had any training, although training and experience are necessary for its strength, growth and due formation. They consider it a constituent element of the mind, as our perception of other ideas may be, as our powers of reasoning, as our sense of order and the beautiful, and our other intellectual endowments. They consider it, as Catholics consider it, to be the internal witness of both the existence and the law of God.[36]

This way of understanding conscience was rooted in St. Paul's claim that all people have God's law inscribed in their hearts (Rom 2:15). Newman was aware that many people had abandoned the traditional Christian understanding of the term, but such people did not make up his audience. He was not trying to prove the Christian notion of conscience; instead, he hoped to show how conscience mitigated against an excessively authoritarian interpretation of the First Vatican Council.

Newman began by demonstrating how papal infallibility should be seen as supporting the inviolability of conscience. The pope's mission, he proclaimed, is to champion, to support, and to strengthen the "light which enlightens everyone that comes into the world" (John 1:9).[37] The pope's authority in theory and his power in fact are, he wrote, founded on the law of conscience and the recognition of its sacredness. Since conscience and the moral sense are the highest forms of knowledge available to humanity, Newman argued it is the least clear type of knowledge for us. Thus, he concluded, it is the pope's raison d'être to champion the moral law found in the conscience. In this way, Newman made it clear that the pope has no jurisdiction over the natural law.[38]

At the same time, Newman conceded that various popes throughout history did not always recognize this limitation on their authority. He explained that Catholics are not bound to any pope's personal character or private acts. Because conscience applies to things that should or should not be done and not to abstract doctrine, Newman concluded that papal infallibility cannot come into conflict with conscience. In short, they have separate realms of jurisdiction. However, Newman conceded that conscience can come into conflict with a pope's legislation, orders, and policies that are not infallible. To prove his point, he asked:

> Was St. Peter infallible on that occasion in Antioch when St. Paul withstood him? Was St. Victor infallible when he separated from his communion the Asiatic churches? Or Liberius when in like manner he excommunicated Athanasius? And, to come to later times, was Gregory XIII, when he had a medal struck in honor of the St. Bartholomew massacre? Or Paul IV in his conduct toward Elizabeth? Or Sextus V when he blessed the Armada? Or Urban VIII when he persecuted Galileo?[39]

Overstating his case a bit, he concluded that no Catholic has ever pretended that these were infallible acts.

In the end, Newman concluded that Catholics can legitimately oppose the pope when his dictates or policies violate their conscience. Nonetheless, he outlined a type of examination of conscience that must take place before a Catholic can legitimately oppose the commands of a pope. First, he said that one must be convinced that obeying the pope would be a sin. Further, the person in this situation should be certain that he or she is not acting out of willful selfishness, mean spiritedness, or presumption. Once these conditions had been fulfilled and the person was fully persuaded that the pope was commanding something contrary to God's law, he or she would sin by being obedient to the pope.[40]

As with his other efforts at reforming the extreme positions toward which the church was leaning, Newman grounded his defense of intellectual freedom and freedom of conscience in history. Both the *Apologia* and *A Letter to the Duke of Norfolk* helped to rebuild his reputation and led to his eventual elevation by Pope Leo XIII to the rank of cardinal. Newman's use of apologetics against the Catholic Church's detractors as a means to present his reform agenda proved to be quite successful. In fact, his rhetoric concerning the perfection or infallibility of the church allowed the magisterial hierarchy a way to recognize the church's imperfection and need for reform and ensured that his statements on the laity would be recovered in the twentieth century.

Newman's Legacy

The aspect of Newman's reform agenda that had the most impact on the church was the restoration of the role of history. His advocacy for freedom of conscience, the active role of the laity, and intellectual freedom all rested on this foundation. Even his ideas concerning the development of doctrine, which he found in the works of other Catholic writers, were fortified by his insights into the nature of history. By identifying the perfection of the church with its ability to adapt to new situations and contexts without losing its essential identity, Newman reinvigorated the idea that the church can make progress in its self-understanding and in its comprehension of divine revelation. Though these positions were contrary to the doctrinal positions espoused by the magisterial hierarchy throughout most of his career, his efforts to reform the church's doctrine were adopted by Pope Leo XIII. To signal the change in ecclesial direction, Pope Leo XIII named Newman a cardinal in 1879.

Newman's efforts at doctrinal or theological reform had broad implications and were carried forward by Leo XIII. In 1883, Leo published a letter to the directors of the Vatican Library calling for true and impartial history drawn from the sources. The first duty of the historian, according to Leo, was not to tell a lie, and the second duty was not to be afraid of the truth. In 1889, a year before Newman's death, Leo directed church historians to "keep back nothing of the trials she [the church] has had to experience in the course of the ages through the frailty of her children, and sometimes even of her ministers."[41]

This new commitment to the importance of history generated a great recovery of medieval and patristic sources by scholars in the late nineteenth and early twentieth centuries. Among these new historians were the leading theological reformers of the twentieth-century church, including Yves Congar, Henri de Lubac, Gerhard Ladner, and many of the experts at the Second Vatican Council, including George Tavard, Joseph Ratzinger, and Hans Küng. The two agendas that drove much of the Second Vatican's work, ressourcement (a return to the historical sources) and *aggiornamento* (an attempt to modernize the Catholic Church), were prefigured in Newman's mission to reform the church.

In 1991, Pope John Paul II declared Newman "Venerable," which is a step in the process of canonization At the end of his papacy, John Paul reemphasized the importance of historical accuracy with his calls for a purification of the church's memory by admitting and apologizing for the various evils performed in the name of the church by its members. While much work remains in the mission of recovering an accurate historical account and assessment of the church's history and its significance for reform and renewal, Newman's contribution to the cause of reform cannot be ignored.

9

Ɖorothy Ɖay and the Catholic Worker Movement

With twenty-five dollars from a benefactor, twenty-one dollars of the editors' money for gas and electric bills, a ten-dollar donation from a New Jersey priest, and a dollar from a Georgia nun, Dorothy Day and her editorial board started an engine for social justice called *The Catholic Worker*. She identified her readers as those who were sitting on park benches to warm themselves, those who were huddling in shelters to avoid the rain, those who were looking for work, and those who had lost hope. The purpose of the paper, she wrote, was to call attention to the fact that the Catholic Church had a social program and that there were people in the church working for their material as well as their spiritual welfare.

Day defined the paper's purpose as responding to radical papers whose aim was to convert people to radicalism and atheism. She asked her readers to consider the following questions: "Is it not possible to be radical and not atheist? Is it not possible to protest, to expose, to complain, to point out abuses and demand reforms without desiring the overthrow of religion?"[1] The mission of the paper would be to popularize and disseminate the encyclicals of the popes on social justice. By grounding the paper's mission in the authority of the papal encyclicals, Day was able to defend *The Catholic Worker* and the movement associated with it against the attacks from more socially conservative Catholics. Many members of the clergy came to embrace the movement as providing an alternative to communism and other forms of atheistic socialism.

Dorothy Day had been a Communist sympathizer and a radical before becoming Catholic. Her pacifist commitments prevented her from joining the Communist Party; but she was impressed by their advocacy for the poor and the oppressed. From 1917 until 1920 she lived in

Greenwich Village and was a part of literary circles that included writers like Eugene O'Neill. At twenty-one she was pregnant with the child of Lionel Moise, a newspaperman whom Ernest Hemingway idolized. Moise refused to take responsibility and Day, as a result, had an abortion in 1919. Seeking comfort, she entered a marriage in the spring of 1920 that lasted less than a year. In 1925 Day entered a common-law marriage with Forster Burke. When she became pregnant in June 1926, she began to experience a conversion and started praying at a Catholic chapel. After the birth of her daughter, Tamara, in 1927, Day felt called to commit to the faith, and both she and her child were baptized. This aggravated Burke, who was an avowed atheist and an anarchist; shortly thereafter, Burke and Day separated.[2]

From 1928 until 1933, Day struggled with finding her place in the church. Increasingly she felt ashamed by the way the church was behaving during those tumultuous years following the onset of the Great Depression. She did not, however, convert with her eyes closed to the nature of the church. She described her conversion this way:

> I had no doubts about the church. It was founded upon St. Peter, that rock, who yet thrice denied his Master on the eve of His crucifixion. And Jesus had compared the church to a net cast into the sea and hauled in, filled with fishes, both good and bad. "Including," one of my non-Catholic friends used to say, "some blowfish and quite a few sharks."[3]

What bothered her was watching all the wealth possessed by the members of the church being wasted on luxury. The self-satisfied statements made by priests and bishops concerning labor issues and the poor particularly galled her because the clergy lived in lavish houses and ate ample meals.[4]

Day was also scandalized by the behavior of wealthy Catholics who were indifferent to the plight of the poor. She increasingly found it difficult to reconcile the wealth of Manhattan Catholics, who adorned themselves with furs and tailored suits, and the church's teachings concerning social justice. How could Catholics live in such luxury when they saw the hundreds of hungry and destitute people walking the streets of New York? Reflecting on this period, she said:

I wanted the churches to open their doors, to let the poor and the hungry and the homeless come inside, to feed them, to give them shelter. I wanted all the gold and the furs, all the fancy jewels worn by the princes of the church, the prelates—all that to be sold, so men and women and children could get a meal and not shiver and get sick on the streets, with no place to go. When I wasn't becoming ashamed of my church, I was becoming ashamed of myself. I remember the envy I felt toward my radical atheist friends; they were fighting on behalf of the poor, and I was a Catholic and praying for the poor, and I believed it was important to keep praying, but I wanted to be out there helping in some concrete way....[5]

Though she wrote articles for *Commonweal* and *America*, she did not feel as if she was doing enough to call attention to the struggles of the poor. In December 1932, Day found a way to put Catholic social teaching into practice.

The Catholic Worker Movement began after Dorothy Day covered the Hunger March in December 1932. The march had been staged by Communists, but most of the marchers were not members of the Communist Party. According to Day, the Communists were leaders by default. They were the only people willing to draw attention to the plight of the workers. They also maintained discipline even after police in Wilmington, Delaware, beat the marchers with clubs and arrested some of their leaders.

As the three thousand marchers approached Washington, the city went into a near state of hysteria. There were riot drills of the Marines at Quantico, additional guards were posted all over the city, and the National Guard was mobilized. The city even armed and deployed members of the American Legion and firefighters. Dorothy Day observed that various women's organizations, pacifist groups, Quakers, and others had come out to protest against this show of force. She also noticed that there were no Catholic groups or organizations supporting the workers' right to march in Washington. After the march was completed peacefully, she described her thoughts this way:

I watched that ragged horde and thought to myself, "These are Christ's poor. He was one of them. He was a man like other men, and he chose his friends amongst the ordinary workers. These men feel they have been betrayed by Christianity. Men are not Christian today. If they were, this sight would not be possible. For dearer in the sight of God are these hungry ragged ones, than all those smug, well-fed Christians who sit in their homes, cowering in fear of the communist menace."[6]

Day recognized that a fear of Communism was paralyzing the church on social issues. Nonetheless, she did not participate in the demonstration because it had been organized by Communists.[7]

The day after the march was the feast of the Immaculate Conception. Since the National Shrine is in Washington, Day went there to pray for guidance. She asked for a way to open up that would allow her to work for the poor and the oppressed. When she returned to her home in New York, the French philosopher Peter Maurin was waiting for her. Maurin still wore the suit he had slept in the previous night, resembling more the members of the "ragged horde" she had observed in Washington than an intellectual.[8] Day was impressed by his program for social reconstruction, which was grounded in the papal encyclicals *Rerum novarum,* or *On Capital and Labor* (May 15, 1891), and *Quadragesimo anno,* or *On Reconstruction of the Social Order* (May 15, 1931).

Social Justice and the Papacy

As we have seen, the enormous political changes of the nineteenth century led most of the popes of this period to be distrustful of democracy and modern science; but economic revolutions represented another and arguably deeper challenge because they fragmented the members of the church. The stratification between the rich and the poor in societies that had become capitalist and industrialized led many thinkers such as Karl Marx to see class warfare as the natural result of property rights. The only way to end such class warfare and its attendant injustices, according to Marx, would be through a revolution that would socialize all industry and end all private ownership of land. While Marx's drastic solution has fallen into almost universal disfavor, his economic theories did identify ways that a society's economic system could be judged as unjust.

Initially, the popes responded to these economic ideas as simply another aspect of modernism to be rejected. Communism and its more peaceful counterpart, socialism, were interpreted as just another attack on the pope's monarchical and territorial claims or as an assault on the church's claims to temporal property. But the extreme poverty and social dislocation caused by industrialization was a fact that could not be denied. Pope Leo XIII, who supported a renewal of historical studies and the idea that the church's doctrine develops to contend with new situations, decided to address the issue of social justice.[9]

To make his case, Pope Leo offered a scholastic-style argument based on natural law. First, he claimed that anyone who works for wages is doing so in order to obtain property for themselves and to hold that property as their own. Since human beings have the capacity to foresee future needs and to store up provisions accordingly, he argued that the right to acquire property is grounded in human nature. This right to private property was observed, according to the pope, throughout the ages by everyone, was attested to in the civil laws, and was found in the divine law of scripture as well. Since human nature comes before the state, Pope Leo declared that the right to own property cannot be removed by the state.[10]

What was true of the individual's right to property could been seen even more clearly, Pope Leo argued, in the rights of the family. He proclaimed that no human law can "abolish the natural and original right of marriage."[11] Since marriage is a type of society older than any existing government, he claimed it had rights prior to and independent of the state. One of the duties of married people is to provide for their children, even in the eventuality of their own deaths. The only way to fulfill this goal, he argued, is through the ownership of property that can be transmitted through inheritance. Thus, Pope Leo declared that the family has "at least equal rights with the state in the choice and pursuit of things needful to its preservation and its just liberty." The only time the pope would allow the civil government to intrude upon family affairs was when a family is in "exceeding distress, utterly deprived of counsel of friends, and without any prospect of extricating itself." [12]

While Leo XIII was interested in preserving the independence of families by restricting state intrusions, he did argue that the state had a duty to provide for the poor and to ensure just wages and healthy working conditions. Secular governments should recognize the interests of all citizens as equals and see that the members of the working classes have the same rights as the rich. Further, Leo advised secular governments to be aware that the members of the working classes represented a vast majority of the citizenry.[13]

Pope Leo's list of considerations clearly tilted towards the concerns of the urban poor even as it admitted some of the concerns of property owners. He justified showing special consideration to the poor this way:

> The richer classes have many ways of shielding themselves, and stand in less need of help from the state; whereas the mass of the poor have no resources of their own to fall back upon, and must chiefly depend on the assistance of the state. And it is for this reason that wage-earners, since they mostly belong in the mass of the needy, should be specially cared for and protected by the government.[14]

If employers fail to be just, then he proclaimed that the government must act because it is both unjust and inhuman to grind people down "with excessive labor as to stupefy their minds and wear out their bodies."[15]

In addition to addressing the deplorable working conditions, Pope Leo forcefully presented a papal teaching on a matter of morality, namely, the matter of fair wages. The pope declared that people who claimed that wages are only regulated by free consent were absolutely wrong. Further, he condemned their claim that when the employer pays what was agreed upon he has done enough to be just. Pope Leo outlined several important considerations for determining whether wage agreements are just. First, he explained that the goal of all labor is to work for obtaining the necessities of life for the worker. Second, he demanded that Catholics recognize that human beings are commanded to work in Genesis 3:19. Labor is therefore personal, he concluded, insofar as it is the exclusive property of the one who acts, and it is necessary because of natural and divine law.[16]

Since labor is not truly free, because it is necessary for survival, Pope Leo XIII concluded that wage agreements cannot simply be regulated by free consent and market forces. He proclaimed:

> Now, were we to consider labor merely in so far as it is personal, doubtless it would be within the workman's right to

accept any rate of wages whatsoever; for in the same way as he is free to work or not, so he is free to accept a small wage or even none at all. But our conclusion must be very different if, together with the personal element in a man's work, we consider the fact that work is also necessary for him to live: these two aspects of his work are separable in thought, but not in reality. The preservation of life is the bounden duty of one and all, and to be wanting therein is a crime. It necessarily follows that each one has a natural right to procure what is required in order to live, and the poor can procure that in no other way than by what they can earn through their work.[17]

In addition to freely agreeing upon the wages, he taught that wages must also be sufficient "to support a frugal and well-behaved wage-earner." He proceeded to declare that when an employee is forced to accept a less than fair wage or worse working conditions simply because an employer will afford him no better, the employee is the victim of force and injustice.[18]

Given these inequities, Pope Leo decided to support the labor unions and other forms of associations that represented the interests of working people. He saw the labor unions as being analogous to the medieval guilds, which provided him with an argument from antiquity in favor of the unions. As in the other cases, Pope Leo grounded his support of unions in natural-law theology, in scriptures, and in the authority of Thomas Aquinas. These scholastic-style arguments reveal the amount of resistance he expected from within Catholic circles to the support of unions and the rights of workers. As it turned out, so many Catholics rejected the authority of *Rerum novarum* that Pope Pius XI had to reaffirm the teaching in his encyclical *Quadragesimo anno*.

Quadragesimo anno refers to the fact that Pope Leo XIII's encyclical had disturbed many people. It was seen as suspect among many Catholics. Pope Pius complained about some members being "slow of heart" and thus disdaining to study this new social philosophy. He described others as being timid. Another group of dissenters he identified were the Catholics who rejected Pope Leo's teaching that workers should form unions and other associations to represent them.[19] Pope Pius said that he intended to defend Pope Leo's doctrine on the social and economic question against its critics and to develop it more fully on certain points.[20]

Pope Pius declared that the common good or interest of all should be a principle governing the distribution of property. He defined this principle as a law of social justice which entailed that it is forbidden for one class to exclude another from sharing in the benefits of economic growth through industrialization. The distribution of wealth in 1931 was, according to Pope Pius, laboring "under the gravest of evils" due to the huge disparity between the rich and the poor. Thus he concluded that societies needed to be "called back to and brought into conformity with the norms of the common good, that is, social justice."[21]

Since labor must be considered in social as well as individual terms, Pope Pius concluded that wages must take account of social conditions as well as individual circumstances. This led him to provide three principles that should govern how employers establish their wages. The first was that workers should be paid a wage sufficient to themselves and their families.[22] He delineated the characteristics of a sufficient wage as being high enough that workers could, by wise management and thrift, increase their property so that they could more easily bear the economic burdens of family life. Further, he taught that the wage should allow workers to save so that they could provide in some measure for their heirs.[23]

The workers Pope Pius had in mind were men, and his frame of reference was the father's ability to provide for his family. He denounced situation's where the father's wage was so low that mothers and children were forced to work so the family could meet its basic needs. While his claim that mothers must be home to ensure the proper rearing of children is clearly a product of the times, the principle that parents should be able to devote time to raising their children is still valid.

Pope Pius's second principle balanced the concerns of workers with those of employers. He asserted that a just wage must also take account of the condition of the employer, because it would be unjust to demand excessive wages that could bankrupt a business to the "consequent calamity to the workers" as a group. Pius laid out the following exceptions to the general rule:

> If, however, a business makes too little money, because of a lack of energy or lack of initiative or because of indifference

to technical and economic progress, that must not be regarded as a just reason for reducing the compensation of the workers. But if the business in question is not making enough to pay the workers an equitable wage because it is being crushed by unfair burdens or forced to sell its product at less than a just price, those who are thus the cause of the injury are guilty of a grave wrong, for they deprive workers of their just wage and force them under the pinch of necessity to accept a wage less than fair.[24]

In these types of cases, he advocated that public authorities intervene in order to aid workers and employers overcome these types of inequities. Thus Pope Pius advocated a type of regulated market as opposed to a free market in terms of wages and working conditions.

The final principle governing wages was that they must be adjusted to the public economic good. Pope Pius saw this public economic good as being manifested in full employment. He affirmed that everyone who was willing and able to work should be able to find employment. Social justice demands "that wages and salaries be so managed, through agreement of plans and wills, insofar as can be done, as to offer the greatest possible number the opportunity of getting work and obtaining a suitable means of livelihood."[25]

Pope Pius believed that governments must be involved in the regulation of labor conditions, but he placed more emphasis on workers and employers reaching agreements. He defended the existence of labor unions and professional associations and praised Catholics who were working to help alleviate the difficulties of working people. These Christian unions, organizations, and associations should have working relationships with priests who would see to it that the workers and the poor could participate in study groups and in spiritual retreats. A year after this encyclical was published, Dorothy Day and Peter Maurin began putting together an organization that sought to incarnate the agenda spelled out in *Quadragesimo anno* in an American context.

Genesis of the Catholic Worker Movement

As Day returned to New York from the Hunger Strike, she must have been meditating on her prayer to find a way to work for the poor and the oppressed, but she probably did not expect such a rapid response to her petition. Day claimed that without Peter Maurin there would not have been a Catholic Worker Movement. Maurin had heard about Day's work writing for *Commonweal* and had decided to enlist her aid. In turn, what appealed to her was his personalist philosophy.

Maurin believed that social reform had to begin with the person considered in his or her totality. A person's physical, social, psychological, and spiritual dimensions were all aspects that must be considered to create a just society.[26] Maurin's emphasis on the person did not, however, imply radical individualism because he held that a person always exists within a broader communal context. He was so distrustful of those who sought to organize people as groups without considering the needs of the person that Day said he sounded like an anarchist. She later confessed that if she had not just come from the Hunger March, had not prayed at the National Shrine, and had not been reading the lives of the saints, she probably would have listened politely to Maurin but would have dismissed his program.[27]

Instead of dismissing the eccentric Frenchman and his ideas, Day took the time to truly consider his reform agenda. Maurin's program, like the papal encyclicals on social justice, was modeled on medieval reform movements and institutions. Like the Franciscan and Dominican reformers, he advocated a life of poverty and a commitment to the works of mercy such as feeding the poor and caring for the sick as the means of evangelizing the masses. He believed that the efforts to teach or propagandize workers by means of newspapers, pamphlets, and leaflets was insufficient and had to be supplemented by acts of mercy. Clothing the naked, sheltering the homeless, and assisting the oppressed were, Maurin claimed, a means to instruct the ignorant, counsel the doubtful, and comfort the afflicted. Thus the most effective means of propaganda would include action as well as communication.[28]

There was also a theoretical side to Maurin's thought, but it was not systematic. He expressed himself in a series of short theses that were, at times, reminiscent of slogans. An example of his sweeping theses was his claim that the study of history allowed a person to discern how ideas had been persuasive in different cultural environments. His conclusion that the study of history was both the catalyst of tradition and the means to humanize the Catholic tradition was equally grand. He would write slogans such as "Be what you want the other fellow to be," or "We should be announcers, not denouncers."[29] His use of easy-to-remember slogans was part of his method of disseminating ideas in a format appropriate to mass communications.

The Catholic Worker Movement, as Maurin envisioned it, would use the methods of mass communication hand in hand with a life of poverty and service. Maurin needed Day to manage the communication side of his program and her guidance in translating his ideas into an American context. The movement would provide service by creating houses of hospitality based on the medieval institution of the hospice. Maurin described their agenda in verse:

> We need houses of hospitality
> to give the rich
> the opportunity to serve the poor.
> We need houses of hospitality
> to bring the bishops to the people
> and the people to the bishops.
> We need houses of hospitality
> to bring back to institutions
> the technique of institutions.
> We need houses of hospitality
> to show what idealism looks like
> when it is practiced.
> We need houses of hospitality
> to bring Social Justice
> through Catholic Action
> exercised in Catholic Institutions.[30]

His stanzas reveal something of the rhetoric of the movement. Under the affirmations to serve the rich, the bishops, institutions, and intellectual idealists, each stanza implied a criticism. They criticized the rich for not serving the poor, the bishops for not practicing solidarity with their people, the institutions for losing their sense of serving the person, and the idealists who do not act.

Maurin tied the idea for his houses of hospitality to the church's tradition. Because the Council of Carthage urged bishops to set up hospices in conjunction with their churches, he was obliquely claiming that the bishops should support the houses of hospitality. Just as those hospices had priests designated to administer spiritual and temporal needs, the houses of hospitality would provide vocational training, reading rooms, and catechesis. Just as the papal encyclicals directed, the Catholic Worker Movement would wed Catholic thought to Catholic action.[31] In conformity with Pius XI's *Quadragesimo anno*, Maurin also supported the idea that workers should return to the land by operating agricultural communes.[32]

Dorothy Day embraced most of Maurin's vision, though she ultimately de-emphasized the desire to return to a more agrarian form of life. Whereas Maurin thought that efforts to organize strikes, to push for better wages, and to reform labor conditions were a waste of time, Day concerned herself with the immediate issues facing poor workers.[33] It was the idea of producing a labor paper that would popularize the papal teaching on social justice that fired her imagination. Finally, she saw how she could apply her Catholic faith and her talents to the cause of rebuilding the social order. Day adopted Maurin's conviction that the work of aiding the poor was more important than writing about helping the poor. Adapting Maurin's maxim on the works of mercy, she wrote, "It has always been through the performance of works of mercy that love is expressed, that people are converted, that the masses are reached."[34]

Given that both Maurin and Day believed that the work of serving the poor in houses of hospitality should have precedence, it is ironic that the movement began with the paper. The paper, *The Catholic Worker*, generated the publicity the movement needed to raise money to establish its first house of hospitality. It was the creation of the paper that first brought the movement under ecclesiastical guidance, which also provided the movement with important contacts. *The Catholic Worker* drew activists and poor people to Day and Maurin and, in this way, produced a new reform movement in the church aimed at reforming both a predominantly Protestant society as well as American Catholics who opposed papal teachings on social justice.

The Early Years of the Catholic Worker Movement

After the first issue of *The Catholic Worker* was published and distributed in May 1933, the movement grew exponentially. Day had overseen all phases of the paper's content while Maurin was away. The issue published one of Maurin's poetic essays, took up the question of cooperatives, exposed the racism faced by African Americans, advocated for trade unions, and discussed the problems of the unemployed. Enough contributions were received to keep the paper going for a second edition. It also generated some disagreement between Day and Maurin.

Maurin believed the paper was too general and did not reflect his personalist philosophy. He was not happy with the paper's declaration of solidarity with the worker and its intention of fighting social injustice. It sounded too much like class warfare to him. In the second edition, Maurin published a brief statement that he wanted to be taken off the editorial board, though he would continue to publish his personalist essays in *The Catholic Worker*. He explained that the revolution he wanted to foster would only occur when "gentle personalism" overcame middle-class values and the ideology of class struggle. Privately he chided Day, saying, "We are more concerned in standards of loving and not in standards of living." Rather than fixing the inequities of an industrialist and urban society, Maurin's goal was to return society to an agrarian way of life to relieve the dehumanizing effects of industrialization.[35]

As editor of *The Catholic Worker*, Day stuck to her agenda, but she continued to support Maurin's agenda and to incorporate his philosophy into her approach to social reform. In six months of operation, the paper went from a circulation of 2,500 to 20,000. This growth allowed the paper to take on a large staff, which was mostly made up of men who were out of work. The paper acquired housing for these men. Since it was a monthly paper, the staff also spent time helping people who had been evicted from their apartments, assisting the unemployed in getting relief checks, cooking for the hungry, demonstrating at strikes, and answering correspondence. By the seventh issue, Day announced that the Catholic Worker Movement was opening a house of hospitality for women, which generated even more donations of money, furniture, and time.

Catholics applauded the new movement as a force against Communism. The hospitality houses were so successful at helping the poor and at catechesis that many of the bishops wanted them in their dioceses. In a six-year period, twenty-three houses of hospitality were feeding five thousand people a day and small groups of the paper's readers were practicing voluntary poverty and the works of mercy around the country. Further, the movement had four farming communes where Maurin frequently lectured on his philosophy of personalism.[36]

Personalism also guided Day's understanding of social reform. Her approach to personalism had a more American feel insofar as she stressed the role of individual responsibility as the starting point for reforming society. She wrote:

> I do feel strongly that we must put everything we have into the work of embracing voluntary poverty for ourselves. It is only when we do this that we can expect God to provide for us. If we do everything we can ourselves, He will supplement our efforts. This is one of the fundamental points of our work in stressing personal responsibility before state responsibility. It is only when we have used all of our material resources that we feel it is permissible to call upon the state for aid, that in good conscience we can demand and expect help from the state.[37]

Her position was not to deny the role of the state, which had been affirmed in the papal encyclicals on social justice, but to emphasize personal initiative and action. "When our brother asks us for bread," Day explained, "we cannot say, 'Go be thou filled.'" Rather than sending someone from agency to agency, she demanded that Christians must first care for the person in need as much as they can.[38]

Although Day stressed personal responsibility, some people were denouncing her as a Communist as early as March 1935. The charges were coming from some very important and well-connected people. Father Joseph McSorely, her advisor at Paulist Press, was concerned enough to bring the matter to Day's attention. In his letter to Day, he explained that a drama critic from the *Catholic World* had heard a prominent New York socialite publicly attack *The Catholic Worker* in an address given to a women's club. McSorely wrote that this socialite saw the paper as giving proof "that the Catholic Church had gone Bolshevik and said that the Episcopal Church was the only remaining bulwark of the social order (this apparently was not intended as a joke)." With prophetic insight, McSorely closed his letter wishing her well and reminding her that she would have no lack of crosses as a true disciple of Christ.[39]

Some of Day's crosses were church officials who were so committed to certain political agendas that they attempted to use their ecclesial authority to browbeat her into submission. One example was the attempt to have her retract her support of the Child Labor Amendment in Congress, a bill that most Catholics opposed. Monsignor Thomas Scanlan, her official church censor, reprimanded Day and *The Catholic Worker* for their support of a law aimed at restricting child labor. Day responded quite forcefully in a letter dated March 16, 1935. First, she listed a number of priests and theologians who shared her sentiments. Then Day took a more theological approach and wrote: "It is after all, a matter of opinion, and it has nothing to do with faith or dogma, so we did not think we were treading on dangerous ground in upholding this piece of legislation." To his credit, Scanlan dropped the matter.[40]

From 1936 until 1939 the Catholic Worker Movement continued to expand as it advocated for workers and started hospitality houses and farming communes. The movement's support of strikers was a continual source of friction. The Seaman's Strike of 1937 caused the Catholic Worker Movement to go into debt because their readers, now over 100,000, refused to donate to help the strikers. Undeterred, the paper also advocated for steelworkers, marble workers, sharecroppers, stockyard workers, fishermen, autoworkers, and others.[41]

Day was frequently called upon to respond to the criticisms presented by priests and bishops. Her responses could be quite biting. Replying to a Father Haskins, who had said that the autoworker strikes in Michigan were immoral because they were illegal, Day wrote:

> I suppose you have seen the statement made by Attorney General Murphy recently that accused the sit-down strike of being illegal. That does not necessarily mean it is immoral. I was scandalized to find on my speaking trips throughout the country that many of our lay people think in terms of sin when they hear immoral. They picture men and women locked up in a factory, night and day, for weeks on end, dancing and carousing. It seems a shame that they should take so stupid an attitude.[42]

On the other hand, she would be much more conciliatory if she believed that a criticism might be justified.

In cases where Day felt that she or the movement had made a mistake, she had a three-pronged response based on the authority of the bishops. First, she quoted Cardinal Hayes as having said that the Catholic Worker Movement would make mistakes, but that the thing was not to persist in them. Then she would assert her faith that the bishops "will not allow us to fall into any error without calling it to our attention." Finally, she affirmed her obedience to her local bishop and the authority of the church.[43] Whereas this strategy worked as a defense against ecclesiastical censures, it did little to assuage the opposition she engendered from Catholics in general.

The social-justice positions espoused by Dorothy Day on labor issues, racism, and anti-Semitism all caused reactions from different Catholic quarters, but she was able to diffuse criticism by grounding her positions in sources that the church recognized as having authority, such as scripture, works of Catholic theology, and papal encyclicals. By 1939 the movement had helped to organize workers and had begun to shift Catholic attitudes in America over labor issues, but the movement was about to face a real test in its support of civil rights during the Red Scare.

Dorothy Day and the Red Scare

While the Catholic Worker Movement was initially cast as a Catholic alternative to Communism, Dorothy Day found herself in the position of defending the rights of Communists. The blockading of Berlin by Soviet troops in 1948, advances made by the Communists in China, and the first Soviet nuclear test in 1949 heightened fears in America over the "Red Menace." The Vatican was also concerned and released a decree in 1949 chastising Catholics for collaborating with Communists on labor issues. Many priests and bishops in the United States took the Vatican decree as giving them license to openly abuse the "Christian Left" from their pulpits.[44] The decree also set the stage for direct conflict between Day and Cardinal Francis J. Spellman, the archbishop of New York.

The conflict began late in 1949 over a labor dispute between the gravediggers of Calvary Cemetery and the Trustees of St. Patrick's Cathedral in New York. The gravediggers were all Catholics and were members of the CIO labor union. When the trustees of the cathedral refused to give the men a just wage, they went on strike and started a picket line in front of Cardinal Spellman's office. Claiming the strike was inspired by the Communists, the cardinal refused to meet with the men and brought in his seminarians to break the strike. Day wrote that the cardinal's decision to use force against a handful of poor workmen "was a temptation of the devil to that most awful of all wars, the war between the clergy and the laity."[45]

Day's decision to join the picket line was more than Cardinal Spellman could stand. Soon after she started picketing, a diocesan official emerged to invite her into the chancery. Rather than meeting her personally, Spellman sent a monsignor to inform her that she would have to take the name *Catholic* off her newspaper or cease publication. Day told the monsignor that they would change the name rather than cease publication. The monsignor advised her to consult with the staff at *The Catholic Worker* before making a final response.

After taking some time to calm down and to consult her staff, Day composed a letter to the monsignor that convinced Cardinal Spellman to drop his demand. She began by expressing her organization's obedience to the church and its gratitude to the Archdiocese of New York for the many times it had defended *The Catholic Worker* against its critics. While she was willing to change the name of the paper, she informed the monsignor that no one on the staff wanted to change the name. Day offered some concessions such as her willingness to put a box under the paper's title that would state the paper's opinions were not to be confused with official Catholic positions. She assured him that the paper was prepared to pay attention to all disciplinary directions and theological censures they received. Most importantly, she promised *The Catholic Worker* would "try to be less dogmatic, more persuasive, less irritating, more winning."[46]

The affirmation of obedience to the church' s teaching authority and the promise to be less irritating served to highlight the problem of suppressing the paper. Day warned that the suppression of *The Catholic Worker* would have negative consequences. First, it would result in a tremendous scandal to its 63,000 readers. Second, she warned it would be used as a weapon against the church by its enemies. Day explained that both Communist papers such as the *Daily Worker* and conservative ones such as *The New Republic* would use the controversy to further their own agendas. Faced with the choice between allowing a paper that was submissive to ecclesiastical authority to continue operation or suppressing it and creating scandal, Cardinal Spellman decided to drop the diocesan order.[47]

Because of episodes like this, Day had to defend herself against the charge of being a Communist throughout the 1950s. When the junior senator from Wisconsin, Joseph McCarthy, sparked hysteria by claiming that he had evidence that more than one hundred Communists had infiltrated the State Department, Day and *The Catholic Worker* were among the first voices to denounce the senator and his methods. When ten leading Communists were imprisoned on the charge of conspiring to overthrow the United States government, she protested that the defendants should be allowed freedom on bail so they could prepare for their trials. She called the incarcerated Communists "brothers" and credited them with helping her to find God in the poor. Dorothy wrote that she rejected their materialism, atheism, and doctrine on class warfare; but she still affirmed their rights as a minority group in this country.[48] Finally, her support of Castro's revolution in 1959 deeply undermined her credibility among Catholics.

Day and her movement were at a low point as the 1960s began, but the country's total rejection of McCarthy's agenda and the war in Vietnam began to change the national sentiment. As the civil rights movement and the peace movement began building some momentum, Day's movement began to restore its image among American Catholics. Lyndon Johnson's war on poverty and his project to build "The Great Society" made Day's positions on social justice seem less threatening and more winning to many Catholics.

Conclusion

After the Second Vatican Council, which marks the terminus of this study of reform, Dorothy Day and the Catholic Worker Movement continued their fight for social justice and for peace. They opposed the nuclear arms race, advocated civil disobedience on the draft, supported efforts to organize immigrant farmworkers in the West, and continued to operate houses of hospitality. Day died on November 29, 1980, but her movement has continued. Now there are 185 Catholic Worker houses of hospitality around the world and the paper's circulation is about 100,000. Shortly after her death, Cardinal John O'Conner of New York requested that the Vatican consider her cause for canonization. The Vatican accepted this request and Day is currently being considered as a candidate for sainthood.

At this time, it is impossible to assess the more lasting effects of Dorothy Day's reform agenda because reform movements can take centuries to implement. Her efforts did help to reform labor conditions in America and her movement has directly assisted thousands of people in need. The social-justice agenda she advocated has met with less success among American Catholics — even though it was founded upon papal teachings that were received by the Second Vatican Council. It is evident that most American Catholics neither know nor actively support the church's teaching on social justice. Even the institutions that officially claim to support a family wage, such as Catholic schools, parishes, and dioceses, frequently fail to practice what they preach when it comes to paying their employees a just wage.

There are troubling signs for the social-justice reformers who wish to carry forward Dorothy Day's attempts to reform society to be more just in accordance with the teachings of Leo XIII and Pius XI. Laws regulating working conditions are being rolled back in a frenzy of deregulation, support for mothers with dependent children has been cut dramatically, more and more people are falling through the cracks in a profit-based health-care system, and the unions are steadily declining in power as globalization presents new challenges to working people.

Day's advocacy of indiscriminate love and pacifism have also fallen out of favor. The terrorist attacks in 2001 and our response to them show that most Americans believe that violence is the best, most expedient means to solve conflict. The protection of the civil rights of religious and ethnic minorities, especially of Muslims, has eroded to the point of the suspension of some civil liberties by the Congress. Even our politics have become less civil. Civic discourse has been replaced by ranting ideologues on the radio and the twenty-four hour "news" networks. The Internet has further added to the Balkanization of society because it allows people to avoid sources of information and opinions that contradict their own position. Rather than generating dialogue, the Internet seems to be promoting a series of disconnected monologues. Increasingly, politics are about creating wedge issues that provoke the type of class warfare Dorothy Day opposed.

Rather than embracing the personalist revolution, which began with the person as a subject rather than an object, our society treats the person as an object understood in economic terms. The value of a person is weighed in terms of what they can produce or consume. The American social order continues to depend on profits and has exported free-market capitalism around the globe. Because market forces do not assign value to a person's relations with his or her family, role in the community, or spiritual gifts for the society, traditional cultures around the world have been disrupted. The disruption of traditional cultures has, in turn, generated a host of fundamentalist movements that are responding with violence to the dehumanizing aspects of globalization.

Dorothy Day would not see these challenges as a reason to be discouraged about the ongoing project of reforming society. She never shied away from a difficult fight. William Miller described her as having "an incomparable passion for what she called the hard contest."[49] Day advised her followers to take St. Teresa of Avila's advice to concentrate on their own efforts to be holy and just and to ignore whether or not others followed suit. She wrote:

> Do what comes to hand. Whatsoever thy hand finds to do, do it with all thy might. After all, God is with us. It shows too much conceit to trust to ourselves, to be discouraged at what we ourselves can accomplish. It is lacking in faith in God to be discouraged. After all, we are going to proceed with His help. We offer Him what we are going to do. If He wishes it to prosper, it will. We must depend solely on Him. Work as though everything depended on ourselves, and pray as though everything depended on God, as St. Ignatius says.[50]

Conclusion

Catholic reform starts with a desire to enhance the church's ability to evangelize by purifying its defects. Our history offers us numerous examples of how reformers have effectively generated change for the better. Church history reveals how reform came to encompass many facets of our faith, including individuals, institutions, systems, church governance, social injustice, corrupt teachings, and even reinterpreting traditional doctrines for new contexts. When reform was extended to new areas, it always generated opposition. The way that reformers respond to opposition distinguishes between those who are quite literally canonized by the church, those who are viewed with suspicion, and those who are rejected. This leads me to conclude that their strategies for responding to opposition are a more helpful way of approaching Catholic reform than trying to identify a set number of essential categories. There are six different strategies that these reformers used to effect change.

First, they established their authority through their service to the church and its pastoral mission. Their input carried weight because they had accumulated personal credibility from their years of service to the church, which demonstrated to people that they had the institution's best interests at heart. Gregory the Great linked his authority as a pope and as a reformer to service. Following Gregory's example, later reformers insisted that all Christian authority is based on service to justify their reform agendas.

Second, the reformers communicated their concerns and proposals clearly and persuasively to their audiences. They used language and categories that the members of the church understood and recognized as having authority. In other words, they framed their agendas and justified their actions by drawing upon the teachings of scripture and tradition. When would-be reformers used language that the members of the broader church either did not understand or accept, they failed.

Third, effective reformers in the past established their moral authority by responding to their adversaries with mercy and charity. When they faced tribulations with patience and fortitude, their authority was enhanced in the eyes of the church. Conversely, moral or spiritual failures detract from a reformer's authority as can be seen in the careers of Jean Gerson and Jan Hus. Both men had a great deal of virtue and accomplished much, but Gerson's lack of mercy and Hus's lack of prudence limited the reach of their reforms.

Fourth, they emphasized the legitimacy of diversity within the unity of the church. This was particularly helpful for responding to internecine fighting among different reform groups. The great reformers like Bernard of Clairvaux or Catherine of Siena insisted that their followers accept the truth that not everyone in the church was going to follow their path, employ their methods, or have their concerns. After stressing this point to their own disciples, they also tactfully reminded the reformers who were opposing them to embrace legitimate diversity. This strategy helped to bring various groups and organizations together and to limit the destructive tendency of reform movements to attack each other.

Fifth, they accepted that the church is comprised of flawed human beings. By making it clear that they loved the church as a visible, organic society on earth, they disarmed many of their opponents. This strategy was also important because it dismissed romantic or idealistic notions or attitudes about the church, and it worked to persuade people to see that adherence to abstractions and rigid ideologies impeded solutions to practical problems.

Finally, and most significantly, they linked institutional, legal, organizational, or social reforms to the conversion of hearts. Institutions, laws, and organizations can only be effective if people embrace their goals, implement the measures necessary to prevent complacency, and take responsibility for their role in the ongoing reform of the church. They believed that the ultimate measure of accountability is found in the great commandment: to love God with all of your heart and soul and to love your neighbor as yourself. The mission of the church, the care of souls, emerges out of this commandment to love.

The reformers' commitment to the idea that we will be held accountable for truly loving God and our neighbors reveals the fundamental problem facing the Catholic Church today, namely, that there are serious problems with accountability throughout the orders of the Catholic Church. The notion of accountability to God and neighbor was traditionally grounded in the spiritual gift of the fear of the Lord. Unfortunately, the connection between fear of the Lord and accountability has largely been severed in current magisterial teaching.[1]

Traditionally, the fear of the Lord did not simply mean that God was grand or awesome; instead, it was interpreted in light of the scriptural and creedal affirmations that Christ will return as judge. Because they believed in the authority of scripture, they held that the measure of the final judgment will be whether we loved God with all our heart and our neighbors as ourselves. They accepted that those who fail to commit themselves to love and mercy will be punished, as Christ warned, even for the thoughtless words they use (Matt 13:36). Fear of the Lord gave the reformers the courage to obey God rather than people, customs, laws, or institutions; and, at the same time, it kept them from making their ideas and agendas absolute. While there are many issues that need to be addressed in the church today, the loss of any sense of accountability seems to be one of the root causes behind the current crisis facing the church over sexual abuse.

Peter Damian warned that a cleric who lacked the fear of God could only be restrained by the fear of losing his position. This principle has been applied to priests who have abused minors, but it has not been applied to the bishops and leaders of religious orders who knowingly moved sexual predators from parish to parish or between dioceses. Their actions demonstrated that they did not understand the mission of the church and that they lacked a sense of accountability before God. Just as we have zero tolerance for such priests, Peter Damian advised we should have zero tolerance for such bishops. To restore credibility, the leaders must be held most accountable to the church's mission and should be punished most publicly for their sins against the community. If they refuse to reform themselves, which seems to be the case, then Peter Damian advised the laity to collaborate with members of the religious orders and with reform-minded clergy to strip them of their authority and power.

How can we reform the bishops if they refuse to reform themselves? Since they seem to be unaccountable under canon law and since the popes have been unwilling to discipline them, we need to write secular laws that will put bishops into prison if they conspire to cover up such crimes. This will have the effect of removing such bishops from ministry without involving canon law. This would be a more effective strategy for reforming the bishops because suing dioceses and withholding donations will not deter most bishops. Such lawsuits have no effect on them personally. When they are sued, bishops just cut resources going to the poor, fire lay employees, sell off their diocesan patrimonies, and ask for more money to balance their budgets. Others simply declare bankruptcy, but you can be certain that bankrupt bishops have a much more comfortable lifestyle than most Catholics. Finally, this approach would prevent Rome from spiriting wicked bishops, like Cardinal Law of Boston, away from the consequences of their actions.

The problem with passing new laws in the church such as the Dallas Charter and setting up institutions like the National Lay Review Board is that the bishops have wide jurisdictional powers to dispense with canon law and to ignore review boards. The unwillingness of the bishops to have any checks on their governance of the church was most shockingly revealed to me in the fourth draft of the new *Program for Priestly Formation,* which was given to me for review in August 2003. The document provided a list of reasons to refuse to admit a man to the seminary and to holy orders. It included items such as insanity, heresy, abusing drugs and alcohol, self-mutilation, and sexually abusing minors. Immediately after listing these impediments to admission, the document stated: "If any of these conditions exist, then prior to admission, appropriate dispensations must be obtained or appropriate remedies must be applied."[2]

While I have been assured that the loophole for child molesters has been closed, it is significant that this document was drafted a year after the Dallas Charter was passed and two years after the sexual-abuse scandal broke in the papers. The fact that some bishops were able to insert a loophole for sex offenders into this draft and that the rest of the bishops failed either to notice or to protest exposes perniciousness, sloth, and blind presumption. In fact, there is nothing protecting dioceses from unworthy priests other than the whims of the local bishop.

Problems with accountability are evident in the priesthood as well. This can be seen in many areas, including the preparation of homilies, parish administration, and in personal behavior; but the clearest example that they fear adversity more than they fear the Lord is their complicity in the sexual-abuse scandal. The bishops were not alone in covering up crimes and transferring predators. Many of our priests knew what was happening and failed to stand up against the unjust policies of the bishops. As the great reformers have shown us, priests have a duty to speak out publicly when their ecclesiastical superiors are sinning in a way that will cause scandal. They cannot justify their failure to speak out by pointing to obedience. Bishop's have no right to command their priests to sin and most priests know this principle very well.

The effects of losing our sense of accountability can also be seen in the activities of the laity and the religious. As Christians, we have a duty to be discerning when it comes to our leaders. By teaching our children that they should always obey priests and bishops, both parents and those who had teaching roles left generations of our people vulnerable to abuse and manipulation. Like the priests, there were many laypeople and members of the orders who allowed this scandal to unfold by their silence. They worked in diocesan or parish offices, as therapists, as lawyers, as social workers, and as judges. Rather than bringing the abuses to light, the laity and the religious have their own share of responsibility for the scandal. Again, their sin was to fear the bishops and not the Lord.

For the victims, the loss of the sense of accountability to God makes it more difficult to heal their wounds. God's justice is a mercy for those who have suffered real evil. It is trusting in God's justice that allows us, over time, to let go of anger and pain. A deep appreciation of humanity's accountability before God can even lead people to imitate Christ by weeping over the sins of those who hurt them. Divine justice teaches us that we must attempt to save those who have sinned against us.

This is not to say, however, that the priests and bishops who have betrayed us can avoid being strongly disciplined by being stripped of their ecclesial offices and required to make public satisfaction for their sins. If they refuse to correct themselves, then the laity and the religious must act to reform them before they squander the rest of our remaining resources in addition to their spent credibility. Ultimately, we should aim to restore episcopal credibility rather than to subvert it, to aid the bishops by making them accountable, and to restore a proper sense of unity between the clergy and the rest of the church.

While our current crisis over accountability calls for the disciplinary approach of a Peter Damian, it is more likely to succeed if it is employed in conjunction with other traditional approaches to reform. Some of us will have to employ the gentle approach of a Clare of Assisi while others may follow Catherine of Siena's example of publicly shaming the bishops. Theologians can follow Newman's example by attacking the corrupt magisterial teachings underpinning resistance to reform; and negotiators with diplomatic skills, such as Gasparo Contarini, can contribute by coordinating different reform movements so that they do not set off on collision courses with one another. Leaders like Dorothy Day need to continue to remind us not to lose sight of the mission to change people's lives for the better through our direct service to them and to remember that we must reach out beyond the church to fight injustice.

The imperfections of the church and of its members should not surprise or scandalize us. Jesus Christ warned us to expect ongoing problems and wicked members of the church. Even as we work to address sin in the church, the Messiah taught us to leave judgment to him. To console those who have been wronged and to urge people to convert, Christ vividly drew out the consequences of malice and complacency with his parables. Reformers should keep the Lord's description of the church in mind to avoid presumption and discouragement:

> Again, the kingdom of heaven is like a net that was thrown into the sea, and caught fish of every kind; when it was full, they drew it ashore, sat down, and put the good into baskets but threw out the bad. So it will be at the end of the age. The angels will come out and separate the evil from the righteous and throw them into the furnace of fire, where there will be weeping and gnashing of teeth. (Matt 13:47–50 NRSV)

The fact that the pilgrim church contains both the bad and the ugly within her communal life is no reason to lose heart and to reject her ability to fulfill her mission, nor should the mixed nature of the church lead us to despair of ever experiencing the healing sweetness of justice.

Even as we struggle with ongoing problems, we should not lose sight of the progress we have made. Over time, we have deepened our understanding of the meaning of conversion and how far it extends. Certainly we must continue to move forward because a fragile hanging ladder, as Bernard of Clairvaux put it, is no place to stand still. Either we move forward or we fall away. One thing is sure: God will continue to call his church to an ever-deeper conversion and an ever-clearer conformity to the selfless gifts of love revealed in the trinitarian life and the incarnation. New reform initiatives may take some time to digest, but we believe as an article of faith that legitimate expressions of Christ's call to repent and to embrace the hope of salvation will be assimilated into the body by the action of the Spirit, and will ultimately lead the church to experience the fontal fullness of the Father's love.

ℜotes

Introduction

1. *Lumen gentium*, 8, in *Decrees of the Ecumenical Councils*, vol. 2, ed. Norman P. Tanner (Washington, DC: Georgetown University, 1990), 855: "...ecclesia in proprio sinu peccatores complectens, sancta simul et semper purificanda, poenitentiam et renovationem continuo prosequitur."

2. This recognition of the need for reform was stated in *Unitatis redintegratio*, 6, in *Decrees of the Ecumenical Councils*, vol. 2, ed. Norman P. Tanner (Washington, DC: Georgetown University, 1990), 913: "In its pilgrimage on earth Christ summons the church to continual reformation, of which it is always in need, insofar as it is an institution of human beings here on earth."

3. Yves M.-J. Congar, *Vraie et fausse réforme dans l'église* (Paris: Les Éditions Du Cerf, 1950), 57, note 50.

4. Ibid., 7–12, 49–54. Congar provided some specific examples of things that could be improved such as simplifying the liturgy, establishing a better connection between the needs of the people and preaching, and reinvigorating the exterior forms of pastoral organizations. He also extended this idea to social structures.

5. Ibid., 34–35.

6. Cited from Congar, *Vraie et fausse réforme*, 37.

7. Ibid., 39–43. The four characteristics of true or actual reform must be distinguished from the four conditions for reform without schism that Congar discussed later, which include the following: primacy of charity and pastoral care, maintaining communion, preserving patience in the face of delays, and a return to tradition. For more information, see Congar, *Vraie et fausse réforme*, 231–352. I accept the vital importance of charity and the other conditions for avoiding schism.

8. For a recent example of the ongoing influence of *Vraie et fausse réforme*, see Avery Cardinal Dulles, "True and False Reform," *First Things: A Monthly Journal of Religion and Public Life* 135 (August/September, 2003): 14–19.

9. Peter Damian's name does come up in Congar's text, but none of his works or ideas are cited and he is not included in the index. For an example, see Congar, *Vraie et fausse réforme*, 248.

10. See Gerhard B. Ladner, "Gregory the Great and Gregory VII: A Comparison of Their Concepts of Renewal," *Viator* 4 (1973): 1–27.

1. Gregory the Great

1. The citations of the various imperial laws are drawn from the first chapter of John Meyendorff's *Imperial Unity and Christian Divisions: The Church 450–680 A.D.* (Crestwood, NY: St. Vladimir's Seminary Press, 1989), 5–38. The critical edition for the decrees is *Theodosiani libri xvi cum constitutionibus Sirmondianis et leges novellae ad Theodosianum pertinentes*, 2 vol., ed. T. Mommsen and D. M. Meyer (Berlin, 1954).

2. Jeffrey Richards, *Consul of God: The Life and Times of Gregory the Great* (London: Routledge & Kegan Paul, 1980), 109. This has become the standard biography for St. Gregory and was the source of most of the biographical material in this chapter.

3. Ibid., 230.

4. Gregory the Great, *Pastoral Care*, 2.6. The critical edition is *Règle pastorale / Grégoire le Grand*, ed. Floribert Rommel, trans. Charles Morel (Paris: Editions du Cerf, 1992). The English translation is *Pastoral Care*, trans. Henry Davis (New York: Newman, 1950). See also *Moralia in Job*, 21.15.22. The critical edition for the *Moralia is S. Gregorii Magni opera: Moralia in Job libri i–x*, ed. Marci Adriaen, *Corpus Christianorum series Latina*, vol. 143 (Turnholt, Belgium: 1979). There is an English translation that is more than a little archaic in style: *Morals on the Book of Job by St. Gregory the Great* (Oxford and London: Parker & Rivington, 1844–50).

5. As evidence of this wealth and its potential for abuse, Meyendorff pointed to St. Cyril of Alexandria's use of up to 2,500 pounds of ecclesial gold to bribe Roman officials to drop charges against him for acts of brutality to his opponents. Meyendorff, *Imperial Unity and Christian Divisions*, 14.

6. Ibid., 17–18.

7. John Chrysostom, *Six Books on the Priesthood*, trans. Graham Neville (Crestwood, NY: St. Vladimir's Seminary Press, 1996). The works of Chrysostom are widely available in translation in the following series: *A Select Library of the Nicene and Post-Nicene Fathers of the Christian Church*, ed. Philip Schaff (Grand Rapids, MI: W. R. Eerdmans, 1956). This series will hereafter be cited as *NPNF*. Gregory of Nazianzus, Orations, 1–2, vol. 7, *NPNF*, 203–27. Dionysius the Areopagite's *Ecclesiastical Hierarchy and Celestial Hierarchy* was pivotal to developments concerning the nature and the purpose of the church in the Middle Ages. The critical edition for all of

Dionysius's works is *Corpus Dionysiacum/ Pseudo-Dionysius Areopagita*, ed. Beate Regina Suchla (Berlin: de Gruyter, 1990). The English translation is *Pseudo-Dionysius: The Complete Works*, trans. by Colm Luibheid (New York: Paulist Press, 1987).

8. The accounts of these events can be found in Joannes Diaconus, *Vita Gregorii*, 1.39–40 and Gregory of Tours, *Historia Francorum*, 10.1. The best Latin editions for source work are *Vita Gregorii Magni*, ed. J. P. Migne, *Patrologia cursus completus series Latina*, vol. 75 (Paris: 1841–64), 59–242; *Historia Francorum*, ed. Wilhelm Arndt, *Monumenta Germaniae historica scriptores rerum Merovingicarum*, vol. 1 (Hanover: Impensis Bibliopolii Hahniani, 1885). There is a translation of Gregory of Tours's work: The *History of the Franks, by Gregory of Tours*, trans. O. M. Dalton (Oxford: Clarendon Press, 1927). Jeffrey Richards has a discussion as to why Gregory of Tours is more credible than the later accounts in *Consul of God*, 42.

9. Richards, *Consul of God*, 16.

10. Ibid., 81.

11. Gregory the Great, *Forty Gospel Homilies*, trans. Dom David Hurst (Kalamazoo, MI: Cistercian Publications, 1990), 147. The critical edition is Gregory the Great, *Homiliae in Evangelia*, ed and trans. Raymond Etaix, *Corpus Christianorum Latinorum*, vol. 141 (Turnhout: Brepols, 1999). The Latin text is also available in vol. 76 of the *Patrologia Latina*. Since the numbering of the homilies in the Latin and English editions differ, I am simply referring to the page numbers of the English edition.

12. Gregory the Great, *Moralia*, 1.3.3.

13. Bernard McGinn, *The Growth of Mysticism: Gregory the Great through the 12th Century*, vol. 2, *The Presence of God: A History of Western Christian Mysticism* (New York: The Crossroad Publishing Company, 1999), 77. This work is a great starting point for research due to the extensive notes. Some of the material in this section was originally published in "Bonaventure and the Sin of the Church," *Theological Studies* 63 (2002): 667-89.

14. Gregory the Great, *Moralia*, 9.11.15: "Urgente etenim mundi fine, superna scientia proficit et largius cum tempore excrescit."

15. John Cassian, *Conferences*, 14.8. The translation is from *John Cassian Conferences*, trans. Colm Luibheid (New York: Paulist Press, 1985), 161.

16. Augustine, *De doctrina christiana* (hereafter cited as *De doctrina*), 3.31.44–3.32.45. The critical edition is Augustine, *De doctrina christiana*, ed. J. Martin, *Corpus Christianorum Latinorum* 32 (Turnholt, Belgium: 1962), 1–167. I am working from the new translation: Augustine, *Teaching Christianity: De doctrina christiana*, trans. Edmund Hill, OP, ed. John E. Rotelle, OSA (Hyde Park, NY: New City Press, 1996). Augustine described

the spotless bride this way: "Ecclesia quippe sine macula et ruga, ex omnibus gentibus congregata atque in aeternum regnatura cum Christo, ipsa est terra beatorum, terra viventium, ipsa intellegenda est patribus data, quando eis certa et inmutabili dei voluntate promissa est, quoniam ipsa promissionis vel praedestinationis firmitate iam data est, quae danda suo tempore a patribus credita est, sicut de ipsa gratia, quae sanctis datur…. Datam dixit gratiam, quando nec erant adhuc quibus daretur, quoniam in dispositione ac praedestinatione dei iam factum erat quod suo tempore futurum fuerat, quod esse dicit manifestatam. Quamuis haec possint intellegi et de terra futuri saeculi, quando erit caelum novum et terra nova, in qua iniusti habitare non poterunt" (*De doctrina*, 3.34.49).

17 See Gregory the Great, *Moralia*, 1.26.37.

18. Ibid., 3.18.33–3.19.35, 4.11.18.

19. Gregory the Great, *Forty Gospel Homilies*, 343–46.

20. Gregory the Great, *Moralia*, 3.24.47.

21. Bernhard Schimmelpfennig notes that the *defensores* were minor clerics who were able to marry in *The Papacy*, trans. James Sievert (New York: Columbia University Press, 1992), 60–61. This book gives an excellent historical account of institutional developments within the papacy.

22. Richards, *Consul of God*, 111.

23. Ibid., 114–15. Richards develops a full account of these issues and others in his biography.

24. Ibid., 116–17.

25. Ibid., 141.

26. Ibid., 57.

27. Gregory the Great, *Forty Gospel Homilies*, 30.

28. Ibid., 32.

29. Richards, *Consul of God*, 96.

30. Gregory the Great, *Pastoral Care*, 2.7.

31. Richards, *Consul of God*, 96.

32. Gregory the Great, Epistle 1.36 and 3.5 (*NPNF*). There is a newer translation that was published after I finished my research: Gregory the Great, *The Letters of Gregory the Great*, trans. John R.C. Martyn (Toronto: Pontifical Institute of Medieval Studies, 2004). The critical edition is *S. Gregorii Magni registrum epistularum libri*, ed. Dag Norberg, *Corpus Christianorum series Latina*, vol. 140–140A (Turnhout: Brepols, 1982). See also Jeffrey Richards, *Consul of God*, 90.

33. Gregory the Great, Epistle 5.41 (*NPNF*).

34. Gregory the Great, *Pastoral Care*, 2.4. Part one of this work is full of warnings about bad pastors.

35. Some examples of warnings about false leaders in the church in the Pastoral Epistles include: Romans 12:1–21; 2 Corinthians 11:1–15;

Colossians 2:6–23; 1 Timothy 1:3–11, 4:1–5, 6:1–10; 2 Timothy 3:1–9; 2 Peter 2:1–22; 1 John 2:18–28, 4:1–21; and Jude 1:1–23.

36. Gregory the Great, *Pastoral Care*, 1.2.
37. Gregory the Great, *Forty Gospel Homilies*, 148.
38. Gregory the Great, *Pastoral Care*, 2.2.
39. Ibid., 2.2–3.
40. Ibid., 2.4.
41. Ibid., 2.4, 2.8.
42. Ibid., 2.8.
43. Ibid., 2.6.
44. Ibid., 2.6. Bernard McGinn has an excellent but brief discussion of Gregory's understanding of ecclesiology in his *Growth of Mysticism*, 43–45.
45. See Conrad Leyser, "Expertise and Authority in Gregory the Great: The Social Function of Peritia," in *Gregory the Great: A Symposium*, ed. John C. Cavadini (Notre Dame and London: University of Notre Dame Press, 1995), 38–61. I found this article quite helpful for clarifying issues surrounding the apologetics of humility.
46. Gregory the Great, *Moralia*, 7.35.53–54.
47. Gregory the Great, *Pastoral Care*, 3.4.
48. Gregory the Great, *Moralia*, 7.35.53.
49. Ibid., preface.5.12—6.13.
50. Gregory the Great, *Forty Gospel Homilies*, 83. For a discussion of how adversity brings the virtues to light, see *Moralia*, preface.2.6. Gregory explained the importance of patience in *Pastoral Care*, 3.9.
51. Gregory the Great, *Moralia*, 3.24.47—3.26.50.
52. Gregory the Great, *Pastoral Care*, 3.4.
53. Gregory the Great, *Moralia*, 3.11.19.
54. Carole Straw, *Gregory the Great: Perfection in Imperfection* (Berkeley, CA: University of California Press, 1988), 201–4.
55. Gregory the Great, *Pastoral Care*, 3.28; *Forty Gospel Homilies*, 140; *Moralia*, preface.5.12. For lay authorities and the church, see Richards *Consul of God*, 219.
56. Gregory the Great, *Pastoral care*, 3.4.
57. For more information on the bond of love, see Carole Straw, *Gregory the Great: Perfection in Imperfection*, 91–105.
58. Gregory the Great, *Pastoral Care*, 3.9.

2. Peter Damian: The Doctor of Reform

1. Though canon law was seen as having absolute authority, the diversity of laws had led people to assume it was impossible to observe them. Abbot Siegfried of Gorze wrote in 1043: "[I]t is sure and undoubtedly true

that the authority of the canons is the law of God." The quote is from Colin Morris, *The Papal Monarchy: The Western Church from 1050–1250* (Oxford: Clarendon Press, 1989), 30–31. Heinrich Fichtenau points out that the general attitude in the tenth and early part of the eleventh centuries was that it was impossible to follow all the details of canon law in *Living in the Tenth Century: Mentalities and Social Orders*, trans. Patrick J. Geary (Chicago: The University of Chicago Press, 1991), 118. Much of the material in this chapter was originally published in "When Magisterium Becomes Imperium: Peter Damian on the Accountability of Bishops for Scandal," *Theological Studies* 65 (December 2004): 741–66.

2. Morris has an extensive discussion of the roots of the reform movement in the first chapter of *The Papal Monarchy*.

3. Morris, *The Papal Monarchy*, 103.

4. Peter Damian, Letter 61.3. All the English translations of the letters are from the series Peter Damian: Letters, vol. 1–7, trans. Owen J. Blum and Irven M. Resnick, *The Fathers of the Church: Medieval Continuation* (Washington, DC: The Catholic University of America Press, 1989–2005). I have largely followed Blum's translation except where inclusive-language issues arise. The numbering of the letters in the translation follows the critical edition *Die Briefe des Petrus Damiani*, ed. Kurt Reindel, *Monumenta Germaniae historica: Die Briefe der deutschen Kaiserzeit*, vol. 1–4, (1983). The critical edition will be cited as *MGH*. I will provide the pages and the volume of the critical edition in addition to the English translation when I provide the Latin in the notes.

5. Peter Damian, Letter, 61.4: "Porro autem nos contra divina mandata personarum acceptores in minoribus quidem sacerdotibus luxuriae iniquinamenta persequimur, in episcopis autem, quod nimis absurdem est, per silentii tolerantiam veneramur" (*MGH*, vol. 2, 208–9).

6. Morris, *The Papal Monarchy*, 45.

7. Ibid., 83.

8. Bernard Schimmelpfennig, *The Papacy*, trans. James Sievert (New York: Columbia University Press, 1992), 139.

9. Ibid., 138–39.

10. Peter Damian, Letter 65.5.

11. See Morris, *The Papal Monarchy*, 87, and Schimmelpfennig, *The Papacy*, 132–33.

12. See, for example, John Calvin, "Prefatory Address to His Most Christian Majesty," in the first edition of the *Institutes of the Christian Religion*, or Martin Luther, "Article Four," in the *Smalcald Articles*. For an excellent treatment of the problem, see George Tavard, *Holy Writ or Holy Church: The Crisis of the Protestant Reformation* (London: Burns & Oates, 1959).

13. Tavard, *Holy Writ or Holy Church*, 196–209. The fathers at the Council of Trent limited tradition to matters of apostolic faith on faith and morals in the first decree of the fourth session of the council. They deliberately excluded disciplinary matters, which compose canon law, from the authority of tradition.

14. Owen J. Blum, *St. Peter Damian: His Teaching on the Spiritual Life* (Washington, DC: The Catholic University of America Press, 1947), 19–22.

15. Morris, *The Papal Monarchy*, 90–94.

16. Ibid., 92.

17. Peter Damian, Letter 31.7: "Et nisi quantocius sedis apostolicae vigor occurrat, non est dubium, quin effrenata nequitia cum restringi voluerit, a cursus sui impetu desistere nequeat" (*MGH*, vol. 1, 287).

18. Peter Damian, Letter 31.7. Peter associated the language of satanic rule with the bishop's role in either commanding boys and men under his authority to commit acts of sodomy or in allowing his priests to do so.

19. Peter Damian, Letter 31.50. He is taking this idea directly out of Gregory the Great, *Pastoral Care*, 1.10–11. The critical edition is *Règle pastorale / Grégoire le Grand*, ed. Floribert Rommel, trans. Charles Morel (Paris: Editions du Cerf, 1992). The English translation is *Pastoral Care*, trans. Henry Davis (New York: Newman, 1950).

20. Peter Damian, Letter 31.50–58. See Gregory the Great, *Pastoral Care*, 1.11, 2.2.

21. Jean LeClerq, *Saint Pierre Damien: ermite et homme d'église* (Roma: 1960), 68–69.

22. Peter Damian, Letter 40.76–77.

23. Peter Damian, Letter 31.9:"Quae proculdubio impia pietas non vulnus amputat, sed ut augeatur, fomitem subministrat, non perpetrati illiciti ausus praebet amaritudinem, sed perpetrandi potius tribuit libertatem. Carnalis quippe cuiuslibet ordinis clericus formidolosius expavescit in conspectu hominum despici, quam in superni iudicis examine condemnari. Ac per hoc mavult quamlibet districtae, quamlibet annosae penitentiae, quam sui gradus periculo subiacere. Et dum per indiscretam discretionem non timet statum sui honoris amittere, incitatur ad inexperta praesumere et in hiis, quae inulte praesumpsit, diutius permanere, atque, ut ita dixerim, dum illic non feritur, ubi acrius dolet, in eo quo semel corruit, coenosae obscoenitatis volutabro molliter iacet" (*MGH*, vol. 1, 288).

24. Peter Damian, Letter 31.13–14.

25. Peter Damian, Letter 31.18.

26. Peter Damian, Letter 31.21–22.

27. Peter Damian, Letter 31.25; Letter 61.11.

28. Peter Damian, Letter 31.25.

29. Peter Damian, Letter 31.38. Peter is citing Burchard of Worms, *Decretorum libri xx*, 17.35. The only printed edition that I am aware of is in J. P. Migne, *Patrologia cursus completus series Latina*, vol. 140 (Paris: 1841–64), 537–1058.

30. Peter Damian, Letter 31.39–40.

31. Peter Damian, Letter 31.4: "Sed nos humanius agentes eos, qui vel propriis manibus vel invicem inter se semen egerunt vel etiam inter femora ceciderunt, et non longo usu nec cum pluribus, si voluptatem renfrenaverint et digna penitudine probrosa commissa luerint, admitti ad eosdem gradus, in quibus in scelere manentes non permanentes fuerant, divinae miserationi confisi volumus atque etiam iubemus, ablata aliis spe recuperationis sui ordinis, qui vel per longa tempora secum sive cum aliis vel cum pluribus brevi licet tempore, quolibet duorum feditatis genere, quae descripseras, maculati sunt, vel, quod est horrendum dictu et auditu, in terga prolapsi sunt" (*MGH*, vol.1, 286).

32. Peter Damian, Letter 61.13.

33. Peter Damian, Letter 61.14.

34. Peter Damian, Letter 61.4. See also Letter 40, Letter 112, and Letter 162.

35. Peter Damian, Letter 61.4.

36. Peter Damian, Letter 61.9. For his source, see Gregory the Great, *Commentary on Kings*, 9.215.

37. Peter Damian, Letter 61.9.

38. Schimmelpfennig, *The Papacy*, 132.

39. Peter Damian, Letter 40.4: "Qui enim divini muneris non Deo sed homini se debitores existimant, tamquam a sui fontis irrigatione siccati necesse est, ut deficientes arescant" (*MGH*, vol. 1, 394).

40. Peter Damian, Letter 40.5. See Augustine, *Homilies on the Gospel According to St. John*, 6.6 and 7.3. The critical edition is *In Iohannis evangelium tractatus CXXIV*, in *Corpus Christianorum series Latina*, vol. 36, (Turnholt: Brepols, 1954), 56–68.

41. Peter Damian, Letter 40.5.

42. Peter Damian, Letter 40.76–77.

43. For more information on this group see R. I. Moore, *The Origins of European Dissent* (London: Basil Blackwell Ltd., 1985; repr., Toronto: University of Toronto Press, 1994), 52–63. The Patarines became more radical over time and eventually ended up as heretics.

44. Schimmelpfennig, *The Papacy*, 141.

45. Peter Damian, Letter 65.12.

46. Peter Damian, Letter 65.10.

47. Peter Damian, Letter 65.12.

48. Peter Damian, Letter 65.26.

49. Moore, *The Origins of European Dissent*, 61.

50. Blum has argued Peter's opposition to the idea that the clergy are not accountable to the laity was a consistent component of his theology. He provided evidence that Peter was not opposed to the intervention of secular, political power in regard to episcopal nominations and that he was not even opposed to lay investiture as long as simony was not involved. See Blum, *St. Peter Damian*, 22, 173. LeClerq has also noted the very active and collaborative role of the laity in Peter's reform theology in *Saint Pierre Damien*, 111–17. Morris focused on Peter's acceptance of the legitimacy of lay investiture as an issue that drove a wedge between Peter and Hildebrand, who became Pope Gregory VII, in *The Papal Monarchy*, 94–107. There are, however, some recent scholars who interpret Peter Damian as being hostile to the laity and to reform. Michel Grandjean has argued that Peter Damian was globally hostile to the laity in *Laïcs dans l'église: regards de Pierre Damien, Anselme de Cantorbéry, Yves de Chartres* (Paris: Beauchesne, 1994), 50–51. Phyllis Jestice claimed Peter was actually an opponent of pastoral reform because he contended that hermits and monks should not take up the mission of preaching. See Phyllis Jestice, "Peter Damian Against the Reformers," in *The Joy of Learning and the Love of God: Studies in Honor of Jean LeClerq*, ed. E. Rozanne Elder (Kalamazoo, MI: Cistercian Publications, 1995) 67–94. Schimmelpfennig, on the other hand, writes that it would be wrong to imagine these hermits as persons who had completely turned their backs to the world and that they were reforming by gathering supporters, over whom they had influence, in *The Papacy*, 139.

51. Peter Damian, Letter 40.109–14.

52. Blum, *St. Peter Damian*, 27.

53. Peter Damian, Letter 54.12–16.

54. Peter Damian, Letter 54.13. The scripture translation is from the New Revised Standard Version.

55. Peter Damian, Letter 54.13.

56. Peter Damian, Letter 54.14–16.

57. Peter Damian, Letter 114.2.

58. Peter Damian, Letter 114.2.

59. Peter Damian, Letter 114.4.

60. Peter Damian, Letter 114.5–8.

61. Peter Damian, Letter 114.8.

62. Peter Damian, Letter 114.9.

63. Peter Damian, Letter 87.8.

3. Bernard of Clairvaux:
The Impossible Reformer

1. Bernard of Clairvaux, Letter 80.10 (78). Bernard is quoting Gregory the Great, *Homilies on Ezekiel*, Homily 7. All the English translations of the letters are from *The Letters of St. Bernard of Clairvaux*, trans. Bruno Scott James (Kalamazoo, MI: Cistercian Press, 1998; first edition, London: Burns and Oates, 1953). The critical edition for all Bernard's works is S. *Bernardi opera*, vol. 1–8, ed. Jean Leclercq and Henri Rochais (Rome: Editiones Cistercienses, 1957–77). The translation and the critical edition have different systems for numbering letters. Further, the two editions of James's translation have different page numbers. As a result, I decided to follow James's system of numbering the letters, which is consistent between the English translations. Further, I have placed the critical edition's number for the letter in parentheses when the number of the critical edition differs. I have checked the accuracy of the cross-referenced list in the English edition, and it is usually accurate; however, it is not accurate in this case. This letter is supposed to be 365 in the critical edition, but it is not.

2. Bernard of Clairvaux, Letter 80.7 (78).

3. Jean Leclercq is an exception to this tendency. He linked Bernard's impossible nature to his success in reform work in "St. Bernard on the Church," *The Downside Review*, vol. 85 (July 1967): 274–94. A more recent study that emphasized Bernard's reforming career is Gerhard B. Winkler, *Bernard von Clairvaux: Die eine und umfassende Kirche—Einheit in der Vielfalt* (Innsbruck: Tyrolia, 2001), 57–73. The limitation with Winkler's study is that it essentially approaches Bernard's reform efforts in light of Reformation-era categories.

4. Gerhard B. Ladner, "Terms and Ideas of Renewal," in *Renaissance and Renewal in the Twelfth Century*, ed. Robert L. Benson, Giles Constable, and Carol D. Lanham (Cambridge, MA: Harvard University Press, 1982; repr., Toronto: University of Toronto Press, 1999) 14–15.

5. Bernard of Clairvaux, *Sermons on the Song of Songs*, 33.15. Cited from Franz Posset, *Pater Bernhardus: Martin Luther and Bernard of Clairvaux* (Kalamazoo, MI: Cistercian Publications, 1999), 344. The standard English translation is Bernard of Clairvaux, *On the Song of Songs*, trans. Kilian Walsh and Irene M. Edmonds, 4 vols. (Kalamazoo, MI: Cistercian Publications, 1971–79).

6. Bernard of Clairvaux, *Sermons on the Song of Songs*, 33.16.

7. Bernard of Clairvaux, Letter 218.1 (178).

8. Bernard of Clairvaux, *On Consideration*, preface. The translation I am using is *Five Books On Consideration: Advice to a Pope*, trans. John D.

Anderson and Elizabeth T. Keenan (Kalamazoo, MI: Cistercian Publications, 1976).

9. Bernard of Clairvaux, Letter 94 (91).

10. Ibid.

11. Ibid.

12. See Jean Leclercq, "The Renewal of Theology," in *Renaissance and Renewal in the Twelfth Century*, 78–79, 84–85; Bernard McGinn, *The Growth of Mysticism: Gregory the Great through the 12th Century*, vol. 2, *The Presence of God: A History of Western Christian Mysticism* (New York: The Crossroad Publishing Company, 1999), 165–77; and Marsha L. Dutton, "Intimacy and Imitation: The Humanity of Christ in Cistercian Spirituality," in *Erudition in God's Service*, ed. John Sommerfeldt (Kalamazoo, MI: Cistercian Publications, 1987) 33–69.

13. Bernard of Clairvaux, *On Consideration*, 3.5, 4.5. Discussing the pope's legal ability to grant exemptions in dioceses other than Rome, Bernard expressed his doubts about the law's validity. See *On Consideration*, 3.16: "It is not a good tree that produces such fruit: arrogance, dissoluteness, dissipation, deception, scandal, hatred, and what is cause for greater grief, serious hostility and discord among the churches.… Forgive me, but I am not easily convinced that this is lawful which produces so many unlawful results."

14. For more information, see G. R. Evans, *The Mind of St. Bernard of Clairvaux* (Oxford: Clarendon Press, 1983), 138–47; Edward Little, "Bernard and Abelard at the Council of Sens, 1140," in *Bernard of Clairvaux: Studies Presented to Dom Jean Leclercq*, ed. M. Basil Pennington (Washington, DC: Cistercian Publications, 1973), 55–71.

15. Leclercq, "Saint Bernard on the Church," 284–86.

16. Ibid., 280–81.

17. Colin Morris, *The Papal Monarchy: The Western Church from 1050–1250* (Oxford: Clarendon Press, 1989), 36–38.

18. Ibid., 60–62.

19. See Chrysogonus Waddell, "Reform of the Liturgy," in *Renaissance and Renewal in the Twelfth Century*, 99–107.

20. My description of the medieval bishop is drawn from Bernard's treatise *On the Duties of Bishops*, which is Letter 42 in the critical edition. James's translation does not contain this letter, but there is a partial translation in Jean Leclercq, *Bernard of Clairvaux and the Cistercian Spirit*, trans. Claire Lavoie (Kalamazoo, MI: Cistercian Publications, 1976), 138–41. A new translation of the whole letter is available in *Bernard of Clairvaux: On Baptism and the Office of Bishops*, trans. Pauline Matarasso (Kalamazoo, MI: Cistercian Publicatons, 2004).

21. Bernard of Clairvaux, *On Consideration*, 3.4–3.5.

22. Ladner, "Terms and Ideas of Renewal," 2. See also Giles Constable, "Renewal and Reform in Religious Life," in *Renaissance and Renewal in the Twelfth Century*, 38–39.

23. Giles Constable, "Renewal and Reform in Religious Life," 39–41. Constable's source is Gerhard B. Ladner, "Erneuerung," *Reallexikon für Antike und Christentum*, vol. 6 (1966), 259–60.

24. I am drawing from Bernard McGinn, *The Growth of Mysticism*, 159–60. McGinn's notes provide extensive references to secondary sources. There are two general sources that place the Cistercians in their context. McGinn particularly recommended: Louis J. Lekai, *The Cistercians: Ideals and Reality* (Kent State, OH: Kent State University Press, 1977) and Jean Leclercq, *Monks and Love in Twelfth-Century France* (Oxford: The Clarendon Press, 1979). Colin Morris is also a very helpful source for placing the Cistercians in the broader historical context.

25. McGinn, *The Growth of Mysticism*, 159.

26. Bernard recited a list of charges against the Cistercians in *Apologia*, 1.1. The English translation is "An Apologia to Abbot William," in *The Works of Bernard of Clairvaux: Treatises I*, ed. M. Basil Pennington, trans. Michael Casey (Spencer, MA: Cistercian Publications, 1970) 33–72. The treatise has an extended introduction by Leclercq that is quite helpful.

27. See George Conklin, "Law, Reform, and the Origins of Persecution: Stephen of Tournai and the Order of Grandmont," *Medieval Studies* 61 (1999): 107–36.

28. Bernard of Clairvaux, *Apologia*, 3.5. In medieval exegesis, Noah was a figure that was seen to represent the clergy, Daniel the monks, and Job the laity. In the notes to the English translation, Michael Casey identified the source for this idea in Gregory the Great's exegesis of Ezekiel 14:14.

29. Bernard of Clairvaux, *Apologia*, 4.7. This idea was well grounded in the *Celestial Hierarchy* and the *Ecclesiastical Hierarchy* of Dionysius the Areopagite. There is an English translation of these texts in *Pseudo-Dionysius: The Complete Works*, trans. Colm Luibheid (New York: Paulist Press, 1987).

30. Bernard of Clairvaux, *Apologia*, 3.6, 4.7, 4.8.

31. Ibid., 5.10.

32. Ibid., 6.12.

33. Ibid., 7.13.

34. Ibid., 7.15.

35. Ibid., 10.24–26.

36. Ibid., 12.28.

37. Ibid.

38. Ibid., 12.30.

39. Bernard of Clairvaux, *On the Duties of Bishops*, 2.7.

40. Ibid., 2.6.

41. Bernard of Clairvaux, *On Conversion*, 18.31. The English translation I am using is contained in *Bernard of Clairvaux: Selected Works*, trans. G. R. Evans (New York: Paulist Press, 1987), 66–97. There is another translation available in *Bernard of Clairvaux: Sermons on Conversion*, trans. Marie-Bernard Saïd (Kalamazoo, MI: Cistercian Publications, 1981), 31–79. I prefer the Evans translation because it is more direct. The critical edition has an excellent introduction that can be found in volume 4 of the *Sancti Bernardi opera*, 61–67.

42. Bernard of Clairvaux, *On Conversion*, 19.32, 21.38.

43. Ibid., 19.33–34.

44. Ibid., 20.36.

45. Ibid., 22.39.

46. Ibid., 22.40.

47. Keenan, "Introduction," in *Five Books On Consideration: Advice to a Pope*, 11.

48. Bernard of Clairvaux, *On Consideration*, 1.1.1, 1.2.2.

49. Ibid., 1.2.3.

50. Ibid., 1.2.3, 1.4.5, 1.6.7. Bernard seems to be using a variant reading in 1.6.7 that incorporates a scribal interpolation, but its meaning is consistent with the NRSV translation of 2 Timothy 2:3–4: "Share in suffering like a good soldier of Christ Jesus. No one serving in the army gets entangled in everyday affairs." Medieval authors worked from many different versions of the Bible containing variant readings. They were aware of the differences, but to the medieval mind they simply expanded the meaning of the text.

51. Bernard of Clairvaux, *On Consideration*, 1.6.7.

52. Ibid., 2.6.10, 2.6.10, 2.6.11.

53. Ibid., 3.1.2.

54. Ibid., 1.10.14: "The case of a widow requires your attention, likewise the case of a poor man and of one who has no means to pay. You can distribute many cases to others for judgment and many you can judge unworthy of a hearing. What need is there to hear those whose sins are manifest before the trial?"

55. Ibid., 3.1.1.

56. Ibid., 5.13.32.

57. See Franz Posset, *Pater Bernhardus*, and William O. Paulsell, "The Use of Bernard of Clairvaux in Reformation Preaching," in *Erudition at God's Service*, ed. John R. Sommerfeldt (Kalamazoo, MI: Cistercian Publications, 1987), 327–37.

58. Discussing his spiritual reading of Bernard's *On Consideration*, John XXIII wrote: "Nothing is better adapted and more useful for a poor pope such as I am, and for a pope at any time. Something of the dishonor that marked the Roman clergy in the twelfth century is always with us. We must

be vigilant, make amends, and persevere." Paul VI, in an address given to the Second Vatican Council on the reform of the curia, drew on Bernard's theology to call them to a program of service, simplicity, poverty of spirit, and an abdication of any ideas of dominance or power. Sources drawn from Leclercq, *Bernard of Clairvaux and the Cistercian Spirit*, 114–15.

4. Clare of Assisi: The Clear Mirror of Christ

1. *The Process of Canonization*, 13.11. All the English translations of Clare's writings and the sources concerning Clare are from *Clare of Assisi: Early Documents*, ed. and trans. Regis J. Armstrong (New York: Paulist Press, 1988). The critical edition for the process of canonization and the resulting bull of canonization is *Santa Chiara di Assisi: I primi documenti ufficiali, lettera di annunzio della sua morte, processo e bolla di canonizatione*, ed. and Italian trans. Giovanni Boccali (Santa Maria degli Angeli: Edizioni Porziuncola, 2002). The best Latin edition of Clare's writings is *Claire d'Assise: écrits*, ed. and French trans. Marie-France Becker, Jean-François Godet, and Thaddée Matura (Paris: Les Éditions du Cerf, 1985). The Franciscan community has developed a consistent numeration system for these texts that I follow. For more information see Ingrid Peterson, *Clare of Assisi: A Biographical Study*, (Quincy, IL: Franciscan Press, 1993), 101–5. See also Margaret Carney, *The First Franciscan Woman: Clare of Assisi and Her Form of Life* (Quincy, IL: Franciscan Press, 1993), 99–109. Carney's study is excellent in content and method.

2. *The Legend of Clare*, 1; *The Process of Canonization* 1.4. The critical edition for *The Legend of Clare* is Anonymous, *Legenda Latina Sanctae Clarae Virginis Assisiensis*, ed. Giovanni Boccali, Italian trans. Marino Bigaroni (Santa Maria degli Angeli: Edizioni Porziuncola, 2001). See also Peterson, *Clare of Assisi*, 91–98. Peterson suggests that the women in Clare's family were similar to communities of lay religious women known as Beguines. While her study helped me to imagine Clare's world, Peterson's method is to interpret Clare, her family, and community in light of sociological studies that explore general trends in medieval society. Such an approach runs the danger of degenerating into the transmission of stereotypes. Even so, her work is invaluable and well documented.

3. *The Legend of Clare*, 9: "They employed violent force, poisonous advice, and flattering promises, trying to persuade her to give up such a worthless deed that was unbecoming of her class and without precedence in her family.... With the increasing violence of her relatives, her spirit grew and her love—provoked by injuries—provided strength. So, for many days, even though she endured an obstacle in the way of the Lord and her own [relatives] opposed her proposal of holiness, her spirit did not crumble and

her fervor did not diminish. Instead, amid words and deeds of hatred, she molded her spirit anew in hope until her relatives, turning back, were quiet."

4. See Marie Anne Mayeski, "New Voices in the Tradition: Medieval Hagiography Revisited," *Theological Studies* 63 (2002): 690–710. This is an excellent article that has the potential of helping Catholic theologians recover the feminine side of the tradition.

5. See Peterson, *Clare of Assisi*, 1–10; Roberta Agnes McKelvie, *Retrieving a Living Tradition: Angelina of Montegiove Franciscan, Tertiary, Beguine* (St. Bonaventure, NY: The Franciscan Institute, 1997), 11–17. Both want to claim that Clare co-founded the Franciscan Order with Francis, but their position does not seem to recognize Clare's own statements in both her *Testament* and her *Rule* that Francis established the form of life the sisters would follow. It would be fair to say they cofounded Poor Ladies or the Poor Clares as they came to be known. Clare and her sisters were known by various names prior to her death, but for consistency's sake I am referring to them as the Poor Ladies throughout the chapter.

6. *Letter of Cardinal Hugolino*, 2–3. The Latin text is in "Chronica XXIV Generalium," *Analecta Franciscana*, vol. 3, 183.

7. Caroline Walker Bynum, "Religious Women in the Later Middle Ages," *Christian Spirituality II: High Middle Ages and Reformation*, ed. Jill Raitt (New York: Crossroad, 1987), 137. I found many valuable sources on the study of women in the Middle Ages in Bernard McGinn, *The Flowering of Mysticism: Men and Women in the New Mysticism—1200–1350*, vol. 3, *The Presence of God: A History of Western Mysticism* (New York: The Crossroad Publishing Company, 1998). I have also generally adopted his hermeneutical principles concerning medieval works written either by or about women as they are spelled out in pages 15–17.

8. McGinn, *The Flowering of Mysticism*, 17.

9. One of the witnesses for Clare's canonization stated that she could recognize Clare's holiness because she knew the legends of many women saints. See *The Process of Canonization*, 7.11.

10. McGinn, *The Flowering of Mysticism*, 15, 21–22.

11. The classic study on these and other movements is R. I. Moore, *The Origins of European Dissent* (Toronto: Toronto University Press, 1994). There were two earlier editions that are widely available; however, the first edition, which was printed in 1977 by Allen Lane, was corrected in the 1985 edition published by Basil Blackwell Ltd.

12. For more introductory information on this movement, see Euan Cameron, "The Waldenses," in *The Medieval Theologians: An Introduction to Theology in the Medieval Period*, ed. G. R. Evans (Oxford: Blackwell Publishers, 2001), 269–86.

13. See Canon 3 of the Fourth Lateran Council. The best translation of the canon can be found in the *Decrees of the Ecumenical Councils*, vol. 1, ed. Norman P. Tanner (Washington DC: Georgetown University, 1990), 234–35.

14. McGinn, *The Flowering of Mysticism*, 11.

15. For an introductory study on medieval preaching, see my book *Christian Eloquence: Contemporary Doctrinal Preaching* (Chicago, IL: Hillenbrand Press, 2004). Despite the subtitle provided by the press, the book is a history of preaching from Augustine until the eve of the Protestant Reformation. The material on Mary of Oignies is largely drawn from *Christian Eloquence*. Overall, I have followed McGinn's discussion of Mary in *The Flowering of Mysticism*, 32–41. As always, McGinn's notes point to a wealth of source materials.

16. See M. D. Chenu, *Nature, Man, and Society in the Twelfth Century*, trans. Jerome Taylor and Lester K. Little (Chicago, IL: University of Chicago Press, 1968), 260–61; McGinn, *The Flowering of Mysticism*, 7–8.

17. McGinn, *The Flowering of Mysticism*, 34–35.

18. For a superb study on the scholars in Paris at the end of the twelfth century, see John Baldwin, *Masters Princes and Merchants: The Social Views of Peter the Chanter and His Circle*, vol. 1 (Princeton, NJ: Princeton University Press, 1970).

19. Beryl Smalley, *The Study of the Bible in the Middle Ages*, 3rd ed. (Oxford: Blackwell, 1983), 196–200.

20. McGinn, *The Flowering of Mysticism*, 34–35.

21. The translation is from *Clare of Assisi: Early Documents*, 245–46. The critical edition is *Lettres de Jacques de Vitry*, ed. R. B. C. Huygens (Leyden: E. J. Brill, 1960), 75–76.

22. McGinn, *The Flowering of Mysticism*, 35.

23. See George Conklin, "Law, Reform, and the Origins of Persecution: Stephen of Tournai and the Order of Grandmont," *Medieval Studies* 61 (1999): 107–36.

24. For the most comprehensive treatment of this question, see Lawrence C. Landini, *The Causes of the Clericalization of the Order of Friars Minor 1209–1260* (Chicago: Franciscan Herald Press, 1968). Landini has pushed scholars to move beyond viewing Franciscan history in dialectical terms between the fidelity to or the betrayal of St. Francis.

25. Much of the material on Francis in this section is drawn from a paper I presented in a symposium at Washington Theological Union on the topic of Franciscan reform, which was published as "Franciscan Reform," in *"Go Rebuild My House": Franciscans and the Church Today* (St. Bonaventure, NY: The Franciscan Institute, 2004), 39–64.

26. "Fragments Inserted into the *Exposition of the Rule of the Friars Minor* by Hugh of Digne," 24. The translation is from *Francis of Assisi: Early Documents*, vol. 1, edited by Regis J. Armstrong, J. A. Wayne Hellmann, and William J. Short (New York: New City Press, 1999), 92–95.

27. See Francis of Assisi, *The Second Letter to the Faithful*, 38; The Earlier Rule, 22:1–2; *The Admonitions*, 9.1–4, 14.4; and A *Prayer Inspired by the Our Father*, 8. All of the translations of Francis's writings are from *Francis of Assisi: Early Documents*.

28. Francis of Assisi, *The Testament*, 24.

29. Francis of Assisi, *The Second Letter to the Faithful*, 33–35.

30. Ibid., 47. I have changed the translation of this passage slightly. The translation in the New City Press edition translates *creaturae* as "creature," but the word can also mean institution. Since Francis was citing 1 Peter 2:13, I think the context demands the word be translated as institution.

31. Francis of Assisi, *The Admonitions*, 11:1–3. See also *The Earlier Rule*, 11:3-4: "Let them not quarrel among themselves or with others, but strive to respond humbly, saying: 'I am a useless servant.' Let them not become angry because whoever is angry with his brother is liable to judgment...."

32. *Fragments from Hugh of Digne*, 28.

33. Francis of Assisi, *The Testament*, 24.

34. Clare of Assisi, *The Testament*, 19–20. There has been a great deal of debate over the last century as to whether this is an authentic work of Clare of Assisi, but most scholars accept it as Clare's. For a review of the debate until the 1980s, see *Claire d'Assise: écrits*, 21–27. For more recent developments in this controversy, see Niklaus Kuster, "Clare's Testament and Innocent III's Privilege of Poverty: Genuine or Clever Forgeries," *Greyfriars Review* 15 (2001): 171–252.

35. *Assisi Compilation*, 20. The translation is from *Francis of Assisi: The Founder*, ed. Regis J. Armstrong, J. A. Wayne Hellmann, and William J. Short, vol. 2, *Francis of Assisi: Early Documents* (New York: New City Press, 2000), 134.

36. Clare of Assisi, *The First Letter of St. Clare to Agnes of Prague (1234)*, 12, 24.

37. Clare of Assisi, *The Third Letter of St. Clare to Agnes of Prague (1238)*, 7–8.

38. Francis of Assisi, *The Second Version of the Letter to All the Faithful*, 50.

39. Gregory the Great, *Forty Gospel Homilies*, trans. Dom David Hurst (Kalamazoo, MI: Cistercian Publications, 1990), 6. This is homily one in the critical edition: *Homiliae in Evangelia / Gregorius Magnus*, ed and trans. Raymond Etaix, *Corpus Christianorum Latinorum* (Turnhout: Brepols, 1999).

40. *The Legend of St. Clare*, 36; *Letter of Cardinal Hugolino (1220)*, 2.

41. Clare of Assisi, *Rule of Clare*, 2.12.

42. The *Form of Life* is no longer extant except for a fragment contained in the *Rule of Clare*, 6.3. Throughout this section I am relying heavily on the first two chapters of Carney's *The First Franciscan Woman*.

43. As quoted in *The Privilege of Poverty of Pope Gregory IX (1230)*, 7. The Latin text is available in *Bullarium Franciscanum sive Romanorum Pontificium Constitutiones, Epistolae, Diplomata Tribus Ordinis Minorum, Clarissarum, Poenitentium a Seraphico Patriarcha Sancto Francisco Institutes ad Eorum Originibus ad Nostra usque Tempora Concessa*, vol. 1 (Rome: Typis Vaticanis, 1898–1904), 50.

44. Brenda Bolton, "Mulieres Sanctae," in *Women in Medieval Society*, ed. Susan Mosher Stuard (Philadelphia, PA: University of Pennsylvania Press, 1976), 149.

45. Carney, *The First Franciscan Woman*, 133–34.

46. Ibid., 66–67. See *The Legend of St. Clare*, 37.

47. Pope Celestine IV was elected between Gregory IX and Innocent IV, but his papacy only lasted thirteen days. Following the death of Celestine, the papacy was vacant from November 10, 1241, until June 28, 1243.

48. Carney, *The First Franciscan Woman*, 77–80.

49. Clare of Assisi, *The Testament*, 18–24.

50. Clare wrote, "When the blessed Francis saw, however, that, although we were physically weak and frail, we did not shirk from deprivation, poverty, hard work,...rather we considered them as great delights, as he had frequently examined us according to the example of the saints and his brothers—he greatly rejoiced in the Lord" (*The Testament*, 27–28). It seems Francis was surprised that these women were every bit as tough as his brothers. Notice also that Clare emphasized the fact that the standard was the example of the brothers.

51. *Bull of Canonization (1255)*, 3.

52. Ibid., 9.

53. Gregory the Great, *Pastoral Care*, 1.2, 2.10. The critical edition is *Règle pastorale / Grégoire le Grand*, ed. Floribert Rommel, trans. Charles Morel (Paris: Editions du Cerf, 1992). The English translation is *Pastoral Care*, trans. Henry Davis (New York: Newman, 1950).

54. *Bull of Canonization* 10. Gregory the Great wrote the bishop must be "pure in thought, exemplary in conduct, discreet in keeping silence, profitable in speech, in sympathy a near neighbor to everyone...." See *Pastoral Care* 2.1 for the entire list of attributes.

55 *Legend of St. Clare*, 56. The author alluded to Acts 3:2, where Peter and John healed a man "who was crippled from his mother's womb." By doing so, he associated Clare's ministry with that of the apostles.

56. *Legend of St. Clare*, 60–61.
57. Carney, *The First Franciscan Woman*, 80.

5. Catherine of Siena: The Insatiable Reformer

1. André Vauchez has a short chapter on women prophets and visionaries that places Catherine of Siena in a broader framework in *The Laity in the Middle Ages: Religious Beliefs and Devotional Practices*, trans. Margery J. Schneider (Notre Dame, IN: University of Notre Dame Press, 1993) 219–29. See also Robert Lerner, "Ecstatic Dissent," *Speculum* 67 (1992): 33–57.

2. For a chronological outline of her life, see *The Letters of Catherine of Siena*, 2 vols., trans. Suzanne Noffke (Binghamton, NY: Medieval and Renaissance Texts and Studies, 1988), vol. 1, liii–lvi; Giuliana Cavallini, *Catherine of Siena* (London: Geoffrey Chapman, 1998), xv–xxvii. Most of the biographies of St. Catherine in English are very old and tend to be more hagiography than history. Cavallini's book is the best overview and introduction to Catherine's theology. The extensive bibliography in Noffke's translation illustrates that most of the scholarship on Catherine is Italian. I find the lack of scholarship on Catherine outside of Italian circles to be inexplicable. At this point, the best way to learn about the details of her life is to read the letters and Raymond of Capua's *The Life of Catherine of Siena*, trans. Conleth Kearns (Wilmington, DE: Glazier Press, 1980).

3. Pus and sin were related in the medieval mind. You may recall that Gregory the Great made that connection in his *Moralia* 3.17.32. See Catherine of Siena, *The Dialogue*, 134 (275–76). The critical edition is *Il Dialogo della divina Provvidenza: ovvero Libro della divina dottrina*, 2nd ed., ed. Guiliana Cavallini (Siena: Cantagalli, 1995); and the English translation is *The Dialogue*, trans. Suzanne Noffke (New York: Paulist Press, 1980). I have decided to cite the chapter number of the critical edition and place the corresponding page numbers in Noffke's translation in parentheses. For more on this subject see Caroline Walker Bynum, *Holy Feast and Holy Fast: The Religious Significance of Food to Medieval Women* (Berkeley: University of California Press, 1987), 167–72. I would recommend that only those with strong stomachs read this material.

4. Catherine of Siena, *Dialogue*, 133 (272): "Now I repeat that, in spite of all their sins and even if they were worse yet, I do not want any secular powers meddling in the business of punishing them. If they do, their sin will not go unpunished unless they themselves atone for it with heartfelt contrition and conversion. Both the one and the other are devils incarnate (clergy and secular powers): In divine justice the one devil punishes the

other, but both are guilty of sin. The secular has no excuse in the sin of the cleric, nor the cleric in the sin of the secular."

5. See Thomas Aquinas, *Summa Theologiae*, 2.2.33.4 reply to objection 2.

6. Catherine of Siena, *The Letters of St. Catherine of Siena*, Letter T28/G191/DT 17 (136). The text tradition for Catherine's letters is very involved, so I have followed Noffke's method of citing the letters and provided the page number from her translation in parentheses. *T* represents the numbering used in the edition of the letters prepared by Niccolò Tommasèo, *Lettere di Santa Caterina da Siena, ridotte a miglior lezione, e in ordine nuovo disposte con note di Niccolò Tommasèo*, vol. 1–4 (Florence: Barbera, 1860); G indicates the numbering system of the edition by Girolamo Gigli, *Opere di Santa Caterina da Siena, nuovamente pubblicate da Girolamo Gigli*, vol. 1–4 (Siena, Lucca: no publisher, 1707–21); and *DT* stands for the numbering used in the edition by Eugenio Dupré Theseider, *L'Epistolario di Santa Caterina da Siena* (Rome: Instituto storico italiano per il medio evo, 1940). The primary source for her life was written by her Dominican spiritual director, Raymond of Capua, *The Life of Catherine of Siena*.

7. For an example of her position, see Letter 209/G2 (vol. 2, 298–300). There is some question about the date of the letter; but you can see this same theme in *The Dialogue*, which was written after the massacre. See *Dialogue*, 115–18 (215–21).

8. Catherine of Siena, Letter 209/G2 (vol. 2, 298).

9. Catherine of Siena, Letter T185/G1/DT54 (vol. 1, 246–48).

10. Francis Oakley, *The Western Church in the Later Middle Ages* (Ithaca, NY: Cornell University Press, 1979), 37. I am generally following Oakley's assessment of the issue surrounding Boniface's career. See also Brian Tierney, *The Crisis of Church and State 1050–1300* (New York: Prentice-Hall Inc., 1964; repr., Toronto: University of Toronto Press, 1988), 172–92; Steven Ozment, *The Age of Reform 1250–1550: An Intellectual and Religious History of Late Medieval and Reformation Europe* (New Haven, CT: Yale University Press, 1980) 146–47; Bernard Schimmelpfennig, *The Papacy*, trans. James Sievert (New York: Columbia University Press, 1992), 195–97.

11. For an English translation, see Tierney, *The Crisis of Church and State*, 175–76; H. Bettenson, *Documents of the Christian Church* (New York: Oxford University Press, 1943), 159–61.

12. For a partial translation, see Tierney, *The Crisis of Church and State*, 178–79.

13. Ibid., 188–89.

14. Oakley, *The Western Church*, 37–38. For a more positive assessment of the Avignon papacy, see G. Mollat, *The Popes at Avignon (1305–1378)*, trans. Janet Love (New York: T. Nelson, 1963).

15. Oakley, *The Western Church*, 40.

16. Walter Ullmann, *The Origins of the Great Schism* (London: Burns Oates & Washbourne Ltd., 1948), 7.

17. Catherine of Siena, *The Dialogue*, 3 (29). The idea that sin is always infinite can be found in Anselm's treatise on the incarnation, *Cur Deus Homo*. Catherine's claim that the human capacity for desire is infinite parallels Augustine's reflections in the first book of his *Confessions*. See Cavallini, *Catherine of Siena*, 42–43. Whether Catherine was drawing upon Anselm or Augustine directly is impossible to ascertain, but the theologians of her time would have seen these parallels.

18. Catherine of Siena, *The Dialogue*, 6 (35).

19. Ibid., 5 (33).

20. Ibid., 14 (50).

21. Ibid., 7 (38).

22. Ibid., 7 (36–37).

23. Ibid., 99 (186).

24. Ibid., 99–100 (186–89).

25. Ibid., 100 (191).

26. Ibid., 102-104 (193–96).

27. Ibid., 102 (194).

28. Ibid., 102 (194).

29. Ibid., 103 (195).

30. Ibid., 103 (195).

31. Ibid., 104 (196).

32. Ibid., 104 (197).

33. Ibid., 105 (198).

34. Ibid., 110–12 (205–12).

35. Ibid., 129 (256). For more on this theme of reforming the head, see Vauchez, *The Laity in the Middle Ages*, 222–23; Oakley, *The Western Church*, 219–30.

36. Catherine of Siena, *The Dialogue*, 113 (213).

37. Ibid., 119 (224).

38. Ibid., 120 (231).

39. Ibid., 119 (223–29).

40. Ibid., 119 (228).

41. Ibid., 121 (231).

42. bid., 121 (231–32).

43. Ibid., 121 (231–32); 126–30 (244–62).

44. Ibid., 121 (232).

45. Ibid., 121 (233).

46. Ibid., 122 (235).

47. Ibid., 127 (249).

48. Ibid., 128 (253).

49. Ibid., 130 (262).

50. Ibid., 130 (262), 132 (266–71). Catherine repeatedly emphasizes that these sinners did not see or recognize their sins.

51. Ibid., 134 (274–75).

6. When Reformers Collide: Jean Gerson and Jan Hus

1. Peter of Mladoňovice, *An Account of the Trial and Condemnation of Master John Hus*, in *John Hus at the Council of Constance*, ed. and trans. Matthew Spinka (New York: Columbia University Press, 1965), 232. The definitive critical edition of this text is in *M. Jana Husi Korespondece a dokumenty*, ed. Václav Novotný (Prague: Komise pro vydávání pramenů náboženského hnutí českého, 1920).

2. The quotation is from Walter Ullmann, *Medieval Papalism: The Political Theories of the Medieval Canonists* (London: Methuen, 1949), 153. I found the subsequent quotation in George Tavard, *Holy Writ or Holy Church: The Crisis of the Protestant Reformation* (London: Burns and Oates, 1959), 47–48.

3. Tavard, *Holy Writ or Holy Church*, 48. Many scholars see the primary issues of the fifteenth century as being issues of papacy and of law. See Walter Ullmann, *The Origins of the Great Schism: A Study in Fourteenth Century Ecclesiastical History* (London: Burns Oates and Washbourne Ltd., 1948), v–vii; Francis Oakley, *The Western Church in the Later Middle Ages* (Ithaca, NY: Cornell University Press, 1979), 25–30; Brian Tierney, *Foundations of the Conciliar Theory: The Contribution of the Medieval Canonists from Gratian to the Great Schism*, new ed. (Leiden: Brill, 1998), ix–xxix.

4. For more detail, see Ullmann, *The Origins of the Great Schism*, 4. For a brief but thorough study on the new powers associated with the cardinals and their relationship with the pope, see Tierney, *Foundations of the Conciliar Theory*, 62–77.

5. I am generally following Ullmann's more detailed discussion in *The Origins of the Great Schism*, 44–68. There are several good treatments of the issues surrounding the election of Urban VI and the beginning of the Great Schism. See Bernard Schimmelpfennig, *The Papacy*, trans. James Sievert (New York: Columbia University Press, 1992), 219–36; Oakley, *The Western Church*, 55–70; Steven Ozment, *The Age of Reform 1250–1550: An Intellectual and Religious History of Late Medieval and Reformation Europe* (New Haven: Yale University Press, 1980), 135–64.

6. Ullmann, *The Origins of the Great Schism*, 48. The original source is a deposition of Bishop Alphonso of Jaën in Raynaldus, *Annales ecclesiastici ex tomis octo, ad unum pluribus auctum redacti auctore Odorico Raynaldo Tarvisino*, vol. 7 (Rome: 1667), 379.

7. John B. Morrall, *Gerson and the Great Schism* (Manchester, England: Manchester University Press, 1960), 34–36. Morrall's historical account is still standard. See also Louis B. Pascoe, *Jean Gerson: Principles of Church Reform* (Leiden: E. J. Brill, 1973), 1–15. I have tried to correlate the historical and concrete aspects of Morrall's study with the more theoretical approach taken by Pascoe. Pascoe's study is the best source for Gerson's thoughts concerning reform and ecclesiology, but he worked under the assumption that the *Tractatus pro unione Ecclesiae* was written by Gerson, when it was not. Giles Deschamps is the most likely author for the treatise. A careful reading of the footnotes in Pascoe's book makes it relatively easy to avoid making the same mistake. There are several studies on Gerson's reform efforts in terms of theology, the university, and the episcopacy, including: André Combes, *La théologie mystique de Gerson*, 2 vols. (Paris: 1963–65); Steven Ozment, "The University and the Church: Patterns of Reform in John Gerson," *Medievalia et Humanistica*, vol. 1 (1970), 111–26; E. Vansteenberghe, "Un program d'action episcopal au début du xve siècle," *Revue de Sciences Religieuses*, vol. 19 (1939): 24–37. For a seminal study on Gerson's ecclesiology that has recently been revised and translated from Dutch into English, see G. H. M. Posthumus Meyjes, *Jean Gerson, Apostle of Unity: His Church Politics and Ecclesiology* (Leiden: Brill, 1999).

8. For a good and brief biography that is widely available, see the Brian Patrick McGuire's introduction to *Jean Gerson: Early Works*, trans. Brian Patrick McGuire (New York: Paulist Press, 1998).

9. Pascoe, *Jean Gerson: Principles of Church Reform*, 17–34.

10. Ibid., 43–44.

11. Jean Gerson, *De auferibilitate sponsi ad Ecclesia*, in *Oeuvres complètes*, ed. P. Glorieux, vol. 3 (Paris: Desclée et Cie, 1962), 300. The translation is from Ozment, *The Age of Reform*, 163. Morrall has shown this is an idea he had basically formulated as early as 1392 in *Gerson and the Great Schism*, 34–35.

12. For Gerson's place in the history of this controversy, see Yves Congar, "Aspects ecclésiologiques de la querelle entre mendiants et séculiers dans la seconde moitié du xiiie siècle et le début du xive," *Archives d'histoire doctrinale et littéraire du moyen age*, vol. 27–28 (1961): 35–151.

13. Pascoe, *Jean Gerson: Principles of Church Reform*, 32.

14. Ibid., 155. See Jean Gerson, *Quomodo stabit regnum*, in *Oeuvres complètes*, vol. 7, ed. P. Glorieux, 991.

15. Pascoe, *Jean Gerson: Principles of Church Reform*, 155–56. Gerson, *Quomodo stabit regnum*, 990–92.

16. Pascoe, *Jean Gerson: Principles of Church Reform*, 58–76.

17. Cited from Ozment, *The Age of Reform*, 161. The source is Gratian, *Decretum*, 40.6. Tierney has a very detailed discussion of this canon and its interpretive history in *Foundations of the Conciliar Theory*, 51–61.

18. This sermon has recently been translated into English. See Pope Innocent III, *Between God and Man: Six Sermons on the Priestly Office*, trans. Corrine J. Vause and Frank C. Gardiner (Washington, DC: The Catholic University of America Press, 2004), 43–50.

19. Pascoe, *Jean Gerson: Principles of Church Reform*, 26–27. For Gerson's statements, see *Propositio facta coram Anglicis* in *Oeuvres complètes*, vol. 6, 132–33; *De auferibilitate sponsi ab Ecclesia* in *Oeuvres complètes*, vol. 3, 296; *Quomodo stabit regnum* in *Oeuvres complètes*, vol. 7, 981.

20. Gerson, *De auferibilitate sponsi ab Ecclesia*, 300.

21. Gerson, *Libellus articulorum contra Petrum de Luna* in *Oeuvres complètes*, vol. 6, 266. Gerson was actually using a form of the argument from piety, which maintained that the theologian should always choose the more perfectly appropriate language about God as true. What is interesting is that he has extended this form of argumentation to the church.

22. Pascoe, *Jean Gerson: Principles of Church Reform*, 43–48.

23. Gerson, *De auferibilitate sponsi ab Ecclesia*, 301. The translation is from Ozment, *The Age of Reform*, 163.

24. Pascoe, *Jean Gerson: Principles of Church Reform*, 72. See Gerson, *De unitate Ecclesiae* in *Oeuvres complètes*, vol. 6, 143–44.

25. Oakley, *The Western Church*, 63.

26. Matthew Spinka, *John Hus at the Council of Constance* (New York: Columbia University Press, 1965), 22–30. I am basically abbreviating Spinka's account. Spinka provided even more detail in *John Hus: A Biography* (Princeton, NJ: Princeton University Press, 1968). Spinka's work remains the best source for information about Hus in English, but the most influential studies on Hus are by Paul de Vooght and include *L'hérésie de Jean Huss* (Louvain: Publications universitaires de Louvain, 1960) and *Hussiana* (Louvain: Publications universitaires de Louvain, 1960). Much of the scholarship on Hus has interpreted him according to Marxist categories. For a review of the historiography on Hus, see Ernest Werner, *Jan Hus: Welt und Umwelt eines Prager Frühreformators* (Weimar: H. Böhlaus Nachfolger, 1991).

27. Spinka, *John Hus: A Biography*, 49–55.

28. Spinka, *John Hus at the Council of Constance*, 32–33.

29. Spinka, *John Hus: A Biography*, 86–87.

30. The translation is from Spinka, who also offers some detailed analysis in *John Hus: A Biography*, 133–36.

31. De Vooght, *L'hérésie de Jean Huss*, 194–96.

32. Spinka, *Jan Hus: A Biography*, 137–40.

33. Ibid., 72.

34. Jan Hus, *Betlemské texty*, ed. B. Ryba (Prague: Orbis, 1951), 63. The paragraphs on *The Six Errors* were drawn from a paper that I presented at the annual meeting of the American Catholic Historical Association in 2006. The material in the following paragraphs was previously published in "A Reappraisal of John Hus in Light of his Medieval Predecessors," *Chicago Studies* 45 (Spring 2006): 16–18.

35. Hus, *Betlemské texty*, 41–42.

36. Ibid., 42–52.

37. Ibid., 53–62.

38. Spinka, *Hus at the Council of Constance*, 42.

39. Peter of Mladoňovice, *An Account of the Trial*, 193–95.

40. Christopher Bellitto, *The General Councils: A History of the Twenty-One Church Councils from Nicaea to Vatican II* (New York: Paulist Press, 2002), 85; Oakley, The Western Church, 64.

41. Gerson, *Ambulate dum lucem habetis*, in *Oeuvres complètes*, vol. 5, 39–40.

42. Ibid., 40.

43. *Decrees of the Ecumenical Councils*, vol. 1, ed. Norman Tanner (Washington, DC: Georgetown University, 1990), 408.

44. *Decrees of the Ecumenical Councils*, vol. 1, 417.

45. Peter of Mladoňovice, *An Account of the Trial*, 106–7.

46. The translation is from Ozment, *The Age of Reform*, 169. For a detailed discussion of this document and of the twenty articles in question, see De Vooght, *L'hérésie de Jean Huss*, 294–305. See also Pascoe, *Jean Gerson: Principles of Church Reform*, 11.

47. Peter of Mladoňovice, *An Account of the Trial*, 166. Jean Gerson described heretics as people who professed to be orthodox Catholic but who use sophistries to escape in *De sensu litterali sacrae scripturae in Opera omnia*, vol. 1, ed. L. E. du Pin (Antwerp: 1706), 7 A–B. See also Pascoe, *Jean Gerson: Principles of Church Reform*, 40.

48. Peter of Mladoňovice, *An Account of the Trial*, 118.

49. Ibid., 142–43.

50. Ibid., 170.

51. Ibid., 171. Brian Patrick McGuire has tried to downplay Gerson's role in *Jean Gerson and the Last Medieval Reformation* (University Park, PA: Pennsylvania University Press, 2005), 249.

52. Peter of Mladoňovice, *An Account of the Trial*, 213–14.

53. Ibid., 214–15.

54. Hus, "The Answer of 'The Father' to John Hus," in *John Hus at the Council of Constance*, 270. The letter is contained in Novotný, no. 137.

55. Hus, "Hus's Answer to This Letter of 'the Father'," in *John Hus at the Council of Constance*, 271. The letter is contained in Novotný, no. 139.

56. There was another brief papal schism with the election of Felix V by the Council of Basle in 1439, but Felix had little support and had to relinquish his claims to the papacy in 1449.

57. Jean Gerson, *The Consolation of Philosophy*, trans. Clyde Lee Miller (n. p.: Abaris Books, 1998), 169. For a comprehensive study on this treatise, see Mark Burrows, *Jean Gerson and De Consolatione Theologiae (1418): The Consolation of a Biblical and Reforming Theology for a Disordered Age* (Tübingen: J. C. B. Mohr (Paul Siebeck, 1991).

7. Gasparo Contarini: Christ's Diplomat

1. Martin Luther, *Luther's Works*, vol. 32 (Saint Louis, MO: Concordia Pub. House 1955–), 112–13.

2. Translation is from Elisabeth G. Gleason, *Gasparo Contarini: Venice, Rome, and Reform* (Berkeley: University of California Press, 1993), 14. Gleason's biography has become one of the standard secondary sources on Contarini, and I have relied heavily on her work in this chapter.

3. Gleason, *Gasparo Contarini*, 132. Her source was Ludovico Beccadelli, "Vita di Monsignor Reverendissimo et Illustrissimo Messer Gasparo Contarino Gentilhuomo Venitiano et Cardinale della S. Romana Chiesa," *Monumenti di varia letteratura tratti dai manoscritti di Monsignor Lodovico Beccadelli*, ed. Giambattista Morandi, vol. 1, part 2 (Bologna, 1797), 47.

4. John P. Dolan, *History of the Reformation: A Conciliatory Assessment of Opposite Views* (New York: Desclee Company, 1965), 229–30. This history is a lot of fun to read, but it lacks footnotes. Much of the material underlying this study and others is from Hubert Jedin's *A History of the Council of Trent*, trans. Dom Ernest Graf, 2 vol. (St. Louis, MO: B. Herder Book Co., 1957). Jedin's work, which was first published in German in 1949, continues to be a central source for historians of the sixteenth century.

5. The translation is from Edgidio da Viterbo, "Address to the Fifth Lateran Council May 3, 1512," in *Catholic Reform: From Cardinal Ximenes to the Council of Trent 1495-1563*, ed. and trans. John C. Olin (New York: Fordham University Press, 1990), 58. The Latin text is in G. M. Mansi, *Sacrorum conciliorum nova et amplissima collectio*, vol. 32 (Paris: Walter, 1901–27), 669–76. The most comprehensive study available in English is John W. O'Malley, *Giles of Viterbo on Church and Reform* (Leiden: Brill, 1968).

6. The translation is from "Adrian VI's Instruction to Chieregati," in *The Catholic Reformation: Savonarola to Ignatius of Loyola*, trans. and ed. John C. Olin (New York: Harper and Row, 1969), 125. The translation Olin selected was done by John Marrone and by an unnamed editor of the Latin text, which can be found in *Deutsche Reichstagsakten*, new series, vol. 3, ed. Historische Kommission (Munich: Gotha, 1893–), 390–99.

7. For a recent and popular account of the papacies discussed in the next several paragraphs, see Eamon Duffy, *Saints and Sinners: A History of the Popes* (New Haven, CT: Yale University Press, 1997), 142–51.

8. For a good general overview, see Steven Ozment, *The Age of Reform, 1250–1550: An Intellectual and Religious History of Late Medieval and Reformation Europe* (New Haven, CT: Yale University Press, 1980), 182–222.

9. Luther, "Letter to Archbishop Albrecht of Mainz October 31, 1517," *Luther's Works*, vol. 48, 46.

10. Ozment, *The Age of Reform*, 212.

11. Olin, *Catholic Reform*, 1–43.

12. Ibid., 35.

13. The idea of rebirth and renewal had been common in earlier periods, but the idea of an almost perfect early church that gradually fell into decline was not as common. The belief in a nearly perfect apostolic church can also be seen in the reform rhetoric of Catherine of Siena and Jean Gerson, but it did not play as prominent a role in their thought. I believe Gerson's language may have been more influenced by the ecclesiology of William of St. Amour than by classical sources.

14. For some examples of this apologetic being used by Roman Catholic reformers, see Savonarola's parable of the fig tree in his sermon, "On the Renovation of the Church," in *The Catholic Reformation: Savonarola to Ignatius of Loyola*, 7–8; Giles of Viterbo, "Address to the Fifth Lateran Council (May 3, 1512)" in *Catholic Reform: From Ximenes to the Council of Trent*, 47–60; John Colet, *Convocation Sermon* (1512), in *Catholic Reform*, 31–39; Archbishop Jacques Lefèvre d'Etaples, "Preface to the *Commentaries on the Four Gospels* (1521)," in *The Catholic Reformation: Savonarola to Ignatius of Loyola*, 113–14. The same theme can be found in Martin Luther's *Babylonian Captivity* and *The Three Symbols or Creeds of the Christian Church*. John Calvin also used this rhetoric in the 1536 preface to his *Institutes*.

15. I am drawing on Olin's translation of *The Office of the Bishop* in *The Catholic Reformation*, 93–106. The Latin text can be found in Gasparo Contarini, *Opera* (Paris: 1571), 401–31. See also James Bruce Ross, "The Emergence of Gasparo Contarini: A Biographical Essay," *Church History* 41 (1972): 33.

16. For more information, see Hubert Jedin, "Contarini und Camaldoli," *Archivio italiano per la storia della pietà*, vol. 2 (1960): 51–117; and Dom Jean Leclercq, *Un humaniste ermite: Le bienheureux Paul Giustiniani* (Rome: 1951).

17. The document, which is in Italian, can be found in Felix Gilbert, "Contarini on Savonarola: An Unknown Document of 1516," *Archive für Reformationsgeschichte*, vol. 59 (1968): 147–49. See also Gleason, *Gasparo Contarini*, 91–92.

18. For example, compare the assessments of Gleason, *Gasparo Contarini*, 93–98, and Olin, *The Catholic Reformation*, 90–92.

19. The English humanists Thomas More and Reginald Pole are two more examples of laymen who were working for reform. Pole was made a cardinal shortly after Contarini.

20. Contarini, *The Office of the Bishop*, 93.

21. The source material for the next several paragraphs is from Contarini, *The Office of the Bishop*, 94–105.

22. Gleason, *Gasparo Contarini*, 49.

23. Ibid., 88. Gleason did not recognize the link between Thomas Aquinas and Dionysian mysticism in her treatment.

24. Ibid., 36.

25. Olin, *Catholic Reform*, 13.

26. For an introduction to the Theatines and for a good bibliography, see *Theatine Spirituality: Selected Writings*, ed. and trans. William V. Hudon (New York: Paulist Press, 1996).

27. Olin, *Catholic Reform*, 16.

28. Gleason, *Gasparo Contarini*, 51–53.

29. Ibid., 107–9.

30. The translation is from Gleason, *Gasparo Contarini*, 106–7.

31. Olin, *Catholic Reform*, 20–21. Gleason does not see the *Consilium* as either a complete program or as a landmark in the history of reform in the Catholic Church. Both Olin and Gleason cite Ludwig Pastor, the pioneering Catholic historian of the nineteenth century, as the source for their divergent assessments. See Gleason, *Gasparo Contarini*, 148. Gleason's notes provide a brief review of the scholarship on the *Consilium*.

32. The primary source material for the next several pages is drawn from John Olin, *Catholic Reform*, 66–79. The Latin text is in *Concilium Tridentinum: Diariorum, actorum, epistularum, tractatuum nova collectio*, vol. 12, ed. S. Merkle (Freiburg: Görresgesellschaft, 1901–38), 131–45.

33. Gleason, *Gasparo Contarini*, 153.

34. Luther, *Luther's Works*, vol. 34, 231–67.

35. Jedin, *A History of the Council of Trent*, vol. 1, 378–79.

36. David C. Steinmetz, *Reformers in the Wings: From Geiler von Kayserberg to Theodore Beza*, 2nd ed. (Oxford: Oxford University Press, 2001), 30. See also Peter Matheson, *Cardinal Contarini at Regensburg* (Oxford: Clarendon Press, 1972), 122–35.

37. Jedin, *A History of the Council of Trent*, vol. 1, 384–85.

38. Unitatis redintegratio, 6, in Tanner, *Decrees of the Ecumenical Councils*, vol. 2, 913.

39. Lutheran World Federation and the Roman Catholic Church, *Joint Declaration on the Doctrine of Justification* (Grand Rapids, MI: Eerdmans, 2000), 15. The text is also readily available online. Some useful commentaries and overviews include: Edward I. Cassidy, "The Meaning of the Joint Declaration on Justification," *Origins* 29 (October 1999): 281–87; Avery Dulles, "Two Languages of Salvation: The Lutheran-Catholic Joint Declaration," *First Things* 98 (December 1999): 25–30; Joseph A. Fitzmyer, "The Augsburg Signing: An Overview on the Joint Declaration on Justification," *America* 182 (February 19, 2000): 17–21.

8. The Most Dangerous Man in England: The Convert Cardinal Newman

1. Sheridan Gilley, *Newman and His Age* (London: Darton, Longman and Todd, 1990), 422. Acton's letter 60 can be found in *Letters of Lord Acton to Mary, daughter of the Right Hon. W. E. Gladstone*, ed. Paul Herbert (London, 1904).

2. Quotations cited from John Coulson, "Introduction," in John Henry Newman, *On Consulting the Faithful in Matters of Doctrine* (Kansas City, MO: Sheed and Ward, 1961), 6–7. A good text for entering into Newman's thought is Ian Ker, *Newman the Theologian: A Reader* (London: Collins, 1990). One of the best studies on Newman is Owen Chadwick, *Newman* (Oxford: Oxford University Press, 1983).

3. John Henry Newman, *The Letters and Diaries of John Henry Newman*, vol. 22, ed. Charles Stephen Dessain, Edward E. Kelly, and Thomas Gornall (London, 1961–72), 293. All references to this multivolume set are cited as Letters. For a discussion of these issues, see *Gilley's Newman and His Age*, 335–51. For a brief and readily available description of the Ultramontane movement see Eamon Duffy, *Saints and Sinners: A History of the Popes* (New Haven, CT: Yale University Press, 1977), 222–35.

4. Newman, *Letters*, vol. 22, 314–15.

5. Duffy, *Saints and Sinners*, 173–75.

6. Ibid., 185.

7. The material on the French Revolution in this and the following paragraphs is drawn from Thomas Bokenkotter, *Church and Revolution: Catholics in the Struggle for Democracy and Social Justice* (New York: Image Books Doubleday, 1998), 7–38.

8. Duffy, *Saints and Sinners*, 220.

9. John Henry Newman, *An Essay on the Development of Christian Doctrine* (Westminster, MD: Christian Classics Inc., 1968), 3–4. There are many editions of this work available.

10. Ibid., 4–5.

11. Ibid., 5.

12. Ibid., 7.

13. Ibid., 40.

14. For an excellent summary of these notes, see Avery Cardinal Dulles, *Newman* (London: Continuum, 2002), 73–76.

15. Ibid., 6–11.

16. Coulson, "Introduction," 8.

17. Ibid., 18–19.

18. Duffy, *Saints and Sinners*, 228–29.

19. Newman, *On Consulting the Faithful*, 54–55.

20. Ibid., 63.

21. Ibid.

22. Ibid., 64–72.

23. Ibid., 75.

24. Ibid., 106.

25. Coulson, "Introduction," 38.

26. Cited from Coulson, "Introduction," 41.

27. Coulson, "Introduction," 20.

28. John Henry Newman, *Apologia Pro Vita Sua: Being a History of His Religious Opinions*, ed. Martin J. Svaglic (Oxford: At the Clarendon Press, 1967), 218. There are many editions of this work available.

29. Ibid., 220.

30. Ibid., 226.

31. Ibid.

32. Ibid., 227.

33. Ibid., 231.

34. Ibid., 232–33.

35. John Henry Newman, *Letter to His Grace the Duke of Norfolk*, in *Newman and Gladstone: The Vatican Decrees*, ed. Alvan S. Ryan (Notre Dame, IN: University of Notre Dame Press, 1962), 132. This edition also contains the original essay by William E. Gladstone.

36. Ibid., 128.

37. Ibid., 132.

38. Ibid., 133: "The pope, who comes of revelation, has no jurisdiction over nature."

39. Ibid., 135.

40. Ibid., 135–37.

41. Citations of Pope Leo XIII are from Thomas J. Shelley, "Whatever Happened to Church History?" *Catholic Library World* 70 (December 1999): 94.

9. Dorothy Day and the Catholic Worker Movement

1. Cited from *A Penny a Copy: Readings from The Catholic Worker*, ed. Thomas C. Cornell and James H. Forest (New York: The Macmillan Company, 1968), 3.

2. My source for the biographical information on Day's early life is William D. Miller, *Dorothy Day: A Biography* (San Francisco: Harper and Row, 1982), 87–179.

3. William D. Miller, *All Is Grace: The Spirituality of Dorothy Day* (Garden City, NY: Doubleday and Company, 1987), 8.

4. Robert Coles, *Dorothy Day: A Radical Devotion* (Reading, MA: Addison-Wesley Publishing Company, 1987), 67–68. Coles explained that Dorothy Day was particularly influenced by Romano Guardini's idea that the church is the cross upon which Christ was crucified. Just as one cannot separate Christ from his cross, one must always live in a state of permanent dissatisfaction with the church. See Romano Guardini, *The End of the Modern World* (Wilmington, DE: ISI Books, Intercollegiate Studies Institute, 1998). This is a reprint with a new preface and introduction of a translation done by Joseph Theman and Herbert Burke in 1956. The German edition is *Das Ende der Neuzeit: ein Versuch zur Orientierung* (Würzburg: Werkbund-Verlag, 1951).

5. Robert Coles, *Dorothy Day*, 68.

6. Dorothy Day, *House of Hospitality* (New York: Sheed and Ward, 1939), xiii.

7. There had been, however, an official statement by the U.S. bishops on social justice issues. Further, there were other Catholic groups addressing labor issues. For example, the U.S. bishops had published a "Program of Social Reconstruction" in 1919, Father John Ryan had been an outspoken advocate for social justice for years, Father Peter Dietz was working with Catholic members of the AFL in the Militia of Christ, and there were many other initiatives taking place. Day was aware of these other social-justice reformers, organizations, and initiatives; nonetheless, she felt that the

broader church was being paralyzed by its fear of Communism. To see how Day fit into the broader milieu, see David O'Brien, *Public Catholicism* (New York: Macmillan Publishers, 1989).

8. Day, *House of Hospitality*, xiii–xvii.

9. *Rerum novarum*, 48–55 (paragraph numbers). I am using the translation provided on the Vatican Web site and its numbering system, which I accessed April 3, 2006; available from http://www.vatican.va/holy_father/ leo_xiii/encyclicals/documents/hf_l-xiii_enc_15051891_rerum-novarum_en.html. The critical edition of the text is *L'enciclia Rerum Novarum: Texto authentico e redazioni preparatorie dai documenti originali*, ed. Giovanni Antonazzi (Rome: Edizione de Storia e Letteratura, 1957). Unfortunately, the numbering systems vary between the critical edition and the Vatican translation. For a recent commentary on the encyclical, see Thomas A. Shannon, "Commentary on Rerum novarum (The Conditions of Labor)," in *Modern Catholic Social Teaching: Commentaries and Interpretations*, ed. Kenneth R. Himes (Washington, DC: Georgetown University Press, 2004), 127–50. The commentary has an excellent bibliography for further research. Pope Leo XIII was drawing on the work of others, including Bishop Wilhelm Von Ketteler of Mainz (1811–77), Cardinal Henry Edward Manning (1808–92), Albert de Mun (1841–1914), and others. For a good introduction to the broader historical context, see Thomas Bokenkotter, *Church and Revolution: Catholics in the Struggle for Democracy and Social Justice* (New York: Image Books, 1998).

10. *Rerum novarum*, 7–11.

11. Ibid., 12.

12. Ibid., 13, 14.

13. Ibid., 32–33.

14. Ibid., 37.

15. Ibid., 42.

16. Ibid., 43–44.

17. Ibid., 44.

18. Ibid., 45.

19. *Quadragesimo anno*, 14, 30 (paragraph numbers). I am using the translation provided on the Vatican Web site and its numbering system, which I accessed April 3, 2006; available from http://www.vatican.va/holy_father/ pius_xi/encyclicals/documents/hf_p-xi_enc_19310515_quadragesimo-anno_en.html. The critical edition can be found in *Actes de S.S. Pie XI: Allocutions Actes de Dicastères, Encycliques, Motu proprio, Brèfs, etc.*, vol. 7 (Paris: Maison de la Bonne Presse, 1936). For a recent commentary with a helpful bibliography, see Christine Firer Hinze, "Commentary on Quadragesimo anno (After Forty Years)," in *Modern Catholic Social Teaching*, 151–74.

20. *Quadragesimo anno*, 15.

21. Ibid., 58.

22. Ibid., 71.

23. Ibid., 61.

24. Ibid., 72.

25. Ibid., 74.

26. Peter Maurin was influenced by the personalist philosophy being espoused by Jacques Maritain and others. For an overview of Maritain's ideas on social justice and on personalism as a philosophy, see Bokenkotter, *Church and Revolution*, 335–401.

27. Day, *House of Hospitality*, xvii.

28. Ibid., xiii-xx.

29. My source for Maurin's ideas and quotes is Miller, *Dorothy Day: A Biography*, 234–35, and 244.

30. Day, *House of Hospitality*, xxiii.

31. Ibid., xxiv.

32. Ibid., xxxv.

33. Bokenkotter, *Church and Revolution*, 418.

34. Day, *House of Hospitality*, 54.

35. Miller, *Dorothy Day: A Biography*, 256–57.

36. Day, *House of Hospitality*, xxxiv-xxxv.

37. Ibid., 60.

38. Ibid., 258.

39. Father Joseph McSorely to Dorothy Day, March 26, 1935, Dorothy Day Collection, Raynor Archives, Raynor Memorial Library, Marquette University, Milwaukee, Wisconsin.

40. Dorothy Day to Monsignor Thomas Scanlan, March 16, 1935, Dorothy Day Collection, Raynor Archives.

41. Day, *House of Hospitality*, 260–61; Miller, *All Is Grace*, 38–39; Bokenkotter, *Church and Revolution*, 417–20.

42. Dorothy Day to Father Haskins, January 17, 1939, Dorothy Day Collection, Raynor Archives.

43. See the March 16, 1935, letter to Monsignor Thomas Scanlan and her letter to Father Whiterbone, written the eve of the feast of St. James (probably 1939) in the Dorothy Day Collection, Raynor Archives.

44. Bokenkotter, *Church and Revolution*, 428–29.

45. William D. Miller, "The Church and Dorothy Day," *Critic*, vol. 35 (Fall 1976): 64. See also Bokenkotter, *Church and Revolution*, 429–30.

46. Day, Letter to Monsignor Gaffney, 1–3.

47. Bokenkotter, *Church and Revolution*, 429–30.

48. Bokenkotter, *Church and Revolution*, 428–29. Bokenkotter's source was William D. Miller, *A Harsh and Dreadful Love: Dorothy Day and the Catholic Worker Movement* (New York: Liveright, 1973), 229.

49. Miller, *All Is Grace*, 39.

50. Day, *House of Hospitality*, 74–75.

Conclusion

1. See the *Catechism of the Catholic Church*, 2nd ed. (Rome: Libreria Editrice Vaticana, 2000), 879.

2. "Fourth Draft of Program for Priestly Formation, Fifth Edition: July 2003," 16. This document was produced by the United States Conference of Catholic Bishops. I have the draft in my possession.

Index

Acton, Lord, 177, 178, 186
Adelaide of Turin, Duchess, 51, 52
Adrian VI, Pope, 153
Agnes, Empress, 37, 44
Agnes of Prague, 93, 98
Alan of Lille, 87
Aleander, Jerome, Archbishop, 169
Alexander II, Pope, 37
Alexander III, Pope, 85
Alexander V, Pope, 131, 136
Alexander VI, Pope, 153, 154, 159
Ambrose, Saint, 3
Anselm of Lucca, Bishop, 47
Aquinas, Thomas, 105, 158, 159, 164, 204
Ariald, 47, 49
Augustine, 9, 10, 27, 39, 46, 64, 138

Badia, Tommaso, Friar, 169
Baronius, Cesare, 179
Barozzi, Pietro, 158
Beatrice of Tuscany, Duchess, 37, 44
Benedict XIII, Pope, 145
Bernard of Clairvaux, xvii, xix, 56–61, 63–78, 147, 219

Bonaventure, Saint, xix
Boniface VIII, Pope, 102, 106–9
Boniface IX, Pope, 134
Burke, Forster, 199
Bynum, Caroline Walker, 83

Calvin, 78
Carafa, Gian Pietro, Cardinal, 166, 168–69, 175
Cassian, John, 27
Catherine of Siena, xviii, xix, 70, 103, 104, 105, 110–22, 126, 147, 219, 223
Charlemagne, 29–30
Charles IV, Emperor, 132
Charles V, Emperor, 150, 164–65
Chrysostom, John, 5
Clare of Assisi, xviii, xix, 78–84, 89–92, 94–97, 99, 101–3, 110, 116, 223
Clement V, Pope, 109
Clement VII, Pope, 125–26, 164–67
Congar, Yves, xiii, xiv, xv, xvi, xvii, xix, 104, 197
Constantina, Empress, 17
Constantine, 2–3, 118, 158
Contarini, Gasparo, xviii, 150–52, 157–76, 223

Cortese, Gregorio, Abbott, 169
Council of Trent, xviii

D'Ailly, Pierre, 127, 144
Damian, Peter, xvii, xix, 30–55,
    60–61, 63–64, 77, 87, 100,
    104, 138, 159, 220, 222
Da Viterbo, Edgidio, 153
Day, Dorothy, xix, 198–201,
    206–17, 223
De Lubac, Henri, 197
De Vitry, Jacques, 87–88
Dionysius the Areopagite, 5, 164

Edict of Milan, 2
Edward I, King, 107
Eugenius III, Pope, 58, 63, 74–76
Eugenius IV, Pope, 148

Ferrer, Vincent, 126
Francis of Assisi, 78–82, 84,
    89–92, 94–97, 99, 101
Fregoso, Federigo, Archbishop,
    169
Fulk of Toulouse, Archbishop, 88

Galileo, 180
Gerhoh of Reichersberg, 61
Gerson, Jean, xviii, xix, 22, 78,
    123–24, 126–32, 139–43,
    145–48, 158, 219
Giberti of Verona, Bishop, 166,
    169
Giustiniani, Tommaso, 159, 173
Gladstone, William, Duke of
    Norfolk, 191, 194
Godfrey of Lorraine, Duke, 37,
    44

Gregory I, Pope, the Great, xvii,
    xix, 1–29, 45, 53, 56, 58, 63,
    77, 82, 87, 94, 101, 105–6,
    114, 129, 138, 218
Gregory VII, Pope, 27, 32, 37, 53,
    57, 61, 64, 138
Gregory IX, Pope, 80, 82, 97–98
Gregory XI, Pope, 105–6, 110,
    122
Gregory XII, Pope, 135–36, 145
Gregory XIII, Pope, 180
Gregory XVI, Pope, 181, 184
Gregory of Nazianzus, 5

Henry III, Emperor, 33, 50
Honorius I, Pope, 129
Hus, Jan, xviii, xix, 22, 80,
    123–24, 126–27, 132–39,
    142–46, 148, 150, 219

Ignatius of Loyola, 175, 217
Innocent I, Pope, 48
Innocent III, Pope, 97, 129
Innocent IV, Pope, 3, 80, 95,
    99–100, 102
Innocent VIII, Pope, 153–54

Jan of Jenstejn, Archbishop,
    133–34
Januarius, Archbishop of Sardinia,
    13
John XXIII, Pope, (Pisan),
    131–32, 136, 140
John XXIII, Pope, (Roman), 78
John the Deacon, 6
John of Salisbury, 61
John Paul II, Pope, 197
Johnson, Lyndon, President, 215

Julius II, Pope, 154
Justinian, Emperor, 6

Keenan, Elizabeth, 74
Kingsley, Charles, 191
Kung, Hans, 197

Ladislas of Naples, 132, 136
Ladner, Gerhard, xx, 63, 197
Langton, Stephen, 87
Laurentius, 7
LeClerq, Jean, 39
Leo IV, Pope, 48
Leo IX, Pope, 34–36, 39, 41–42
Leo X, Pope, 154, 159
Leo XIII, Pope, xv, 196, 202–4, 216
Lippomano, Pietro, Bishop, 160–61
Lombard, Peter, 61
Luther, 70, 146, 150, 152, 155, 157, 160, 163, 165, 167, 175

Manning, Henry Edward, 177
Martin V, Pope, 146
Marx, Karl, 201
Mary of Oignies, 86–88
Maurin, Peter, 201, 206–11
McCarthy, Joseph, Senator, 215
McGinn, Bernard, 8, 64, 83–84
McSorely, Joseph, 211
Moise, Lionel, 199
Moore, R.I., 49

Newman, John Henry, xviii, xix, 177–78, 181–97, 223
Nicholas II, Pope, 32, 37, 42, 44

O'Conner, John, Cardinal, 215

Paul III, Pope, 151, 155, 167–68, 170, 172, 175–76
Paul VI, Pope, 78
Peter the Chanter, 87
Peter of Mladoňovice, 123
Petrarch, 109
Philip the Fair, King, 106–8
Philip IX, King, 107
Pius VI, Pope, 181
Pius IX, Pope, 187
Pius X, Pope, xv
Pius XI, Pope, 204–6, 216
Pius XII, Pope, xiv
Pole, Reginald, 168

Quirini, Vincenzo, 159, 173

Ratzinger, Joseph, 197
Richards, Jeffrey, 13
Roger, Pierre, 132

Sadoleto, Jacopo, Cardinal, 168
Savonarola, 159–60
Scanlan, Msgr. Thomas, 212
Scotus, Duns, 158
Sigismund, Emperor, 132, 142
Simpson, Richard, 186
Sixtus IV, Pope, 153–54
Spellman, Francis, 213–15
Sylvester, Pope, 118

Talbot, Msgr. George, 187, 190
Tavard, George, 125, 197
Teresa of Avila, xvii
Tetzel, John, 152
Theodisius, Emperor, 3

Ullathorne, Bishop, 187
Ullmann, Walter, 110

Urban IV, Pope, 102
Urban VI, Pope, 110, 125–26

Valla, Giorgio, 158
Venerable Bede, 138
Vernazza, Ettore, 165

Wenceslas IV, Emperor, 133–34,
    136–37, 145
Wyclif, John, 134–35, 142, 150

Zabarella, Cardinal, 144–45
Zbyněk, Archbishop, 134–36